Crime Scene Investigator

Crime Scene Investigator

Paul Millen

ROBINSON
London

Constable & Robinson Ltd
3 The Lanchesters
162 Fulham Palace Road
London W6 9ER
www.constablerobinson.com

Published by Robinson,
an imprint of Constable & Robinson, 2008

A copy of the British Library Cataloguing in Publication
Data is available from the British Library

ISBN: 978-1-84529-663-6

Printed and bound in the EU

1 3 5 7 9 10 8 6 4 2

Contents

Contents

To those who seek the truth and to those whose job it is to find it

Introduction

There is no such thing as a perfect crime. For every effect there is a cause, for every contact there is a trace. The detection of crime is dependent on both time and resource. A crime may seem perfect but there is always a victim, an offender and some gain, financial or emotional. There are always witnesses, some unwitting, to events which the offender would wish to conceal. Some crimes may be particularly well planned and elude detection for long periods of time, but detection is never impossible. Persistence and opportunity (some may call it luck) can unlock even the most difficult investigations. The resourcefulness, skill and tenacity of investigators are all that is needed to identify that a crime has taken place and bring the offender to justice.

This is not to say that all crimes are solved. But they can be. All you need to do is ask the right question of the right person and look in the right place.

Crime scene investigation is not what some popular TV programmes would have us believe. Some episodes cram in a lifetime of real endeavour. But in one area TV has it right. Crime scene investigation is more than just the examination of the crime scene and the recovery of forensic evidence. It is about reaching milestones which fix fact into an investigation. Fact from which there is no turning back. Quite often there are key or killer questions (no pun intended), the answers to which are profound. They can mean that certain statements from witnesses or the accused are proven absolutely true or false. They may not come along too often, but when they do they can turn the direction of an investigation. Often it is the little pieces of evidence which build up to give a full picture. It is always necessary to stand back and question the validity of each part and the overall view. Small milestones can often make a case.

Crime scene investigation doesn't usually extend to the interviewing of suspects unless you work in a small department and cover a large area. CSI is about the scientific investigation of crime. It is a contributor to the wider crime investigation and detection. Unlike on TV, it is not carried out by one individual or by a team, each member of which has the same and complete set of skills. The team is varied and diverse. Each member brings his or her skills, investigational, practical and knowledge-based, and through clear communication and good management focus on the common goal, the detection of the crime.

Forensic evidence is just like any other evidence produced in court. It can be accepted or rejected by the judge and jury. It may be strong or weak, it may support a theory or proposition or not. Strong evidence is that which has a high probability of supporting a view, a contact, a presence, an event. Even then it is strong or weak only based on the science as it is understood at that time and in the context of which it is being used. Forensic evidence is never good or bad. That is really dependent on whose side you are on and science doesn't take sides. It only seeks to support the truth so it should only be described as strong or weak. Likewise, whenever I hear that some evidence is 'consistent with' I shudder. It is a question which experts will be asked by ill-informed lawyers. To me it is a trap; it may be unintentional but it is a trap none the less. The evidence may be consistent with some other event or proposition. The expert must also consider these other circumstances and communicate them too. DNA is generally considered strong evidence, foolproof. However, it must be questioned and tested in the judicial process to ensure that it is used in the correct context. DNA evidence, strong though it may appear, does not prove guilt on its own.

Some people are born investigators, others are taught. Both types improve with development, practice, experience and exposure. The last, exposure to a large range of criminal investigations rather than just one type, is very important as it confronts the investigator with a range of experiences on which to do well and also to make mistakes. There is nothing wrong with making mistakes, provided they don't result in miscarriages of justice. The mistakes which I am referring to are ones of approach, technique and recovery. These can be corrected and honed to improve and investigate further crime, particularly more complicated or serious crime. Everything found or recovered should be kept even if its condition could be better. Like any apprentice, I cut my teeth on the basics, improving and developing, learning how to do things better. I embraced the opportunities which technology and changes in legislation gave me.

The ability to think objectively and laterally, to look at objects or scenes in a different way, to look up as well as ahead are all important. I am still horrified by the care which I took to copy and describe some strange writing on an object which had been submitted to the forensic science laboratory early in my career. The font was strange and appeared like hieroglyphics, until I turned it around. To my shock and embarrassment it read simply '1½'. It was a lesson so well learnt that I still remember it thirty years later. And the important thing is to learn and to keep on learning.

There is a tendency to see things not as they are, but as we are. So we make assumptions based on our experience and expectations. There is a constant challenge for the investigator to test those assumptions. Only then can we be sure that the assumption is correct and the answer measured against our understanding and wider accepted knowledge.

Science is the perfect companion and contributor to the

detection of crime. By its own nature, seeking information, observing, questioning, analysing and testing against published criteria and even questioning those criteria, are the meat and drink of science. The discipline is in carefully recording observations, material and tests so that others might see and question. It is the basis of sound scientific endeavour. Important enough in the laboratory or places of learning, it is critical in a court of law where the liberty, reputation and perhaps the very life of the accused may be at stake. It is a sobering responsibility.

Rules often limit the boundaries of our imagination. Prejudices and preconceptions impede our search for the truth because we may not like the answer or what it might reveal.

As a young scenes of crime officer (often known as SOCO), I was sometimes told that, because I was a civilian and not a police officer, I could not examine crime scenes effectively. That was long before I realised that I was actually investigating scenes and with some success too. These unhelpful remarks by some colleagues were the last throes of a dinosaur age where some thought they could protect their jobs through such jibes. These individuals were not detectives in any sense of the word; they had missed the evidence before their own eyes. A questioning mind is not the sole right of any individual; it is an attribute which many people have and use in many walks of life. Later in my service I enjoyed the company of many fine detectives and investigators. For them I opened a door to the resources of the forensic science laboratory and beyond. There they found a wealth of committed and talented scientists who delivered the interpretation of evidence which we had recovered.

Even being without police powers did not stop me doing my duty as any member of the public can. Through being present at the right time I can claim three citizen's arrests on two occasions, although as I recall they were recorded as 'given into custody' on the arrest sheet back at the station. Both occasions were to the amusement and joking congratulations of my police officer colleagues. Even more embarrassing was the occasion I stumbled across a cycle theft which had just taken place and saw two young men re-spraying an impressive new cycle. Calling on my radio for help, the ensuing chase involved a fleet of police cars and the newly acquired and much prized police helicopter. At the end of the chase there was nothing to show but a partially re-sprayed stolen cycle, lots of out of breath and red-faced police officers and one equally out of breath and out of shape, red-faced scenes of crime officer. Later, much later, once I had composed myself, I examined the recovered cycle. I managed to recover finger marks from the spray can used by one of the young men. Once identified, a detective took a more leisurely stroll to the young man's house and arrested him. Now, wasn't that much simpler, I thought.

In writing such a book there is a danger that I might educate career criminals or even someone who plans to undertake a life of crime. I have no desire to do either. My advice to such individuals is, don't bother, you will get caught. Apply your talents to honest living, the rewards are better. So I have focused on how scene investigators undertake their interesting and challenging work and the tools they use, physical, mental and evidential. I hope to offer an insight into how crime scene investigators think and how they seek. I would like to inspire those new to this field and assure the honest reader that the answers are out there. This is not a textbook of forensic science (there are other volumes in print that offer that) but it is about the tools and methods the crime scene investigator applies. This book has examples of some of the scene investigations which I have either undertaken or managed. They offer the reader real examples of how some of these methods can be applied. There are also chapters covering the crime scene sciences themselves. I hope to inspire the reader to realise the limitless boundaries of evidence and to inform those of 'ill will' that their actions are futile. The only lottery is the skill of the investigator who is chasing them. As more and more sound investigators join law enforcement agencies, that aspect is diminishing. To the innocent, and those victims who wait to be healed by the capture of the offender, there is the comfort that the truth is out there. Sometimes justice is delayed, but I hope that it is not denied too long or too often.

My career would take me from a comprehensive school education to working at a bench at a forensic science laboratory, to crime scene investigation and the Flying Squad. I would command my own department in Surrey Police and serve in high office in the Forensic Science Society. Then I graduated to the independent field, defence investigations, training and contributing to TV documentaries in high-profile cases of the moment, ultimately to foreign fields, to Jamaica, the Source of the Nile in Uganda, and to Afghanistan post 9/11. Not bad for a boy from south London who found his science A levels challenging, but through tenacity and a firm sense of purpose passed, and went on to college and ultimately succeeded.

Through these pages I hope to enlighten you on the journey I took and on some of the cases I had the opportunity to investigate. I am hesitant to appear boastful or conceited and I do not want to forget all the fine colleagues who I worked with and those who continue to develop the science and the practice today. I was fortunate to be part of the development of the science at a particular moment in time, a small contribution in the scheme of things but a contribution none the less. I never forgot the victim or why I was motivated to do my job. These emotions did not cloud my responsibility to bring the offender, and only the offender, to justice. Like many of my contemporaries, I helped bring to book individuals who had committed minor and serious crime, all which affected the lives of their victims. I also helped eliminate and exonerate the innocent, of which I am equally and profoundly proud.

I hope that this can be read by the casual reader with an interest generated by the public perception of crime scene investigation and by the professional alike. For the former, I hope that it is not disappointing given the speed and glamour of the TV programmes which bear the name CSI. For the latter I hope that it reinforces the shared experiences and offers at least a little further insight in some areas. The book is written with chapters on biographical experience intermingled with the science which I believe underpins them. I have taken the decision not to include photographs. This is not a textbook and many photographs would be offensive to victims or their families. If any of the material in this book offends or causes pain to any victim of crime, I apologise now. My only hope is that it demonstrates that the truth is out there and it can be found. Wherever possible I have changed the names of many people involved in these cases to protect their identity. The names of some remain unchanged as do the names of police officers and colleagues. So I want you to think and picture in your own mind the work I undertook. I hope the text allows you to do that. If you are happy to read on from an intellectual position driven by interest, I hope this informs.

London, January 2008

1. Young Sherlock

Still holding the gun, I stood in front of the vehicle's shattered windscreen. The glass was everywhere. I was about to get caught, my heart was racing but for some reason my legs were not.

I grew up on a pleasant housing estate in south London and a regular and daily visitor to our street was the Unigate milk float, driven by a rotund, tall, red-faced, jovial and kind milkman who we knew only as 'Milko'. He was a constant and reliable presence who embodied all the best virtues of friendship and neighbourliness as he went about his daily task of delivering fresh milk to all the houses and flats on the estate. He would always be in the background at some time during the day as we played.

Two events as a child had a profound effect on me and probably determined my future professional career.

The first occurred while playing with my friends, Billy, John and Jo-Jo. I had been bought as a birthday or Christmas gift, a cowboy outfit (some might think I was to work for at least one in later life) complete with cowboy hat and belt and toy pistol. Prized amongst the set was a mechanical 'pop' gun. It was of thin metal construction and popular amongst young boys growing up in the 1960s. It had a long barrel rather like a toy rifle or shotgun. At the end was a cork which could be placed in the muzzle and pop out under pressure when the trigger was pulled with an accompanying satisfactory bang. To prevent injury or similar, the cork was attached to the barrel at one end by a chain or piece of string so it didn't fly too far.

Well, this wasn't good enough for Jo-Jo. A year or two older than me, he was the maverick leader of our little gang.

On that fateful day Jo-Jo and I were playing in the driveway of the block of flats where he, Billy and John all lived. Milko was in the flats delivering the milk and Jo-Jo and I were outside. The front of Milko's electric milk float was facing us. Jo-Jo had the idea of replacing the supplied cork with a handful of small stones picked up from the gravel. Placing them in the barrel he pointed it directly at the windscreen of the milk float and pulled the trigger. The sound of the shattering windscreen was deafening. At this point Jo-Jo handed me the gun and shot off like a rocket to hide. I stood there for what seemed to be an eternity, not really understanding what had happened. I don't know if I had intended to run, wasn't fast enough or just plain stupid but in any event I didn't move. Milko quickly emerged from the flats (the fastest I had ever seen this mature man move) where he confronted me. A short blond-haired boy wearing a pair of baggy shorts and a dumb expression was standing at the scene of the crime, holding the offending weapon. I was caught red-handed, 'bang to rights' as I would later know the term to be. The evidence was all around. The offender was still holding the weapon and the shattered glass of the screen said it all.

I was taken firmly by the ear and led by Milko to my house a hundred or so yards away to be greeted by my father. I'm not sure if I had protested my innocence on the way, or had 'grassed' Jo-Jo up by then, but both my father and Milko probably had already realised this was not in my nature. I could sense the wry smiles and hidden amusement on both of their faces as I protested my innocence. I was suitably admonished for the event by embarrassment if nothing else. Between them they sorted out how the damage was to be repaired. I don't suppose my father was too pleased at the prospect of having to fork out for a new windscreen, when we couldn't afford a car of our own at that time. I don't remember any sanctions, but there must have been some. But such was the loving family environment in which I grew up that whatever the punishment, I soon forgot it.

What I did not forget was the feeling of injustice. I had been holding the offending weapon at the crime scene. The evidence was obvious and overwhelming. But it was wrong. From that day forwards I had a sense of the importance of accurately investigating the crime scene so that the guilty were brought to book and the innocent (particularly the dumb innocent as in my case) were exonerated.

The second event was as I sat on the floor of our home in front of the small black and white television. I was small. Well, I have always been small, but I was very young and very small. As I gazed up at the screen the news reporter was telling the story of some heinous crime and the in-depth police investigation. The images of police officers in dark serge uniforms and black police cars flickered across the screen. The reporter then uttered a phrase which totally enthralled me. He said 'and a man is helping police with their enquiries.' Wow, how exciting was that! I thought. My imagination quickly turned to a Sherlock Holmes figure, with pipe and cape, painstakingly sifting through the evidence to bring the case to a successful conclusion. I realised there and then I wanted to be that man. It was some time before I realised the true meaning of the statement I had heard, but by then it was too late and my imagination was hooked.

I didn't have the physique to become a police officer (where my lack of height at that time would have meant certain elimination). I had to use other qualities and attributes. I would be that man who would help the police with their enquiries, and for all the right reasons.

My career in forensic science began in 1978 amid serious competition. I got a job as an Assistant Scientific Officer at the Metropolitan Police Forensic Science Laboratory. I consider myself extremely fortunate as I am sure there were people with far better examination grades amongst those who didn't get through. Perhaps the words 'tenacity' and 'sense of purpose', which occurred in my early school reports, had some effect.

For two years I worked in the Criminalistics, Drugs and Toxicology sections. This was my apprenticeship in forensics and gave me a great underpinning knowledge of the science I was going to use as a tool later. It wasn't just about the science though, it was the people too. I got to know many committed experts in all the fields at the lab, contacts I would use later whenever I needed advice. The lab, however, wasn't for me, and when, in 1980, twelve places became came available as scenes of crime officers, I jumped at the chance. My lab experience gave me an advantage over many other candidates and, following a good interview, I was offered a post.

The hardest thing to do in early life is to decide what you want to be when you grow up. Once you have that vision and goal it only takes time and tenacity to realise it. Although my goals and vision meandered as I grew into adulthood, the events which I had experienced as a child sparked off my imagination and determination.

Throughout thousands of investigations, I found horror and tragedy, humour and fun, life at its worst and at its best.

It was always for me a search for the truth. I didn't concern myself with justice. I quickly realised that was for others. If I used my best efforts to establish truth that would be contribution enough, so that is what I did.

2. First Steps

City Road was the smallest station of the Metropolitan Police's G Division which covered the London Borough of Hackney and included Stoke Newington and Hackney. It was definitely inner city, but City Road bordered with N Division (Kings Cross) and the City of London Police, a small force whose patch was the Square Mile, the financial hub of London. This meant that the lower part of City Road's ground was a strange mix of a gritty inner city and the financial capital.

My first day at City Road Police Station was, like all new beginnings, a nervous one. Scenes of crime officer Grade 2 (SOCO II) Millen queued with a small line of people in the public foyer of the police station. With a little apprehension I identified myself to the young fresh-faced constable who gave me a cheery welcome and let me through, directing me to the CID office on the first floor. I was met by Norman Craig my boss and mentor for the first two weeks of 'going live'. Norman was not my regular boss, that was to be Brian Finch, but Brian was on holiday so Norman had been brought in to accompany me in the first few days.

Norman Astle Hamilton Craig or 'Norm', as he was affectionately known, was a legend. He was a scenes of crime officer (Grade 1), and so was a god to me, such was the hierarchy within the organisation. I was to realise in later life that the first-line supervisor or manager is the backbone, the rock of any organisation. Norm was a consummate professional with a love of real ale and jazz and our friendship was to last until his premature death in the mid nineties. He was someone I always looked up to and I quickly realised that he knew his craft. He had got 'it'.

We made our introductions and then went into the adjoining CID office to meet the detectives I would be working with. It was a small office of about eleven detectives headed by a calm detective inspector and three detective sergeants, the rest being constables.

The area had a history and I was to discover later that nearby Worship Street was once the site of an early Elizabethan theatre. Right next to the police station in Shepherdess Walk was the Eagle public house, which I was to get to know very well in the four or so years I spent at City Road. The Eagle was made famous in the nursery rhyme: 'Up and down the City Road, in and out the Eagle, that's the way the money goes. Pop goes the weasel.'

Our introductions made, Norm and I examined the Crime Book, a record of all reported crime and picked out all new crimes reported overnight that we might be expected to attend. There had been a lot, but we whittled the list down to a priority list of some twenty or so scenes and got on our way. It was going to be a long and busy day and I loved it.

Norm and I gathered my examination case, lamp and clipboard and proceeded to the station yard where we got into a dark green SOCO van. We drove off to my first crime scene a few streets away.

My initial training had taken ten weeks or so at the Detective Training Wing of the Metropolitan Police Training Centre in Hendon, north London. The course consisted of two main portions of Forensic Science and Fingerprints, with a final phase on Law. It is strange to think the course time was equally divided amongst these two main subjects. But the subject of fingerprints was to be the most important single skill in my life as a SOCO in London at that time.

However, times were changing and new opportunities for the scientific investigation of crime were emerging and I and many others had a part to play. So the importance of fingerprint evidence hasn't diminished but rather has been joined and complemented by DNA and a raft of scientific advances in intelligence and evidence which has transformed the way crimes are investigated. Advances in the science would include new methods of finding and recovering fingerprints using chemicals and light sources of variable wavelength. New computer programs and networks would increase the speed at which they can be searched and identified. Whilst DNA technology was still in the dreams of researchers we had to use the available tools of blood grouping, shoe marks, fibres, paint and glass and many more. Many of the new science applications had been emerging for some time. It would be a little big headed to think that people like me helped their development, but I am sure we helped with their application in both minor and major crime investigations.

I saw my role as SOCO to be the eyes and ears of all the scientists and other experts back in the lab, those who couldn't be at the scene. It would be my role to recover material and information, recognise the potential and sell that to the investigator. Alongside these developments would be our thought processes and through these how we identify our purpose, undertake our investigations and how we communicate our findings. Put it all together and I knew it would work.

So now I had to put my initial training and sense of purpose to the test. I had a feeling of great anticipation but the nervous feeling in the pit of my stomach was overcome by an eagerness to make a difference.

My first visit was to an office above a parade of shops in Old Street, the swanky offices of a shipping company or some other commercial business in Shoreditch. A window had been broken at the rear first-floor fire escape and the intruder(s) entered and rifled the offices, stealing cash and anything else of value they could find. They had moved a few bottles of wine. Norm and

I gathered as much information as we could and then worked our way methodically through the scene from the point of entry to the point of exit as best we could determine. We tried to dodge the office workers who were keen to get back to their desks after I had finished. At some point the detective assigned to the case turned up and interviewed the 'loser' and made his enquiries before moving on to his next case. He agreed to call me over the radio if he could reprioritise where I might be needed, and cancel me from those scenes where I was not. Such was the incoming traffic of new crime reports that the list was likely to get longer not shorter.

The term 'loser' was not a derogatory term for the victim, as it might appear to someone reading this today, just merely the jargon of the day, reflecting the person reporting the loss but, looking at it now, it does seem strange.

I was on my best behaviour and doing everything by the book to impress Norm. I took samples of glass and paint from the point of entry, recovered shoe marks and examined everything I could along the apparent path of the offender. I was disappointed to find some glove marks at the point of entry, as these would prove difficult to identify but continued to examine other moved items (moved in the view of the occupants) for finger marks. On a bottle of wine I found a couple of sequences of finger marks. These I brushed and developed carefully with aluminium powder applied with a fine brush, before cleaning out with another brush and then lifting on adhesive tape which I then applied to a plate of clear plastic acetate sheet. This was and remains the standard way of recovering latent finger marks on objects without having to seize the whole item. Having written the details on the acetate, I admired the marks before showing Norm.

I packed, labelled and sealed all the items which I had recovered. I obtained the elimination fingerprints of those who might have legitimately touched the bottle at the office. I completed my notes and diagrams, which took some time, before leaving the scene. This was the discipline which was to become the template for my professional life. My first crime scene examination had taken me well over an hour, nearly two, to complete. If this were to continue I was never going to see home again. As we left, I handed the bottle of wine on which I had found the finger marks back to the owner. He gestured that I could keep it and I said I would give it to the CID. Although there are rules about accepting gifts, this seemed harmless. Despite now being covered in grey aluminium powder and quite unappealing on the exterior, it was certainly drinkable and very acceptable for the CID!

The other crime scenes I examined that day merged into what I can only recall as a long day, at the end of which I had a headache. After our last scene, Norm and I returned exhausted to City Road and to the CID Office. We had examined eighteen crime scenes and had bags of evidence, paint and glass samples, shoe and finger marks. All of which had to be processed and documented before the start of a new day tomorrow. I presented the unopened bottle of wine to the detective inspector, who promptly placed it in the office drinks cupboard.

Two months or so later I got a call over the radio from a detective to say that the marks which I had found on the bottle had been identified. I had received my first 'Ident' and it meant I had to buy everyone a drink, or so I was told, which I duly did. It was all the sweeter because it had been my very first scene. A few weeks later I was asked to write a statement and the officer in the case knew that the bottle and what was or was not left of its contents was in the inspector's drinks cabinet. My statement read (from my notes) how I had found the finger marks 'on a full unopened bottle of wine endorsed "Hock" twelve inches high, the marks were above the front label, seven inches from the base, two inches to the right pointing to four o'clock.' The problem, the detective pointed out, was the bottle was now most definitely open and empty. I was ribbed by the all the detectives in the office for days. How was I to explain how the contents had disappeared in the intervening time? In the end it didn't matter. The bottle itself was never an exhibit, nor did it need to be. In normal events I would have left the bottle at the scene as I had tried to do, relying on my notes and diagrams and the finger mark lift I had taken. That was more than sufficient and quite proper within the law. I reminded myself that the bottle itself was no longer relevant, that it was not recorded as recovered property as there was no evidential reason to record it. That didn't stop the ribbing I received, and I had learnt that I could expect plenty of banter from my detective colleagues and this sharpened my attention to detail.

The ribbing did not overshadow my feeling of success. I had become what many colleagues call a 'thief taker'. Someone was going to be brought in for questioning and I had played an important part in the process. The individual I had helped identify was later convicted of the burglary. The finger mark I had found had been the spark the CID had needed to find more evidence and resulted in the recovery of some small items of property and the solving of the case.

It was probably from that start that I realised I was not just conducting a crime scene examination. I was part of a process of crime scene investigation, where each component plays a part in the overall outcome and I would have to understand and develop my craft to ensure its full impact. It would be a few years before I could convince my colleagues that we were moving from examining crime scenes to investigating them, but I for one had started that day.

3. Forensics: So What's it all About?

Any schoolchild studying science for the first time will quickly understand the principle of scientific experiment and the concept of 'a fair test'. This is a question which constantly challenges and I hope will continue to challenge the modern forensic scientist. Is it accurate? Is it reproducible? If we do it again will we get the same result? Is it based on sound research and review by the scientific community? And what does it mean? To the casual reader this may seem unimportant, but those accused or convicted of crime based on scientific evidence would have a different view. So it is a burden and a responsibility that anyone who practises forensic science should understand and embrace.

Less than a hundred years ago forensic science as we know it was barely recognisable. There are examples of scientific evidence being used in criminal trials going back centuries. An early example can be found in the term 'caught red-handed'. This originates from the sixteenth century, but the earliest printed reference is attributed to Sir Walter Scott in his novel *Ivanhoe*, first printed in 1819. 'Red-handed' indicates finding the blood of the victim on the suspect. The assumption made is that the red liquid is blood, human blood, and from the victim. Even in the 1980s human blood could only be distinguished by a series of independent grouping systems, such as ABO, which a scientist could interpret and only then give, by today's standards, limited statistical probability as to its origin. Not until the introduction of DNA technology in the late 1980s could the discrimination and probability of blood and other body fluids reach any high degree of certainty.

Early attempts by researchers such as Bertillon to identify and catalogue individuals by an elaborate system of anatomical measurement recognised that humans are all different. However, it was overtaken by the much more practical science of fingerprints. Fingerprints could be used to identify individuals and had the added bonus of being recoverable from the scenes of crime.

First used in a criminal case in London in 1902, fingerprints provide a ready and reliable method of identifying individual people. The basis of the system is the premise that no two individuals have the same finger, palm, or footprints. These are the areas of the human body where friction ridges can be found. The ridges are frequently broken by forks or stop at an ending (known technically as bifurcation and ridge endings). These breaks and endings are known as fingerprint characteristics.

Sir Edward Henry introduced the fingerprint system in Scotland Yard in 1900. A collection of inked finger impressions (fingerprints) formed the basis of the method of identifying individual convicted criminals along with their criminal record history. It exists to this day. Finger impressions (finger marks) recovered from crime scenes formed a later collection. At first manually stored and now computerised, these can be searched against the prints of those with previous convictions. It is a powerful tool only to be matched in its impact in the scientific investigation of crime by DNA technology, almost a century later.

The Frenchman Edmund Locard is the modern father of forensic science. In the early 1900s he formulated his 'principle of exchange' which is the cornerstone of the science to this day.

He stated, 'When two objects meet there is a mutual exchange of material from one to the other.' It can be summarised to say 'every contact leaves its trace.' The challenge is to find it.

However, finding it is only the first part of the problem. Once found, we have to consider its meaning. Forensic science can be said to be the science that brings all science together and then brings it into the courtroom. Which is where the term forensic originates, its means 'pertaining to the law'. Forensic science is the science of identification, contact and dynamic events. Above all it is a science of context. Many events which forensic science may detect can be ordinarily found, perhaps innocently, in everyday aspects of human endeavour. What makes these events evidence in a criminal trial is the context in which they are found. The finding of forensic evidence can indicate the presence, actions and consciousness of an individual at a time or place which supports their involvement in the commission of a crime. It can also exonerate, which is often its most important use.

The Metropolitan Police Forensic Science Laboratory opened in 1935 at Scotland Yard and marked the beginning of a planned use of forensic science in criminal investigation in the UK. Home Office laboratories followed to serve provincial forces. By 1959 a new profession of forensic science was establishing itself, prompting like-minded individuals to form the Forensic Science Society. Its aims were to 'advance the study, application and standing of forensic science and to facilitate cooperation among persons interested in forensic science throughout the world'. It has been doing that pretty effectively ever since.

The specialised examination of the crime scene is an even more recent event. Until the 1950s in the UK and North America, the examination of the scene was the domain of the detective. Only rarely, in numbers which could be counted on one hand, would forensic scientists themselves examine a crime scene and then for a single purpose, most commonly for something like blood splashing. Pathologists had for many years examined the scene of sudden or suspicious death but their domain was that of forensic medicine and toxicology. It didn't stop many of them from stepping into areas in which they had no training or experience. In the absence of dissent, their medical expertise in all matters forensic was accepted unopposed.

The regular and routine examination of crime scenes for fingerprints by specialists began with the Metropolitan Police in London with the introduction of civilian fingerprint officers in 1954. Up to that time it was the sole domain of detectives with varying degrees of interest and skill. In 1966 Humberside Police employed the first civilian scenes of crime officers, followed by the Metropolitan Police in 1969. Other police forces in the UK followed suit using a mixture of civilian and police personnel. The term scenes of crime officer or SOCO became synonymous with the role. Other police forces (such as Durham) used the term scientific aids, but soon came in line with the rest of the UK.

The role was seen as one of crime scene examination for a number of years, which belied its full impact within the investigation process. That was not good enough as far as I was concerned because it failed to recognise the integration of science within the whole investigation. Dave Werrett (a pioneer in the introduction of DNA technology into forensic science and who later become head of the UK Forensic Science Service) used the phrase which I always liked. He referred to the 'continuum'. This aptly describes the seamless process from crime scene to court. Many players take part in the process but it should have one purpose and goal. To me it was always a matter of escalation, from the first patrol officer who attended the crime and realised there was something more than they could handle, to the detective and the specialist crime scene person, to the specialist scientist in a particular evidence type. Each adds his or her own knowledge, training and expertise to the problem until a definitive answer can be found. The crime scene investigator is in real terms a compromise. They are the eyes and ears of the expert scientist in every conceivable field. It isn't possible or practical to regularly bring every expert to the scene to conduct their own examinations. This is not to say that experts never attend scenes and examine areas specific to their expertise. They do. They are called as part of the escalation process when the scene investigator establishes that the scene is beyond their own skills. As a crime scene investigator I needed to maintain a crust of knowledge of all the forensic science disciplines and be able to handle new ones. This I could do by holding to core principles whilst seeking advice from wherever I could get it. Compromise may be a harsh description of a scene investigator, but that is how the role started out. It understates the investigative role which has added immense value to criminal investigation and has developed now into the management of the scene investigation process.

The standard text *Techniques of Crime Scene Investigation*, first published in the 1950s, was a bible to me but even it did not demonstrate the application and dynamics of the investigative team and process. This comprehensive textbook fully explores the techniques I would use in crime scene examination, but did not explore the communication and interaction with others that I saw as true investigation. By 1989, when I led the development of the Forensic Science Society diploma, there was no doubt in my mind that we were testing scene investigators and not just scene examiners. So against some resistance (well quite a bit actually, as I will explain later), the Diploma in Crime Scene Investigation was born.

Forensic science is not just about fingerprints and blood, which are often seen as the easy options, giving the highest returns. Any contact trace or residue which can prove a crime has taken place or link an offender should be considered.

So the toolbox of the crime scene investigator is full of technologies and evidence types: paint, glass, shoe marks, tyre marks, bite marks, ear marks, blood, semen, saliva, urine, hairs, fibres, firearms residues, toxicology, poisons, ballistics, pollen, vegetation, fire accelerants, inks, latent marks and impressions, physical and mechanical fit, computers, light sources and many more.

All these technologies are worth nothing without much more important tools. Technologies continue to improve and changes in legislation necessitate finding new ways to enforce our laws and detect when they have been broken. However, the enquiring mind and the ability to listen and question are the most important qualities of an investigator. The answers to questions such as who, where, when and why remain unchanged. When these answers are sought, only then can the quest to methodically search, test, recover, record, review and evaluate evidence begin. The final question is to determine what it all means.

4. A Touch of Spice

The sound of wailing sirens pierced the hot and humid air coming through the office window. It was a balmy sunny evening and I was looking forward to clearing some paperwork. Late turn on G Division meant covering the three police stations in the London Borough of Hackney up until ten pm, after all my colleagues had gone home. Any thought of a quiet evening, perhaps examining a couple of burglary scenes and enjoying a quick pint next door at the Eagle before going home, disappeared when the phone rang.

It was a detective sergeant calling from the CID office at Stoke Newington. He was investigating an allegation of a racial attack on a West Indian woman. It appeared that someone had put a lighted petrol bomb through her door. He asked me to attend. It was serious so I had no hesitation.

I didn't enjoy driving through the weave of traffic as London commuters made their way home. It was only a few miles after all, but it can seem like ten times that and it would probably have been quicker to walk. Stoke Newington was the biggest police station on the Metropolitan Police's G Division. Its CID office boasted about thirty detectives, although only a handful were on duty at any one time. It was a hard place to work and tested every part of your professional existence. It had a very high crime rate and the range of crime tested every part of your training. All life was there. It was a grand area with tree-lined Victorian avenues which had seen many changes. Once the domain of the emerging middle classes, boasting the names of theatre land as its occupants, it had been swallowed up as London expanded and was now most definitely inner city. A large influx of immigrants from Europe and latterly the West Indies made it a racial melting pot. Hassidic Jews, the men in their black robes and brimmed hats covered in plastic to keep them dry, lived in grand houses in areas surrounded by post-war council flat developments.

The area had seen much redevelopment since the end of the Second World War. Although the blocks of pre-war flats with their concrete courtyards still existed, new blocks of large, imposing council flats on green estates were emerging, providing good accommodation with a more pleasing outlook. Even that was not enough to take away the tension of inner city life and the close proximity of neighbours.

I met the detective at the scene. By the time I arrived it was already after eight pm. I parked my van at the foot of the block of flats. The building was a pleasant-looking 1970s-built apartment block. It had about five levels and all the front doors of the flats opened directly out on to the front balcony with an impressive view on to the car park and grass areas below and over the rooftops of older but still well-maintained houses across the way. The scene was on the fourth floor. There was a feeling of space. It was clean and even the lift (which worked) didn't have the usual smell of urine which was the norm in many similar complexes. I sensed that the occupants of this building took care to look after it.

When I arrived at the front door to the flat it was open. I could see some scorching to the outside of the front door around the letter box. The fire damage inside was worse but limited to the rear of the door, with a little smoke damage extending at a high level along the hallway area. Looking inside, down the hallway, I could see the detective sitting at a kitchen table with the victim, a middle-aged black woman. The detective was taking a statement but broke away when he saw me. I apologised for the interruption. He explained to me that the lady stated that she had received some racial threats over a period of time. Today, a lighted object had been pushed through the letter box. The victim was in at the time and had quickly put out the fire. The potential threat was serious as, had the fire spread, it would have been potentially life threatening. Being on the fourth floor and with the hallway on fire, she would have had only the front window as a potential escape route.

The detective then drew my attention to a small, heavily blackened bottle complete with charred paper wick. The contents for some reason had been poured down the drain by the first officer at the scene, apparently for some safety reason which made no sense to me at the time. A note for future training, I thought. There was still a drop of liquid which smelt of spirits.

The detective then returned to the victim to continue with the statement whilst I began to examine the scene.

Although the door was on a public landing it still required examination for finger marks, for accuracy and thoroughness if for nothing else. The contents of the bottle required identification and the bottle and the wick would need fingerprint examination. Although now burnt and covered in spirit this would be very important, as it was a direct link to the offender.

I completed a full visual examination, making some initial notes and diagrams before beginning to preserve the bottle and its contents.

There was something which worried me. The glass bottle was indeed small, but the letter box, although a little larger, was restricted by a poorly fitting flap, which severely reduced the opening aperture. I measured both before offering up the bottle as carefully as I could so as not to disturb any finger marks. It didn't fit and that was obvious. No matter how I tried, this glass bottle was not going to go through the letter box. Nor had it done in the past. This changed the situation completely.

I went into the kitchen and stood by the detective as he sat with the victim at the kitchen table. Looking around, I noticed a neat row of spice jars each one of them identical to the now blackened jar at the front door. And to add to this there was a gap.

Interrupting the officer, I called him outside on the pretext of a question. With very few words and shielding my actions from the victim inside the flat, I offered up the bottle to the letter box. I also drew his attention to the spice rack in the kitchen, for his return. Without a word, he turned and walked purposefully back into the kitchen. His attitude had changed. He remained professional, but he now knew he was no longer dealing with an external attack of racial origin. The door had not been opened during the fire and therefore the agent had to come from within. His caring demeanour gave way to a more direct voice and line of questioning.

I continued and completed a full examination and notes. I may have had to fully account for my examination and findings later. The items would be preserved but not sent to the laboratory at the moment. This took time, but it had to be done. I couldn't see the situation changing, but by that time in my career I had already realised you can't predict the future. At least I could demonstrate my professional and thorough approach to the situation should I be asked in the future.

The officer continued to speak carefully to the lady occupant. He remained courteous, but was now a little more direct. When confronted with the fact that the jar would not fit through the letter box and its obvious implications, she broke down into a flood of tears. It transpired that she was seeking to be re-housed and thought the allegation of racial threats against her would speed up the process. She was a good woman, just a little desperate and misguided. What was a relief to the detective and me was that we, on this occasion were not dealing with a life-threatening racial attack with all its implications.

It was strange because, looking at the spice jar and the letter box, everyone, me included for a short while, assumed that it would pass through. Reconstruction of the events of a crime is an intrinsic part of the crime scene investigation. It is important to recognise, question and test assumptions.

Having completed my work I drove to Stoke Newington Police Station to update the crime report, a report which was soon to be reclassified as a 'No Crime'. I'm sure the detective considered a charge of wasting police time against the lady, but even in circumstances such as this they are rarely pursued. It doesn't do any good; the lady had learnt her lesson and probably felt rather silly. It's strange, as I thought the flats were one of the better developments in the area. But I didn't live there.

I then drove the two miles or so in lighter traffic back to City Road. I think I even managed a pint in the Eagle before going home.

5. Cutting my Teeth

It was in burglary and stolen car investigations that I cut my teeth. Although there was a high volume, I never got bored even if I visited the same premises on subsequent occasions to investigate other crimes. This was because no two crimes, even at the same premises, are the same. Details change, the point of entry and exit, what the offender did and what they took. Previous investigations form a basis of intelligence which the investigator retains in memory or more accurately in their notes.

Science and police investigations share common values so when they come together in crime scene investigation the benefits quickly follow.

At the very beginning of any investigation there is a need to talk: to the police officer who is reporting the crime, to the victim and other witnesses, all who will have a story. Even if they were not present at the time of the crime (as is often the case with burglary or vehicle theft) they will tell you what they found. The broken window, the muddy footprints (shoe marks, I would correct them), the rifled drawers and broken jewellery boxes. This helps formulate a picture of the route of the offender and timeline of the offence. Often, if the scene allows it, a cup of tea and a chat with the victim helps. It is a chance to calm down all the emotion and distress. This helps show concern and also allows the investigator to plan and review the examination they will undertake.

So, imagine a small single-storey bungalow sitting on a quiet road. A white picket fence breaks in the middle and through a gate a path leads to a front door. On either side are bay windows. Flowerbeds skirt the brickwork.

The female occupant had come home from shopping to find she could not open the front door. Her keys worked but the bolts on the inside of the door appeared to have been secured. Looking through a front window she could see the lounge had been ransacked and the television, which occupied a prominent position was missing. Frightened, she went next door to a neighbour who called the police.

The officers quickly attended and checked the premises. Going to the rear of the premises they found a broken pane of glass in the kitchen door. The door was open. Entering, they found that the offender or offenders had long gone, but not before turning furniture over. They had also bolted the front door from the inside, possibly to prevent being caught if the owner returned.

Comforting the female occupant, they ask her to accompany them through the scene, avoiding the broken glass. 'What has been stolen?' they ask. If she tries to pick anything up they express caution in case of fingerprints or DNA. A TV and a camera along with the contents of her jewellery box have been stolen. Then the tears come, at the realisation that a ring, or other item, a gift from a long-dead close relative, is missing. We don't just grieve for people. We grieve about items and the memories which they hold. Being the victim of a crime is a horrible thing.

The description of the scene I have given may not reflect that of gritty inner city crime but the circumstances are the same whether you live in a country cottage or a high-rise flat. There is a scene, a story and a victim.

My job was to find the person or people who committed the offence. The best place to start is at the beginning. This is true of all investigations and not limited to the scene. I would listen to the allegation and talk to victims or witnesses to the events leading up to the crime, the commission of the crime itself and its aftermath. It helped me define the boundaries of the scene and identify the number of scenes. It prompted me to ask questions which I would methodically address. It helped me prioritise the scenes and issues within them so that the urgent ones, those which would change if I did not deal with them first, would become apparent.

The range of issues which would confront me could be large and varied. Even attending the scene of a simple burglary, I would use the same process, considering the type of premises, the boundaries within which to look for signs of criminal activity. The witnesses or victim would always give an indication of what they found, a damaged window, an open door, scattered belongings, missing items.

I would start by trying to confirm or identify the point of entry, then the offender's route through the scene, by the damage or disturbance they had made, and finally where they left the scene. I would not normally wear the white protective suits to prevent contamination, simply because fibres and the other types of evidence which they are there to protect are not normally an issue in these types of scenes. However, I could not forget the issue of contamination. As I walked around the scene with the witness, I looked, observed and reviewed potential areas of evidence, avoiding touching areas which I would need to examine. I would address them in a methodical manner once the initial scene evaluation had been completed.

This would help me identify, for example, a newly washed kitchen floor, to all intents and purposes spotless, but potentially hiding the latent footwear impressions of the offender. I would issue a gentle restraint to prevent the witness stepping too close until I had fully searched it.

The victim would often notice something unusual which would require greater thought, so it's important to listen even to the little asides. On one occasion I heard a cleaner at an office premises say that her washing-up gloves were missing. This prompted me to think that perhaps the offender had not been wearing gloves when they entered and there was a distinct chance of finding their fingerprints, if I looked in the right places. On searching the scene I found a discarded pair of rubber gloves with a torn finger, they didn't belong to anyone at the scene and so seemed to have been left or, more accurately, swapped by the offender. What I did next was a leap of thought. I sent the torn gloves to the fingerprint lab, asking them to try and develop marks on the inside soft fleece surface. The methods which I had available at the scene were not sufficient to achieve this. The lab developed a full set of ten finger marks using gentian violet staining and the offender was identified by an expert fingerprint officer who searched them. It caused a bit of a stir as no one seemed to recall whether this had ever been successful before, although I'm sure it must have been. Perhaps it was just rare.

Following my initial evaluation of the scene, and before I undertook a methodical search, I would have to deal with any priorities. This would include any items which would decay or deteriorate due to inclement weather or other factors if I did not immediately address them. This was also a matter of time management. Casts of marks which may take some time to dry would need to be made early so I wasn't hanging around for them to dry at the end of my examination. To allow me to get on with my job I would encourage the often distressed victim to occupy themselves. 'How about putting the kettle on?' I would suggest. This took their mind off things and gave them something practical to do. By the time my examination was finished the tea would probably be cold, but drinking it often allowed me to gather my thoughts and make my notes before I left. It got to the stage where I would burn my mouth whenever I drank hot tea. One old pro of a detective, investigating a burglary in a 'well-to-do' premises, when offered a cup of tea remarked that he 'didn't drink tea'. Within a minute he was offered whisky in a cut crystal glass. Then offered a cigarette, he stated he 'didn't smoke cigarettes'. Within another moment he was standing there with a glass of whisky and a fine cigar. As my tea got cold, I looked on in wonder at his use of words.

Having dealt with the priorities, I could then make a careful search of the whole scene. Observation is the watch word and a strong lamp a reliable companion.

The first search is usually one which doesn't potentially destroy any forms of evidence. These are the non-destructive techniques which don't swamp further techniques. I would ensure no brushing or the use of powders for developing latent finger or shoe marks for the moment. This would wipe away or cover other delicate items. I would carefully observe, recognise, record and recover fibres, blood or visible fingermarks. Only once this was completed would I examine items with a fine brush and fingerprint powder. This would reveal the latent marks of fingers or shoes.

Fingermarks can be left in deposits of salt, amino acids and other body secretions and also in contaminants picked up by the hands or on the item on which the finger mark is found. Sometimes they are visible and can be recovered by photography or removing the item. On glossy surfaces, such as paint or glass, even the invisible can be revealed. By gently brushing with a fine powder such as aluminium or carbon, the powder adheres to the secretion deposit or contaminant and reveals the detail of the fingerprint of the donor.

Shoe marks can be found in any contaminant, from house dust to dried rain water or blood. If they are visible they too can be photographed or lifted. The invisible may be revealed by an oblique light, the dust giving a true impression of the donor shoe pattern. Once visible they can be photographed or lifted using static electricity or soft gel.

As the scene was searched and items recorded or recovered, my notes would be updated. My contemporaneous notes were a record of what I had observed and the exact measurements of what I had found. My notes would, wherever possible, be accompanied by plans and diagrams. These would be of the whole scene, areas within it or of just individual items. Any photographs would be referred to in the notes to indicate when and where they were taken, and any particular item or area of interest which I wished to highlight would also be noted. I felt strongly that photographs should always be accompanied by notes and diagrams, because without them they meant nothing.

As I recorded and recovered items I would carefully preserve and package them so that the evidence which they potentially contained would not be destroyed or contaminated and compromised before it was examined at the laboratory.

My final action at the scene before leaving would be to review. This would be one final check to see that it all made sense to me or would do so once we got some answers back from the lab. Only when I had searched the entire scene and recorded and recovered all the evidence I had found would I consider the scene examination complete. But the investigation was not. That would only just be beginning.

The end of the scene examination would always raise potential questions in my mind, about where I might find the answers.

I would need to decide what would happen next, perhaps a search of finger or shoe marks against a database or the development of marks by chemical or other methods.

What makes an individual a scene investigator rather than a scene examiner is a matter of responsibility and ownership. No one else may care about the potential outcomes of the scene examination. As an investigator I did. I would pursue or ensure others pursued the evidential potential, the answers. I would ensure that other members of the investigative team understood the meaning and potential of the evidence. The goal of solving the crime and bringing those responsible to court is shared by all those who consider themselves to be investigators.

As a crime scene investigator I attended a lot of crimes, often within a particular area and often over a period of time. So it was quite natural that I would begin to notice patterns, either of offending or in the evidence collected.

It was generally but wrongly considered that criminals keep to one type of offending and within specific geographical areas. The arrival of the DNA database in the UK in 1995 blew this theory apart. Offenders who had been pigeonholed as burglars or robbers were found to commit other crimes, such as theft by deception or, in some cases, sexual offences, and not only within a local area. The national database was able to link criminal activity over a wide area.

Intelligence within the crime scene investigation process begins with the soft patterns which the scene investigator notices. This may be a particular footwear mark appearing at a number of scenes, often within a local area over a period of time. The shoe may be known to be a common pattern fashionable at the time but when it is linked with a type of burglary in a particular area, usually at the same time of day and where the same type of goods are stolen, it doesn't just suggest coincidence.

At one time I noticed a series of burglaries of a similar nature, and I saw the same shoe pattern originating from the offender. After a period of time I had accumulated enough of the pattern to piece it together and identify what the whole shoe pattern and the upper style looked like. I even managed to instantly notice the mark on a very thin strip of wood on a door jamb which had been kicked in. The mark was in dust and revealed all the damage features within the shoe itself. It was not very common. It bore the name 'Banana' on the sole. So I put a few notices around the police station so that police officers could look out for it. Within a few days a police officer called me down to the Charge Room where he had just brought in a young man for another offence. He was wearing shoes of the right pattern. Submission of the shoes and crime scene marks to the laboratory confirmed that in at least one of the scenes these shoes had made the marks which I had found. The pattern and unique damage features were such that no other shoe could have made the same marks.

Intelligence can build up by linking similar events together and supporting the links with some physical evidence. I held a local database of footwear and also instrument marks recovered from scenes within my area.

When physical evidence can be categorised it forms a database which can be searched with evidence collected from suspected offenders. The longest to date is the fingerprint system which has been around for over a hundred years. DNA is a relatively new kid on the block but its success has been overwhelming when used as an intelligence database. Anything which leaves a mark or can be analysed and categorised can be put into an intelligence database. But it is just that – an intelligence database. It is not an evidence database. Once a link has been made, then a comparison to the full evidential standards expected must follow. It is an expert, not a database, who gives their opinion, their evidence, on the findings and its relevance.

Databases can be made of finger, shoe, tool, firearms, tyre and ear marks and of injuries. They can be made from blood grouping and DNA extracted from body fluids found at a crime scene – blood, saliva, semen – and also in hair. Intelligence databases can be made from the manufacturer's information in matters such as fibres. This may indicate the occurrence of such fibres in the garments of the general population. Car manufacturers keep databases of the types of light fittings their vehicles are equipped with, along with details of primer, undercoat and top coat paint colours. These are used when glass and paint are found at collision scenes. By identifying the glass and paint it may be possible to identify a particular model and the year in which the material originated. Databases also exist within crime labs for prescription medicines and drugs of abuse.

All this information forms a web of intelligence which has the potential to be searched and cross-referenced. But the information technology systems must allow this information to be shared.

It is the expert who maintains the databases of DNA and fingerprints so that they, and only they, can access and compare. When they link scenes or suspects, that information is communicated to investigators so they can show the link on their database. Only the link and not the technology on which it is based are communicated.

Intelligence based on other factors, such as the methods used by offenders, are useful but they cannot become evidence themselves. Similar fact evidence has some value, particularly if it is sufficiently unusual, but it has its pitfalls. It is best if similar fact evidence can be used as a means to find even one piece of strong physical evidence which can link an offender to a substantial offence.

I attended a series of burglaries in a particular block of flats over a period of some weeks. In each case the two suspects cut the phone wires above the front door before forcing entry. Once inside, they took jewellery and light items. I managed to find some finger marks and they were subsequently identified and found guilty. Two years later a violent rape occurred in the same block of flats. I was not involved in the initial investigation as I was on leave at the time. But when I returned I was naturally interested. A week into the enquiry no suspect had been identified. Although some fingermarks had been found they were not of enough detail to be searched using the available technology at the time. This meant a direct comparison with a named suspect was the only way they were going to be identified. My ears pricked up when I was told that the phone wires had been cut before the front door was forced and the female occupant raped. Remembering the scene two years earlier, I put the names of those offenders forward for comparison. The marks were quickly identified as originating from the suspects and later examination of the body-fluids evidence supported the rape allegation, for which they were later convicted.

The investigating officer was commended for his investigation but I received no mention. That was normal. I reminded myself that the important thing was that the offenders were caught and quickly. The events did, however, stick in my mind. Later as a manager I always tried to find ways of recognising the good work of committed and hard-working professionals. They may get paid for doing this, but doing well needs recognition, it cost nothing and inspires greater deeds.

Much later in my career as a manager, I would review all the laboratory submissions where the investigating detective thought the answer wasn't helpful. This was mainly to see how we could improve performance, perhaps improve our scene investigation and even alter the sorts of questions we posed for the scientists. On many occasions, the officer's unhappiness was caused by the fact that no evidence was found to link the suspect to the scene or that it actually eliminated them.

On one occasion I was intrigued by a case. A young man had been seen breaking a large shop window in the high street, but his attempt to remove a television was thwarted by the alarm and the appearance of a resident living above a shop opposite who duly called the police. The suspect ran off, but a young man fitting the offender's description was stopped in the next street. The police didn't like the account they got from him and decided to arrest him on suspicion of attempted burglary. Back at the police station the officers seized his clothing and also arranged for a hair combing sample to be taken, to see if there were any fragments of glass in his hair. Samples of glass were obtained from the frame of the window by a scene investigator who promptly attended the scene. Also it was observed, measured and recorded that the break was above head or chest level. This indicated that any glass on the offender would be most likely on head or upper clothing level. There might be glass on the uppers of the footwear but there was no sign that it had been kicked, and any glass found on the soles of the shoe might come from walking past the scene, a common and legitimate defence. The strongest evidence would be if there were small particles of glass on the head and upper clothing of the suspect, indicating that they were within a few metres of the shop window, or similar shop window, when it was broken.

Glass evidence is not as precise as DNA. Glass is generally classified into types and measured by refractive index (RI). This is the amount that a light beam is deflected when it is passed through it. In most cases it will not link the glass solely to a specific window, more likely to one of that type. That may be a sufficient evidential level. When a person stands in front of a breaking window they will be exposed to a shower of tiny particles. The higher the break and the closer they are to it will determine where these particles land on them. What is equally important is that these small particles of glass will fall off exposed skin within an hour and off most clothing within a few hours, only leaving a few fragments in particularly coarse cloth after a long period of time.

In this case, the samples were sent off to the lab: the glass control sample for comparison with any fragments found on the hair combing and the clothing of the suspect. The good news was that thirty fragments of glass were found in the hair combing of the suspect (that is difficult to explain in most circumstances) but the bad news was that none matched the control glass from the scene. The officer unhappily dismissed the case and there it would have stayed had I not reviewed it.

The presence of such a large quantity of fresh glass fragments in the hair of someone tells a recent story. I was about to enlighten the officer about what that story might be. I asked the officer to see if there were any other cases of burglary where a glass window had been broken. There was one. It was right in the next street. It had been reported a day or so after our original crime as the victim had been away. It was investigated by another detective. I suggested that the officer submit the glass samples from that scene to the laboratory, which he duly did. This time the glass matched and the officer's satisfaction increased. It was raised even more when he went to arrest the young suspect. He found an item of property from this second scene at his address. It seemed that, having committed this offence, the suspect hid the stolen property, returning to it later after his release for the first offence. This highlighted to the detective the need to review the answers from scene and laboratory investigations, ask what they mean. The answer is the answer, the question may be wrong. So ask another question. This was a lesson the detective learned and I was glad to be a part of his education, as I too had been educated in the past.

This is an aspect of reconstruction which is useful at the scene, to try and determine an offender's path or the sequence of events. It equally applies to reviewing what is understood about the crime when further information (such as laboratory results) is available.

Reviewing an investigation is a rolling process and needs to take place every time an answer comes back from the laboratory. Answers would inspire in me further questions until who, where, when and how was satisfactorily answered.

It wasn't all serious stuff though. Even in the darkest of moments there was a black humour which kept me in the real world. Finding the funny side of things would keep me and my colleagues human. So whenever there was tension or horror someone would always remind you of a funny incident. Throughout my career it was always my intention to ensure that I investigated crime without becoming a victim of it. By the very nature of the job I could expect to be present at the aftermath of the most awful crimes. This meant I always had a respect for my own safety.

The early 1980s on G Division was the time when the Irish Republican Army was at their most active. I often received reminders to check under my marked police van whenever I got into it, in case a bomb had been placed there. I always listened to the advice and checked. One morning I and my SOCO colleagues received another reminder. Mark Russell, one of the team, dismissed the warning as unnecessary worry. A few hours later, having examined a scene, he got back into his van and slammed the door. Immediately there was the mechanical whirring. Panic overcame him and fearing the worst, he jumped out of the van, ran across the road and dived head-first into a bush, with his hands behind his head. Lying there for a moment he realised that the whirring was still with him. Examining his pocket he found his electric shaver. He got up, nonchalantly dusted himself down in front of the viewing crowd and, with as much dignity as he could muster, he got back into his van and drove off.

6. Needle in a Haystack

'Armed robbery in progress.' The message came across the radio. Police officers dashed into the station yard and sped off at high speed to High Street North in Manor Park, east London.

I quickly made my way to the scene, which was a security vehicle parked outside a building society office. Within a few minutes I was there. Security guards had been transferring bags of cash from the security vehicle to the building society branch office. The guards had been approached by a group of men who made threats at gunpoint and snatched a bag of cash. A struggle had ensued but the offenders ran away and made their escape in a vehicle parked around the corner. Nobody got a description of the vehicle.

Normally at such a crime scene there is little to do. Perhaps a search of the ground to see if anything has been dropped and arrange for the clothing of the guards to be taken in case it could be examined for fibres from any clothing of a suspect seized at a later date.

That situation was different. A female witness who had seen the whole event came forward to say that during the struggle one of the suspects had fallen against the side of the security vehicle and that he had steadied himself with his hand.

I looked at the vehicle. It was very clean. As I made a quick visual examination along the side of the vehicle I immediately saw a glistening hand mark, complete with fingers and palm. It was still wet and it was in the general area in which the witness saw the offender fall against the vehicle. It was so wet that I was concerned that the application of aluminium powder with a fingerprint brush would wipe it away. It is very difficult to age finger marks but what made me believe that these marks were very fresh was the cleanliness of the vehicle (it appeared to have been washed very recently, and we could find out exactly when) and the fact that the marks were visible to the naked eye and appeared to be still moist.

The enhancement of finger marks using aluminium or similar type flake and granular powders is still the most common form of finding finger marks. A visual examination using a good light source should always precede the application of a powder as the latter is a relatively destructive technique. Any marks in dust or delicate material could be wiped away by the brushing with powder.

Finger marks are routinely left by the deposit of sweat from the tips of the fingers and palms. What makes them extremely useful in criminal investigations is that they leave the mark of the friction ridges from the fingers. All of which are unique to the individual donor. These marks can be classified and searched against fingerprint databases held by police forces.

Marks in sweat are generally clear and dry slowly. They leave a deposit in salt and amino acids and other body secretions which cannot be seen with the naked eye. Anyone looking at a clean glass which they have held will see some finger marks, but these generally dry clear over a period of time. There are chemical methods of enhancing salts and amino acids and such like, but the mechanical method of developing marks by lightly applying fine aluminium powder with the stroking action of a brush is the commonest method of enhancement. Referred to by those less in the know as 'dusting', the technique calls for the light application of powder using a squirrel hair or glass fibre brush in one hand whilst holding a good light in the other.

This technique generally only works on solid, smooth, non-porous surfaces such as glass or painted doors and walls. The operator should wear a mask to prevent the inhalation of the powder. This is to prevent 'Silver Bogey Syndrome' which anyone who has used this technique for any length of time will recognise. After the mark is developed it should be cleaned out with a clean brush, again brushing along the lines of ridges to ensure the mark is as clear as possible without any damage to the detailed ridge ending and bifurcations.

The marks can then be photographed but it is more likely they will be lifted with a special clear adhesive tape which can then be preserved for posterity on a sheet of clear and thick acetate film. Details of the location and date can then be written on the sheet to aid identification and presentation at court later.

So there was no doubt in my mind that the position and condition of the marks which I found on the side of the security vehicle were highly significant.

I had to wait a while for the marks to dry before carefully applying the powder. The marks immediately glistened and were easily developed. I continued to search the whole of the side of the vehicle, in case the witness was mistaken in the area in which the suspect fell and also in case there were more finger marks. There were no more.

I recovered the finger and palm marks with adhesive tape, placing them carefully on an acetate sheet, adding my notes and completing my examination report. I arranged for the fingerprints of the security guards to be taken so that they could be eliminated as the donors of the marks.

That evening the marks were on their way to the Fingerprint Branch at New Scotland Yard. It was only a matter of weeks before the marks were identified. A man was quickly arrested and interviewed. Following enquiries by detectives the man was charged with armed robbery.

By the time of the trial I had been transferred to the Flying Squad and was now predominantly examining and investigating armed robbery scenes.

The trial was held at Wood Green Crown Court, which was undergoing extensive refurbishment at the time. The building was an imposing, classic Gothic style, but built within the last century. The number of courtrooms had been significantly reduced and parking was a problem in the cramped car parks and busy side roads.

It was not thought that the trial would be long. The guards and lady witness were the first to give their evidence. I and the fingerprint expert who matched the mark to the now accused defendant were the main prosecution witnesses.

The court buildings were extremely cramped, with little or no space for the separation of witnesses, prosecution and defence lawyers. In fact our courtroom was immediately inside the main door, with only a small passage for all other visitors to the court to pass by.

I checked the court list pinned to the door to see who the presiding judge was. This was not only out of interest but the title would determine how I would address him or her in the court. A high court judge would be referred to as 'My Lord' or 'My Lady' according to gender. A justice would be referred to as 'Your Honour'. If all else failed, and to break the monotony of referring to the judge by title, just plain sir or madam would do. Generally it is the barristers who ask the questions, with the presiding judge clarifying points when needed. But whoever asked the question my reply was always directed to the judge and I finished with the words My Lord, My Lady or Your Honour, as appropriate.

I was called to give my evidence mid morning. The courtroom was small and crowded. The witness box faced the jury only a few yards directly in front of me. Two barristers, both wearing traditional white wigs and black gowns were to one side and the defendant sat in a railed box next to a prison officer. The judge, also wigged and gowned, sat in a high prominent position next to the witness box where I stood. I didn't take much notice of the jury other than a 'note to self' to make sure that, although answering the counsel and the judge's questions, I included them in eye contact when giving my answers. After all, it was they who had to understand the evidence and make their decision based on it. As events unfolded, perhaps I should have made a better note of them.

Having taken the oath, I was asked by the prosecution barrister to explain what I had done and what I had found. This was a simple enough task and I followed the course of my written statement, although I was not allowed to read from it. At the beginning of my evidence, as I normally did, I asked the permission of the judge to allow me to refer to my notes. The usual question, 'When were these notes made?' received my normal and honest reply, 'At the time of my examination, My Lord'.

I described my search of the scene. I stated that my attention was drawn to the side of the vehicle where the offender, whoever he was, fell. This was to avoid my giving 'hearsay' evidence, that is the evidence of another (in this case the lady witness) which I had not directly seen myself. So 'my attention was drawn to' was just fine.

My description of the marks included how they were easily seen, and readily developed. I was asked if the marks were fresh. I would normally be very cautious about answering such a question, but based on my experience and the observation that the vehicle was clean, I stated that in my opinion they were. I added that the marks were likely made since the last time the vehicle was washed, as any thorough washing process would have removed such delicate material.

The questions of the prosecution barrister finished just as lunch approached. This is sometimes referred to as 'evidence in chief' and is the main part of your evidence. What was to follow was the cross-examination by the defence barrister, aimed at testing the evidence on the defendant's behalf. Once that is finished the prosecution barrister is allowed to ask more questions to clarify any points from the defence questioning. But at that stage no new evidence is allowed to be introduced, it is just clarification of the evidence in chief and the cross-examination.

My evidence in chief at an end, the judge decided to take a natural break and to call me back immediately after lunch. However, the judge warned me that as I was between my questioning by the prosecution barrister and the cross-examination by the defence, I should not discuss the case with any of my colleagues during the lunch break, and particularly those who might be called to give evidence later. It is not an uncommon warning, but I took his words seriously as he clearly thought I was going to be tested by the defence after the break and didn't want any situation to arise which might jeopardise the process, prejudice the accused and call for a retrial.

So lunch with my colleagues was out of the question. The decision was then where do I go? I wanted to be careful not to accidentally bump into anyone and exchange even a single word which might be observed and construed as disobeying the judge's words.

I noticed that the defence and prosecution barristers were heading for the communal tea room, just a few paces along the corridor, so I decided to follow. I can't remember much about the prosecution barrister, other than he wore a gown and wig. I do remember the defence barrister, which is probably because they are the ones who will question your evidence and put you through your paces. The defence barrister in this case was a kindly looking man in his thirties. He was pleasant enough and a shock of blond and ginger hair protruded from under his wig. He appeared friendly, but he had a job to do. Due to the refurbishment work, the tea room was truly communal. There were no separate rooms for barristers, witnesses, friends and family, those defendants not in custody, or jurors, for all I could see. It was crowded but I stood in the queue behind the opposing barristers. Having purchased a sandwich and a cup of tea, I proceeded to a table directly in front of where the two barristers had sat and in their full view. Safe, I thought. Whilst they chatted I sat alone, exchanging the occasional but unconcerned glance.

For nearly an hour I sat there, safely out of harm's way and not in danger of even remotely speaking to anyone about the case. The smiling nods of counsel indicated to me that they knew what I was doing.

When they rose after lunch and walked the few yards back to the courtroom, I followed closely behind and I waited outside the court with them for the doors to open and for us all to be allowed back in. We were right by the main front doors to the court building and a stream of people were walking past on their way back to the courtrooms. To my surprise a complete stranger, a lumbering man with a ruddy face and carrying a brown plastic bag walked up to me and commented on how well I was giving my evidence. 'You are doing great in there,' he said, nodding towards the courtroom. 'Oh, thank you,' I replied, not understanding who he was or why he was saying it. He walked off as quickly as he had appeared. The two barristers broke into immediate laughter. I didn't get the joke, but it wouldn't be long.

Within a minute I was called back into the witness box and it was then that the judge recalled the jury. They marched in and took their seats. The last juror in was the ruddy-faced individual who had spoken to me only minutes before outside the courtroom. I got the joke now, but I wasn't laughing, my heart sank. The man then proceeded to take a swig from a bottle inside his brown paper bag.

The defence barrister asked to approach the bench and then asked for the jury to be removed so he could discuss a point of law. The judge agreed and so the jurors marched out as quickly as they had marched in.

The defence barrister then described to His Lordship what

had gone on immediately outside the courtroom, courteously including that I had sat alone and in his view for the whole preceding lunch hour. I was asked if I knew the juror, to which I replied no and then explained what he had said and my reply.

I was asked to step outside the court whilst the juror was called. I understand that the account he gave was less pleasing to the judge, compounded by the contents of the brown paper bag, which clearly contained orange, but probably also included some gin!

The juror was discharged and the judge decided to continue with trial with eleven jurors as is his prerogative. It would save a retrial and all of us going through our evidence with a new jury. The judge could not afford to lose another juror.

When the remaining eleven jurors returned to their seats he explained that one of their number would not be continuing. There were some understanding glances.

Our little lunchtime episode over, we returned to the trial proper and my cross-examination by the defence barrister. It was a courteous but rigorous set of questions. There appeared to be no doubt that the finger and palm marks found on the vehicle belonged to the defendant but the defence's case appeared to be that the marks were deposited there at some other time and location. It was a fair and honest point, and I was careful not to overstate what was fact and be cautious with my opinion.

The experience of examining many scenes over a long period of time can build a database in your mind. You have to be careful that this is not corrupted by assumptions that damage your view.

On the question of 'How fresh is a finger mark?' there are rarely occasions when the answer can be accurate and specific. If a mark were placed on a newspaper or letter which bore a date then that might indicate the mark was made between that date and the date it was recovered. A mark in blood might indicate that it was deposited whilst the blood was still wet, useful if that time were known. Finger marks in sweat dry out in time and in hot conditions.

All I could say in this case was that the finger marks which I found were clearly visible and still wet when I arrived, to the extent that I needed to let them dry, fearing that I could wipe them away as I tried to develop them so that they could be recovered. And dry in my presence they did. The vehicle itself was clean and I suggested that the marks were made since the vehicle had been washed. The detectives were covering this point, as I had suggested they should do. So, were the marks fresh? Yes, based on my experience and observations within the parameters I had described.

Defence counsel then suggested that I had only examined the small area described by the lady witness who saw the offender fall. He went on to suggest that had I examined further areas of the security vehicle I would have found a large number of fingermarks from many other people who had recently touched it. My statement and evidence in chief contained the factual description of the vehicle and where I had found the finger marks. My notes contained a lot more. To his surprise, I stated that I had examined the whole of the pavement side of the vehicle and had found no more finger marks. The sense of incredulity passed over his expression. His eyes frowned and he said, 'But Mr Millen, why did you do that? It would be like looking for a needle in a haystack.' My reply was swift and for once it came to me straightaway. 'Sir, I spend most of my professional life looking for needles in haystacks,' I said. Shocked and surprised by my retort, he sat down with a slump. He appeared mortally wounded. It is unusual for a barrister to ask a question to which he does not know the answer. But this had done it for him.

My evidence finished and with no re-examination by the prosecution counsel, I left the court.

The defendant was found guilty of the robbery. He wasn't

the only one who probably didn't sleep too well that night. I trust one barrister at least was polishing up his technique. As for the ruddy-faced juror with the gin and orange takeaway, he probably didn't care.

7. The Murder of Dr Goss

Friday evening was traditionally a debrief night in the CID office at Forest Gate Police Station. It usually involved a drink and was a good way to unwind and get to know the close colleagues you worked with.

The CID office at Forest Gate was on the first floor of the small Victorian building. The office stretched almost the whole length of the building. My desk was immediately inside the door, and overlooked the small rear yard. The detective inspectors (DIs), of which there were two, shared an office sectioned off on one side.

It was early evening, the rush hour traffic still clogging the Romford Road outside and the 'debrief' was going well. A uniformed officer came into the office and shattered the atmosphere.

Uniformed officers had been called to a house where two bodies were found and a man wielding a blood-stained hammer had been arrested. He too was injured.

The office scattered into action. I grabbed my folder and went straight to my van to make my way to the scene. The traffic was awful. The scene was only a mile or so away but it seemed to take me ages to get through the traffic which clogged up all the side roads.

When I got to the scene, the road was properly cordoned off. Some further details were available. 'It was alleged' (a good old police phrase) that the man under arrest had a severe mental disorder. His name was Alan Wood. His wife (Alice) had called their doctor to visit him at their home. It appeared that for some reason the suspect had then attacked his wife and the doctor with a hammer. Both had received serious hammer wounds to the head. The suspect's wife was dead at the scene. The doctor, although seriously injured, was still alive.

Dr Goss was a well-known medical practitioner in the area. She had run her surgery, serving the people of Forest Gate and Stratford for over twenty years. She was well respected.

The man had been arrested but, given his condition, he was on his way to Whipps Cross Hospital. So too was the injured doctor, but at this stage it was doubtful that she would live.

The scene was preserved, the initial medical response complete and no one else needed to go into the scene at that time. Following a review of what we knew with the DI, I suggested that an immediate priority was to deal with the female victim and the suspect at the hospital. This was based on the fact that the scene could wait (nothing was going to change immediately) but the events unfolding at the hospital could not. I summoned help to attend the scene and then made my way to Whipps Cross as soon as I could. Ideally, I would need a colleague so that one of us could deal with the female victim and one with the suspect. The reason for this is to ensure that there is no contamination between areas which may need examination and comparison later. I did not have that time or luxury. I decided to review that when I got there and see if I could get someone to take steps to advise others so that any evidence was properly preserved for examination later.

When I arrived at the Accident and Emergency department at Whipps Cross the atmosphere was highly charged and sombre. The hospital's Emergency unit covered a large part of northeast London and was always busy. Now it was full of police as well as medical staff.

Dr Goss was well known to the staff at Whipps Cross, after all she was a doctor, one of their own. I identified myself to the medical staff. Both Dr Goss and Alan Wood were in separate cubicles and were being dealt with by different medical staff. This was an important first step to ensure there was no contamination. However, if the paramedics who attended had dealt with both of them at the scene and then transported both in the same ambulance to the hospital, there would be some contamination. I had yet to find that out. Even if they had, we would have to consider what it meant in the light of what we could or needed to prove. There was a lot of action going on. There was serious concern for the condition of Dr Goss. The looks on the faces of the medical staff said it all. They too were in shock. I didn't want to interfere in any aspect of their work or distract them in any way, but I was going to be ready to pick up the pieces as soon as the time was appropriate. Whatever forensic issues I had, I would have to wait for the medical team to finish their work and stabilise their patients. I asked to see the medical staff dealing with Dr Goss and I was directed to her cubicle. I decided I would just stand at the entrance to the cubicle so as not to intrude and also to limit any risk of contamination as I still had to deal with Alan Wood. Drawing back the curtain, I found the cubicle full of medical staff standing around Dr Goss's motionless body. All the attending medical staff were silent and there was little activity. Looking at Dr Goss I immediately realised why. She had a massive head injury, her brain was exposed and there was nothing the medical staff could do. She was alive, but it was only a matter of time, very little time before she died. There was a look of helplessness on the faces of the nurses. Their professional armour breached by the emotion of the situation.

I advised the doctor dealing with Dr Goss that we would need to take some steps to preserve the forensic evidence once she had died, but then I left quietly, respecting the tragedy of the situation that was in its final moments.

As I made my way to the cubicle where Alan Wood was, the doors to the unit flew open and in marched a tall man in his thirties. Scurrying, he looked around frantically. There was fixed horrified gaze on his face. It was Dr Goss's son, himself a doctor and he was about to hear the terrible news about his mother.

I continued to Alan Wood's cubicle. As I opened the curtain I found him lying on a couch, with a nurse attending to him. There were three uniformed police officers with him. He was, after all, under arrest. He was on the edge of unconsciousness. Either through his apparent mental condition, drink or drugs, or possibly all three, he was an extremely troubled man. Occasionally, the officers would have to hold him as he roused. His condition was not life-threatening, but he needed care.

Information from the scene and what we were observing at the hospital indicated that, either before the attack or immediately after, Alan Wood had consumed the contents of a tablet bottle. It was not known exactly how many tablets he had taken as the bottle was now empty. His lack of consciousness indicated to the medical staff that he was under the influence of some drugs and they would have to take action.

One of the uniformed police officers there was a friend, John Cronin. I had known John before he joined the police. He was a friend of my young sister-in-law. John was a big jovial man, always with a smile on his face.

I wanted to recover Alan Wood's clothing as soon as practical. There was also the sticky subject of consent. He was under arrest, but he was also unconscious. The information we had about the whole event was hearsay. That is, it was yet to be determined. As far as I was concerned, I wanted to help establish the truth. For all I knew, the story on which we were basing our actions could be completely wrong. Alan too may have been a victim of an as yet unknown suspect. Taking samples without consent could be seen as contrary to the Police and Criminal Evidence Act. Although not law at that time, it was due to be so within a few months. We were undertaking to work within its guidelines as, for the first time, it offered protection for the rights of detained persons and the police who dealt with them correctly.

Although Alan Wood could not consent due to his condition, recovering evidence could help establish what happened, what was the truth. It could prove or disprove any allegations. Failure to take action to recover this evidence would make it harder to do so. We might not be allowed to use such samples if consent were not subsequently given by Alan Wood or his legal representative to use them. We also had to be careful that we were not accused of assault by taking the samples without his consent. I explained the situation to the senior nurse and to John and his colleagues. I suggested that we (the police) would advise and help recover the clothing and other samples, some which we would need and some medical staff would need and some we would both need. In order to allow any legal argument regarding the right of the police to take and retain these items, they would all be preserved but left in the secure possession of the hospital staff. This I confirmed with the medical staff and hospital administrator. It was a tightrope walk between the rights of the unconscious Alan Wood and the quest for evidence, evidence which I hoped would establish what had happened, and establish the truth about the events and even the medical condition of Wood at the time of the attack.

At the very least, I would be seeking to retain Wood's clothing, any blood stains on him (he had no wounds himself) and samples of blood grouping, drugs and urine. Normally these samples would be taken by a forensic medical examiner, but the casualty officer was happy to assist. Any external swabs I could direct or take myself, mindful still that I had no consent, although I did obtain, by phone, the authority of a superintendent. This allowed me to take external (non-intimate) samples of a suspect in a serious arrestable offence, where evidence was likely to prove or disprove involvement. It gave me some protection, although that could be tested in court.

The medical staff indicated to me that they wanted to pump

out Alan Wood's stomach. This seemed like an opportunity to establish not only if he had taken any drugs but what they were and how much. I think when I indicated that I wanted a sample they thought that I wanted just a small pot. I had decided that I wanted the lot. This I found out was likely to be a couple of gallons as they would force water into his stomach through a tube in his mouth and then pump the contents out. I quickly obtained three large clean glass jars from my van. They were designed for debris from fire scenes but they would do for this purpose.

As we began, we got the sad but inevitable news that Dr Goss had died. It was a sobering moment. I ensured that her body would be preserved so that we could examine her and prepare for a post-mortem examination. The Home Office pathologist was going to be busy.

The dynamics of the room changed when the stomach pumping began. I realised that John and his two colleagues moved from around Wood's head to his feet, whilst the nurse and I found ourselves at the business end of the procedure. I glanced at John and got a knowing smile. We got on with it. We filled nearly all three jars before the nurse was happy that there was nothing left in his stomach.

I recovered some blood-staining from Wood's forearms as well as his clothing. The medical staff also took the blood samples for blood grouping and also one for drugs. I also managed to persuade the doctors to take a second blood sample for drugs an hour after the first. This, I hoped, would help determine the effect of the drugs on Wood's action at the time of the attack. Had he taken the drugs before or after? I thought two samples with a known time in between might determine the length of time the drugs had been in his system, indicating whether the levels were increasing or decreasing in his blood. Further timed samples would be better still, but that would be asking a little too much. A urine sample was also needed but that would have to wait until Wood awoke or the medical staff decided to empty his bladder by other means if he remained unconscious. Two blood samples for drugs was one more than the toxicologist normally got.

As the events unfolded in the following days, the story was confirmed. There was no objection to the examination of all the items I had taken and so I submitted them to the forensic science laboratory.

Wood pleaded guilty to the manslaughter of his wife and their family doctor on the grounds of diminished responsibility. His plea was accepted. The toxicological examination of the blood and stomach contents helped his defence. He had been under the influence of his medication at the time of the attack and he had tried to kill himself after realising what he had done.

It was a tragic story for his family and the family of Dr Goss. Wood was committed to a secure hospital. Within two years he was seen in a main shopping area where someone recognised him. He had been released back into the community. There was a lot of strong opinion about it, and I too felt, at the very least, surprise. I reminded myself that, whatever the judgement of the court, his subsequent treatment and release was the job of others. Mine was to help establish the truth and I think I did that.

8. The Flying Squad

I used to watch the TV series of *The Sweeney* during my years at school and college. The stories, involving fast cars, hardened detectives and tough criminals within the underworld, were popular and entertaining but seemed a million miles away. I had no ambition to become a police officer and so it never occurred to me that one day I would be a part of the real thing.

The Flying Squad had been formed in the 1920s within the Metropolitan Police. It was an élite group of detectives who were given the job of investigating violent crime. The mobile and proactive nature of the squad with its wide geographical remit caused a *Daily Mirror* reporter to refer to it as a flying squad of detectives and so the name stuck.

In good old cockney rhyming slang it became known as the Sweeney, after Sweeney Todd, the fictitious demon barber of Fleet Street.

In the 1970s the Squad's role was redefined to investigate the increases in armed robbery, kidnappings and kindred offences. It proactively targeted those gangs who committed armed robbery rather than waiting for them to commit the offences and catch them after. It became the Central Robbery Squad but this was not a name to match the romantic and macho Flying Squad which it soon re-adopted.

The Sweeney immortalised the Squad for a generation. DI Jack Regan and his sidekick Detective Sergeant Carter inspired young boys and coppers alike. They were earthy and tough with laddish lifestyles but they were also professional and honourable. And so it was in real life.

In the mid 1980s the Squad was C8 Branch with its main office at New Scotland Yard. Four branch offices in the north, south, east and west of London each contained about fifty officers. They were mainly detectives but there were also also surveillance officers and the famed Flying Squad drivers who were the cream of the Met's Class 1 drivers. It was their job to get the detectives into the thick of the action as fast and as safely as possible, which they did regularly with heroic bravery and skill.

For over sixty years the Flying Squad had targeted London's most dangerous and ruthless criminals, those who carry guns and commit violent armed robbery. The stakes were high with terms of imprisonment of fourteen years and upwards for those caught.

In reality it was called just 'the Squad'. There was only one and everyone knew it. In the early 1980s the detectives and drivers were joined for the first time by civilian scenes of crime officers, of which I was to become one.

By 1982 two scenes of crime officers were attached to the Squad's five offices covering the four corners and central area of London. Their success meant that by 1984 each of the four outer offices had their own with a manager based at the central office at the New Scotland Yard. I eagerly applied for the northeast London office post, but it was given to a SOCO who was a retired police officer many years my senior. He didn't last too long in the post and I didn't have to apply the second time. I was given the job. It would not be the last time I was second choice for a job, but that didn't hold me back and it was to prove both enjoyable and successful, with a lot of hard work thrown in.

My appointment to the Squad was probably hastened by my performance in a case which occurred in my last year at City Road. The Squad descended on City Road Police Station with four prisoners in their custody. The men had been arrested for conspiracy to rob and I got actively involved with the examination of the suspects. This involved the taking of hair combing samples amongst other things. When it came to the trial at the Central Criminal Court in London, I was asked by the prosecution barrister to demonstrate how the sample was taken. As I stood in the witness box I showed them how I opened out a kit containing a sheet of white paper and a comb, the teeth of which were seeded with a strip of moistened lint. Showing how I would ask the subject to bend their head forward, I bent my own head forward and demonstrated the thorough combing action, allowing fibres to be caught in the comb or fall onto the sheet. Placing the comb in the paper, I folded the paper around it before placing it in a bag. Looking up I could see all the court, the judge, barristers, defendants, jurors and officials laughing, many with tears steaming down their faces. My bald head had been the focus of everyone's amusement as I demonstrated how to take a hair combing. Wiping his eyes, the judge composed himself and apologised for himself and on behalf of the court. I replied that I quite understood, but offered that I 'hadn't resorted to wearing a wig yet'. The judge's face changed abruptly and, lowering his head, he looked over the top of his spectacles and told me, 'I'll allow you to get away with that, Mr Millen.' Everyone except the judge and barristers continued to laugh.

The greatest prize for the Squad was catching a team of robbers 'on the pavement', as they committed their offence literally outside a bank or similar premises. Months, sometime years of investigation, surveillance and planning would turn the robbers' world upside down. The adrenalin rush felt by all those who witnessed such events would never be forgotten. And they would be accompanied sometimes by the bravest and often seemingly reckless pieces of police action, when unarmed police officers would tackle and arrest armed criminals.

The Squad detectives all had experience on local police divisions and all had talent and ability. There was, however, a core of the finest, most talented and hard-working investigators I was ever to come across in one place. I was moving from a minor league to the top division and I knew I had to work hard and competently.

The élite and hard view which some people had of the Squad drew its problems. There would be allegations of corruption. The allegations are understandable. When police officers deal with hardened criminals, use informants and recover large quantities of cash the allegations will not be far away. History had shown that some detective succumbed to these temptations or abused their power and position. However, that is not an excuse to abandon the police response. It would take committed, honest and ruthless detectives to overcome even the hint of allegations and demonstrate to anyone who needed to know that the job was done right.

I quickly realised that my role as the only civilian scene of crime officer attached to the north-east London branch office of the Squad was to have many facets. Yes, I was to examine and investigate every armed robbery scene, getaway vehicle and prisoner I could get to. But there was more. I would have to use as a resource all the officers on the Squad as well as SOCOs based locally on division. As well as recovering evidence, I would have to encourage and ensure the preservation of evidence recovered by others. Giving advice and instruction was the best way to counter allegations of corruption or just plain poor practice and engineer it out. So items would be preserved, labelled and sealed and these facts documented at the very earliest opportunity. Through this we would not only preserve evidence but preserve the integrity of the investigators. Poor practice and the allegation of or opportunity for accidental contamination or deliberate planting would be removed. Sometimes it would be a matter of protecting officers from their own eagerness, such as arresting a suspect and then going to the crime scene before it was preserved or examined.

Key to this was dealing with 'prisoners'. Now I could use the more politically correct term of 'detained' or 'arrested persons', but prisoner was the accurate term used at the time for some-one in police custody. For those merely suspected of a crime the word 'suspect' is accurate. Defendant refers to someone who has been charged with an offence and will stand trial. I remember one prisoner being unhappy at being referred to as such by a police officer. His reply, 'I'm not a prisoner, I'm a free man,' is a direct quote from the Patrick McGoohan character in the TV series *The Prisoner*.

The prompt and full examination of prisoners was always an important priority. Firstly, clothing and samples had to be taken to stop any loss of evidence. Secondly, the prisoner would be examined before interview so that they could not use any opportunity to destroy evidence as the case against them became clear. Finally, by securing and preserving this evidence at an early stage, the chance of contamination and planting is removed. In my first few weeks on the Squad, whilst at a police station dealing with a prisoner, I overheard one officer say, 'Boy wonder has sealed all the exhibits.' Well, I was the boy wonder and I was going to do that every time and at the earliest opportunity. I thought that my time on the Squad might be short lived, but that was not the case. The officer who I suspected made the remarks was soon moved. It would be naïve to think that there are not corrupt officers. Discipline and professionalism, however, will thwart and expose them. Over the coming years I would demonstrate to many, if anyone was in any doubt, that by doing the job in a professional manner the result followed. Some of the hardest and most ruthless of detectives would equally champion the high standards which I proposed.

For almost four years I worked out of the back of a car. I had an office and a desk back at the Flying Squad office and I would spend a lot of time there. It was, however, the need to be mobile and work in any environment that made the nature of the job, demanding, challenging and very enjoyable. The office did have one amusing aspect. Its name was 'the Gannetry'. It was a large room suitable for the collation of sealed exhibits. Occasionally, I might examine items (if appropriate within the conditions) on an examination bench to confirm a description or make a search. This would normally be to screen a large number of clothing items from a single location (important to avoid contamination) for traces of blood prior to submitting positive items to the lab for detailed examination. One particular operation codenamed 'Gannet' (the name picked randomly from a book of birds) generated a large number of exhibits which occupied my attention and that of a small number of detectives for a long time. Being a keen birdwatcher myself, I started referring to the room as the Gannetry (as a place where gannets roost) and it stuck. Some years later I returned to visit the building; all my former colleagues had long since gone. One label on the door and another on the alarm panel caught my attention. It referred to 'Gannetry'. 'Everyone calls the room the Gannetry but we don't know why,' one detective told me. I just smiled.

Examining vehicles would also prove an important part of the job. Often the way in which a vehicle was stolen, prepared and stored as a getaway car would say a lot about an armed gang. So I spent a lot of time examining vehicles. To many scene investigators this was seen as a chore. For me it was a challenge. The benefit of personally investigating most of the vehicles used in robberies over a large geographical area was that you could build up a picture based not only on obvious items but on small nuances. The way the vehicle was stolen, the way its stolen identity was disguised told a story. I would also look over the examinations made by colleagues when I was not available. However, this wasn't too often. A vehicle once preserved could wait a day if necessary.

On a cold evening just before Christmas in 1986 two armed robbers attacked a red Post Office security van which had been collecting and delivering high-value gold to the jewellery trade in the Kings Cross area. The gang was well informed. As the van stopped at a business premises in City Road the three post-men, all approaching sixty years of age, opened the cab door and were confronted by two armed masked men. They heard violent and very loud threats and one of the robbers opened fire. Almost immediately all three postal workers had been hit and were immobile. This completely halted any hope of the robbers getting any money as it was all safely locked in the rear security compartment. The robbers fled empty handed.

The postal workers had serious gunshot injuries, but by luck all survived. Between them they thought that no more than three shots had been fired. They had just heard a maximum of three bangs around the shouts and confusion. It appeared at first that each bullet had hit and gone through at least one person, as some had entry and exit wounds.

I had information relayed to me from the hospital where they were being treated. I went to the scene and made an examination of the area around the security vehicle. It was dark, not ideal conditions. The suspects had got away in a stolen vehicle and that had yet to be found. I found one shell case from an auto-matic pistol. This is the part which is ejected from an automatic weapon once a shot is discharged and the gun reloaded. These shell cases had a rim which is pulled out by lever hooks to eject them. They are noticeably different from revolver shell cases, which have no such rim. Revolver cases are only removed by the user opening the revolving chamber and allowing the cases to fall out, often on the floor. It is for this reason that only when automatic pistols are used are you guaranteed to have a chance of finding spent cases.

The spent case I found was outside the cab door on the floor. There was a fair amount of blood and gunshot damage inside the cab which would take a long time to examine. I was not happy to undertake the examination in the street. I secured the vehicle and waited until it could be towed to the yard at City Road Police Station, a short distance away.

Once there, I made a detailed examination of the cab. With

constant updates from the hospital it was clear that they had recovered four bullets from the injured men. My examination revealed a further two. One was a different calibre to the rest and indicated that it was from an automatic weapon. So it was clear that two weapons were used, both discharged and one was an automatic. The other could be a revolver; the fact that only one shell case had been found suggested that the other weapon was likely to be a revolver. Most revolvers hold at least six bullets. It was likely that this weapon was responsible for at least five of the bullets.

During my examination I was joined by Mark Godfree who was the SOCO 1, and my immediate line manager. He came along to see how I was doing and to assess my performance. By the time he arrived I had already begun to reconstruct the shooting, but I was not happy. The victims had only heard three shots, but we had already accounted for six, from at least two weapons. Even more confusing was the number of exit wounds on the victims and areas of damage inside the cab. I carefully reconstructed the shots and this seemed to fit a total of six shots. By now Mark had forgotten he was there to assess me and rolled up his sleeves to get involved. I wasn't happy with a total of six shots. Looking again we managed to account for all six but there was a final piece of damage which could be a ricochet on the door and frame edge but could also be another hole. If this was the case there would be another bullet in there somewhere. With the Post Office security manager present we opened the secure door and there, in the runner of the sliding door, was a seventh bullet. Elated by the successful reconstruction, Mark and I danced a jig around in the yard to the bemusement of the security manager.

Having completed our examination, it was clear that the valuable contents of the van were intact. In fact no attempt had been made to physically remove them. Shortly before dawn I told the Post Office security manager we were finished with the van. A standby crew got in and drove off. As it disappeared with its valuable cargo Mark said to me, 'You do know those guys, don't you?' Luckily for him (and for my assessment) I did. I had already obtained the authority to release the vehicle to the manager as soon as my examination was complete.

The first few months on the Squad were busy and breathtaking. I was using every bit of my training and experience in everything I did. As the only specialist in my role at my Squad office, I had the opportunity to advise and influence the way investigations developed. My input concerning the evidential potential of cases and how that evidence could be secured was always welcome and quickly became expected. I never wanted to say, 'Well, I thought of that,' after something had gone wrong. A colleague had made that unfortunate remark at another office. He didn't last too long. So I made sure my voice was heard clearly at the earliest opportunity. Almost always my advice was taken and acted upon. It may seem strange that it wasn't universally accepted. Not for any unethical reason, you must understand, but because of clear investigative needs. Often after an armed robbery an item is recovered which may potentially contain some forensic evidence and need some search to evaluate where it needs to go. It may also have some recognition potential. The press are only interested in the case in the first few hours or days so the chance to show some item and appeal for witnesses who might know who owned it, or where it came from, is important. Examinations are slow and the press lose interest quickly. So the investigator might forgo the forensic evidence in favour of a quick response from potential witnesses. It is the detectives' call, it's their case.

The long hours I worked and the amount of overtime I built up was a source of ribbing and perhaps concern amongst my managers. When I announced that my wife was pregnant with our second child, one manager jokingly suggested that, according to my overtime sheets, I had not been home. According to him, my daughter's conception had occurred during busy periods at work. She was born in a busy period too. I fondly remember that she was conceived in (Operation) Pisces and born in (Operation) Taurus.

Working on the Squad also meant that I could not use a marked police van, such as I had done when I was a divisional SOCO. So I was given a mileage allowance to use my own car, which was fitted with a police radio. My patch was north-east London, my boss, Mark Godfree, covered the whole of London. By rights, he claimed, he should get a higher mileage allowance than me as he should incur more miles at work. Whenever I called him to tell him I was off to some distant part of the south-east of England on an operation he remarked he would have to drive around the M25 a few times to catch up. When I eventually left the Met in 1992, I tried to present my car keys to my boss, saying that they should be given to the Commissioner. By my reckoning he had paid off the car at least once.

During my time on the Squad, I was blessed to work with a team of gifted and professional forensic scientists at the Metropolitan Police Forensic Science Laboratory and fingerprint identification experts at New Scotland Yard. Although I delivered the crime scene investigation, it was they who delivered the forensic science and fingerprint evidence. They were a part of the team and the success of the investigations.

I took a great deal of time preparing the laboratory submissions to make their job as easy as possible. The investigations were often more complicated than murder investigations. The great bulk of the laboratory work fell on the forensic biologists Ann Priston, Geoff Roe, Liz Wilson and Dave Scaysbrook who made a massive contribution. I remember one statement being received and served on the defence eleven months after the arrest. It gave twenty-four areas of independent corroboration in support of the police case. That very night two defendants decided it was too much and mounted a successful escape from their high-security prison.

In other cases, Robin Keely and Geoff Warman examined

hundreds of items for firearms residues, and Pam Hamer examined footwear and the occasional tooth mark. There wasn't a member of the Gun Room team who was not involved in Flying Squad cases. The number of cases was great and so was the quality of their examinations. Enda Ayres and his fingerprint expert colleagues at Team 9 of the Fingerprint Branch at New Scotland Yard had every right to groan when I walked in the door or they heard my voice on the phone. Long before the computerised fingerprint search facilities common today, marks had to be searched manually with what seemed unending permutations. Team 9 always rose to the challenge and, although armed robbers went out of their way not to leave finger marks, my crime scene colleagues found them and Team 9 had a sound success rate in identifying them.

Armed robbers are, by their very nature, hardened criminals. Unlike those who assault or murder out of plain evil or malice, their goal is serious financial gain. This focus they share with terrorists (who commit crime for political gain), and they plan, often well. Unlike terrorists, those who commit armed robbery have often been through the criminal justice mill. They may have served apprenticeships committing lesser crime, learning how to avoid detection, although that is never totally possible. Even when they think they are ahead of the game, there is always the ability of the police to be yet one step ahead of them. One team of robbers under surveillance were noticeable by their clothing, plain and common. They had been caught by valuable fibres evidence in a previous case some years before and so they tried to limit the chance of detection by wearing clothes with low amounts of transfer and low evidential value. The Flying Squad detectives got to hear about this and told me. I contacted the Traps and Markers section of the Metropolitan Police Laboratory. They had a range of markers developed for other uses. With the help of two dedicated scientists, Brian Gibbins and Anne Welch, we adapted these markers to invisibly stain the getaway car the suspects had hidden away. Its whereabouts were known to the police. The use of markers is extremely delicate as it is effectively a method of positive contamination. The marker itself is specifically prepared and formulated for the case. It is unique. Once deployed, the source must be returned to the laboratory so no trace exists except on the target vehicle and whatever it comes into contact with. So as a team we developed the marker and decided where it was to be applied to show the most evidential contact between suspects and stolen vehicle. The presence of the marker and other characteristics of it would be incriminating, provided there was discipline in how the vehicle and potential suspects were handled. On the first occasion I had used this technology the lab supplied me with a white one-piece suit, crime-scene style, to avoid contamination. When I explained that I was going to enter a stolen car, parked in a quiet but still public east London street within sight of the suspect's house, the penny dropped. With their help I used suitable dark disposable overalls. I was protected by armed officers whilst I marked the car. Once a stolen car is found by the police it is no longer considered stolen. The Squad had the authority not to recover this vehicle because of the serious offence for which the officers believed it was going to be used. This was an ideal opportunity for the police to be one step ahead in a potentially major crime. Once I had completed my marking, the residual marker and all the other materials which I had used were taken straight to the laboratory.

On a later occasion I had to mark another vehicle, this time parked up in a small lock-up garage overlooked by a block of flats. Again with the authority of a chief police officer and with armed officers covering me, I entered the small garage to mark the stolen vehicle inside. The marking was not a problem. However, once inside I noticed a bag in one of the foot wells. Looking carefully inside in low lighting, I could see a sawn-off shotgun (a prohibited weapon) and automatic pistol. This was a 'Happy Bag', the tool kit of the armed robber. Radioing this information, I got the next question, which I was dreading. Are they loaded? Well, there was only one way to find out. Taking each in turn I unloaded and then reloaded them with as little handling as possible. I noted what information I could about the weapons before placing them back as I had found them. I then set about marking the vehicle. Once outside and away from the garage I made my notes. Firstly, there was my scene investigation report, a copy of which would go to the laboratory. I also made a second set of notes which I referred to and cross-referenced in my report. This was in my pocket book and gave details of the weapons and their finding, information which was too sensitive, and not relevant to the information which the laboratory was to receive. All these notes would help me give my evidence whenever I was asked later. With this information, the detectives knew they were dealing with a dangerous team. Hasty discussions were held at chief officer level to determine whether the suspects should be arrested as soon as they went to the car or allowed to run, with the full resources of the Flying Squad following their every move. They were allowed to run and they were arrested as they committed their robbery. The marker evidence helped prove the charges made against them.

During the long hours and regular late nights I was often confronted with problems which required novel solutions. One night I had to examine a vehicle recovered in an area on the other side of London. I recovered a large number or items including a large quantity of cash left by the robbers in the car. At the completion of my examination I went to the local police station and made sure all the property was listed there. Having counted the cash once during my examination, I was made to count it again with the station sergeant. As I sealed it for a second time it was now the early hours of the morning. I had to be back at the Flying Squad office with the bags at nine am and I still had an hour's drive home. I elected to take the items, including the cash, to the police station near to my home and deposit the sealed bag there for safekeeping until the morning. The bags, forensically sealed now, also had police property security seals on them. When I arrived at my local police station I expected the station officer to accept the sealed bags as just that, sealed bags, and place the cash in the safe. He was just signing for a sealed bag, I was guaranteeing the contents. However he insisted that the cash be counted again. This would take at least another hour and made the exercise futile as I would get no sleep at all before needing to return. So I took the bags home, put them under my bed and went to sleep. The items, I could honestly say, remained in my possession the whole time and within a few hours were lodged in property office at the Flying Squad office.

The rewards for working with dedicated detectives and expert scientists on complex and long cases were great. Our resources were finite, but they were used well and for a period certain types of armed robbery actually stopped. In reality all those committing the crime were behind bars and the crimes would not start up again until some were released, many years later. It seemed that armed robbery was a career for some violent men even if it were interrupted with terms of imprisonment, which they seemed to accept as an occupational hazard.

Sometimes it was a family business. At one time three brothers from the same family had been arrested in separate investigations. A fourth brother who undertook legitimate work as a market stall holder made sure he had a prominent pitch outside a busy London underground station. Whether it was intentional or not, it provided him with a constant and reliable alibi. Perhaps rather unkindly, one of the Flying Squad teams was considering sending the boys' unfortunate mother a rather small turkey for Christmas. Detectives often display a warped sense of humour, it helps keep them in the real world, but I don't think even they would have seen this heartless deed through.

Being part of the investigative team was a drug. The combination of forensic evidence and good detective work produced a focus and team spirit which was hard to match.

Guile and cunning are useful traits, provided they are ethically used. Following a long surveillance operation, the Squad pounced on a team of robbers just as they got out of their cars and began to enter a jeweller's. Although armed, they were overpowered by the police and arrested on a charge of conspiracy to rob. It would be necessary to prove association of all the suspects and the false-plated getaway vehicle at the scene and change-over cars scattered at other locations. The forensic evidence would be used to corroborate the surveillance testimony offered by detectives. The arrest went off without any shots being fired and so there was no priority for me to examine any suspects. The recovery of clothing was dealt with by detectives I had trained and instructed along with police surgeons. One suspect was sitting in a change-over car bearing false number plates, a few streets away. He realised something was up and simply got out and walked away from the car. He was arrested fifty yards away but denied any involvement. The vehicle was in the street and I went to give it a screening search so that it could be brought in for full examination later. The screening would ensure that there was nothing in the vehicle, like weapons or masks, which the detectives should know about before they conducted any interview. On the driver's seat I found a pack of branded cigarettes and a lighter. This I removed and packaged so the vehicle could be taken away by a tow truck. I went to the police station to enter the items I had found on the custody sheet of the arrested man. As I was doing so I overheard a detective who was about to interview the suspect say that the suspect was asking for a cigarette. Showing the detective the sealed exhibit bag, I suggested that the suspect might sign for the ones I had found in the vehicle. If he did he would unwittingly associate himself with the vehicle. I had sealed the item with a view to fingerprinting them later. If the suspect signed for them he would save me the trouble of associating them with him. Although probably well handled, there was no guarantee that I would find his fingerprint so I opened the bag and gave the contents to the detective. Within a minute the suspect had signed for them and the job was done. He was later to plead guilty to conspiracy to rob.

Being an expert in a particular field within a diverse team comes with its responsibilities. There were times when I needed to say something that was uncomfortable. On one occasion, whilst covering the south-east London Squad office, I was called to assist them when they arrested a team of robbers as they committed an robbery. I noticed that one overzealous officer new to the Squad had arrested one of the suspects away from the scene but went back to the scene later and recovered an item. There was a potential risk of contamination of the evidence we were seeking. In a crowded briefing, I told the senior investigator, a detective inspector. There was silence, it was an awkward moment. It was not the news he or any of the officers present wanted to hear. Nothing could be done to undo the problem. There was one small crumb of comfort though, and I offered that. Although there was a risk of contamination from the suspect to the scene, there was none from the scene to the suspect as the officer had only gone one way. So, although a two-way transfer of evidence was unsafe, a one-way transfer was still worthy of investigation. The detective inspector accepted the advice. The scientist who undertook the laboratory examination was given the full facts and this was also disclosed to the defence. It rather deflated any of the usual allegations of planting of evidence which were often made by the defence. In any event, the suspect later pleaded guilty.

I was fortunate to receive commendations from the Commissioner of the Metropolitan Police and his deputies on a number of occasions. I have received kind comments and congratulations from the best of detectives with whom I have worked. To me they worked as motivators, and gave me comfort that

I was doing my job well. It was, however, some words spoken by a young detective, one who did not know me, of which I am proudest. I had received a call to an armed robbery at a bank in Romford in Essex. Shots had been fired and I was only a mile or so away when the call came out. I responded to the call and informed the control room that I would make my way there. When I arrived at the scene a local detective was already there. I showed my identification and told him I was from the Flying Squad, but he must have assumed that I was a detective (if a short one), or perhaps I didn't make my introduction clear. Looking at the scene, he told me how the armed robber had threatened the bank staff as they ducked behind the counter. He said that the suspect had fired a long-barrelled pistol and the officer pointed at the screen to indicate where it had struck. I looked at the mark on the screen and then in front of it on the floor I saw a piece of plastic wadding (which he had not seen) hidden on the patterned carpet. Both indicated to me that the weapon was a shotgun type weapon and not a pistol. I told the young detective that the weapon was more likely a small-gauge shotgun and indicated the glass damage and wadding. 'Oh that's great,' he said. 'I'm glad we sorted that out before your SOCO got here. He's on his way. I've heard that he's shit hot and that would have been embarrassing.' On the inside I felt my chest rise and I pulled myself to my full five feet seven inch stature. I quietly and proudly told him, 'I am the Flying Squad SOCO.'

9. The Robber Who Bit Off More than he Could Chew

The crime scene is thought by many to be the most productive area for finding forensic evidence. That is not always the case. Often other locations associated with the crime are much more useful. Arriving at the getaway car, this was going to be one of these occasions.

The crime scene itself was unremarkable. Two armed men had threatened a security guard as he was transferring a wages bag between his security van and a small factory. There was no struggle and nothing had been dropped at the scene. There were no shoe marks on the ground to indicate anyone's presence, criminal or otherwise.

The suspect had jumped into a small saloon car popular at the time and driven off at speed. The guards gave chase in the security vehicle and, having caught up, they were threatened with a gun for a second time. Naturally, the suspects escaped.

The car was found, engine running, doors open, a mile or so away, near some garages and an alleyway leading to an open area of waste ground and dwellings beyond.

I picked up the call on the police radio channel. Central 857 a Flying Squad car crewed by Dick Kirby and his driver Tony Freeman ('Freeburg' as Dick often referred to him) also answered and they beat me to the scene.

Dick and Tony were all that epitomised the professional Flying Squad. Dick was the tenacious maverick detective, Tony was the expert driver who would get Dick into and out of situations with calm professionalism.

Tony could make even the smallest car sing. With the right tool, and on the Squad he had the right tool, he was at his professional best. One of my earliest investigations on the Squad was when I was asked by Kevin Shapland (who I was later to realise was the most complete detective I would ever work with) to drive from the office in east London to Heathrow Airport to examine a car. Like most SOCOs at that time I had previously covered only a small geographical area. At first I thought it was a wind up. Heathrow was well outside the East End of London which my Flying Squad office covered. Kevin and Tony were going to meet me there. It took me well over an hour to get there through the traffic. I knew that Tony was still at the office some thirty minutes after I left as he had been called back to the office radio set as he was leaving to receive another message. This increased my fears of being the brunt of a practical joke.

To my amazement, as I arrived at Heathrow, Tony and Kevin arrived too. I confirmed that the drive, which had taken me well over an hour through the central London traffic, had taken Tony precisely thirty-five minutes. Much later, when travelling in the car with him, I realised that he quickly and safely got his crew to where it mattered without fuss and in a condition where they could quickly get on with their job.

Back at our robbery scene, a quick examination revealed that there was little for me to do at the robbery location itself so I jumped back into my car and went to where the getaway vehicle had been found.

A police officer protected the car. It was my intention to undertake a preliminary examination of the vehicle so that it could be removed for a comprehensive and much longer examination back in the privacy of a police station. I would also search the alleyway down which a witness had seen the two suspects run.

My first thoughts were to secure any evidence around the vehicle, perhaps a shoe mark in the mud or item dropped. I would then search the vehicle for large items which it would be important to know about immediately, perhaps the stolen money bag or a loaded firearm. I would then examine the driver's area for fibres and then any other areas (gear stick, hand brake) which would have to be touched to allow the removal by tow truck to the police station.

The engine was still running when the vehicle had been abandoned and there was a key in the ignition. On closer examination it was not the original manufacturer's key. It was a new key, that was obvious from its clean undamaged appearance. At one end (the end which one would attach to a key ring) was a plastic covering that contained the inscription 'Curtis', which was a replacement car key brand. In my initial observation of the car I had also noticed that the boot lock was missing. Things were coming together. From examining many similar vehicles I had realised something that the criminals also knew. On this particular model of this particular car the specific number to the ignition key was marked on the boot lock barrel. So it was common in such cases for thieves to remove the barrel from the parked car, go to a local replacement key supplier, give the number and get a key. They would then return to the vehicle and steal it. I am glad to say that such an opportunity was removed in later designs.

I also saw on the key, before thinking of how to remove it, some scratches. They looked like the indentations made when someone bit a semi-hard plastic. Which in fact, they were. They were teeth marks.

It was the scratches which particularly intrigued me. They were only small but I had on many occasions used evidence resulting from when a screwdriver or similar implement is used to force open a metal cash box or the like. The screwdriver leaves scratches or striations which are unique to the tool which made them. Even a new screwdriver can leave striations from the milled or ground edge and these will show up under a microscope. When a tool is damaged from regular use, the resulting pitting leaves a wave of striations which makes the evidence all the more obvious. So although I was sure that the marks looked like bite marks, it was the striations from the damaged end of the donor's teeth that immediately struck me as evidential.

I also had to consider the possibility that as these were teeth marks I could assume the presence of saliva. This was before the days of DNA but saliva could in some case reveal the blood group of the donor. Although not totally specific it was a useful investigative tool. It could include or certainly eliminate a suspect. There was also a smooth area which was worthy of fingerprinting, although I decided not to at this early stage for fear of damaging the saliva and the bite-mark evidence.

The vehicle, duly preserved, was removed to the local police station for my full examination later. That would take at least another four hours and I still had the alleyway to examine.

The alleyway led directly from the open door of the getaway vehicle behind some garages to an open waste area and dwellings beyond. The usual amount of litter and vegetation could be found and would make the examination complex. What made things a little easier were the presence of a few items of clothing left almost in sequence along the path. I recorded the location of each before making a very delicate examination and then placing each item in separate exhibit bags. I would normally have completed a more in-depth inspection of each, before packaging and sealing the item there and then at the scene, but these items needed more attention and careful search. I was unwilling to do this in an open space where fibres and other evidence would be lost. Once they were sealed, I would be unwilling to disturb the items before their submission to the laboratory without a very good reason; such is the proper concept of integrity.

I placed each item in separately labelled bags and secured

the closure to prevent any contamination. The items I found included two black motor-cycle type gloves, one bearing the handwritten number 558 on an inside label, and a denim jacket bearing the manufacturer's label 'Manto'.

Having recovered all the items from the alleyway I stood at the point where it opened out on to the waste ground behind and the dwellings beyond. Much, much later I was to find out from Dick that the suspects had dropped the bag of stolen money in a waste bin a few hundred yards away. They returned later that night to claim their booty. To me the choice of where to go at the end of the alley was too large, the ground opened out in all directions and for me the trail ended there. The search area was getting too large and the trail weak. It still pains me to think there was a prize clue still within my grasp. It had always been my practice to look, as without looking you won't find, but this was one step too far, even for me.

Mind you, looking does sometimes have its downside. My first investigation with Dick had been on my very first day on the Flying Squad. A robbery had taken place in the very high street of the area where I lived. The suspect, having left the bank he had just robbed, ran around the corner to his getaway vehicle. I traced his route and noticed a litter bin attached to a lamp post. Checking to see if he had dumped the gun (always an incriminating piece of evidence if found on you), I gingerly lifted the uppermost contents and had a good look. I then noticed one of my neighbours standing in front of me, an elderly lady from my street. She had a horrified and quizzical look on her face, which quickly turned to pity as I turned red with embarrassment. 'Poor dear, what has this come to?' she must have thought before marching off clutching her bag whilst turning her head to look back at me. She had no idea what I did for a living and I had no time to explain. The situation wasn't helped by the fact that all the Squad officers were in plain clothes and drove unmarked vehicles. For many years she gave me a wide berth whenever I saw her.

Having completed the lengthy examination of the car, which revealed a large number of potential pieces of evidence (including fibres and finger marks), I returned all the items I had collected to my office.

I then carefully opened, searched and examined the items I had recovered from the alleyway, making more detailed notes about them.

Looking once again at the key, I was convinced that it contained a bite mark. I also prepared a note to Dick to make sure that he knew that he should investigate which shop had supplied the 'Curtis' key, in case that might lead to a suspect.

The gloves were indeed heavy duty but revealed nothing further. The jacket was much more interesting. It was a bomber-style denim jacket with outside waist pockets. In one pocket I found two smoked cigarette ends, in the other I found a Yale-type front door key. I documented both before packaging them separately.

In the days that followed, Dick pursued every line of enquiry he could. Dick was a consummate and complete detective. A small wiry guy, he just about made the five foot ten inch height requirement to join the force. He was sometimes referred to by his colleagues as Nipper. This reflected his tenacious nature but was also in honour of his Flying Squad hero Leonard 'Nipper' Read from the 1960s. He was thorough, skilled and hard working. He oozed commitment and a sense of justice, rough justice in some cases. He knew how to deal with criminals in a way they would understand. He never cut corners and always took advice once he knew that you were just as committed as he. Dick has gone on to become a successful writer. When I read *Rough Justice* and *The Real Sweeney*, both written by him, I hear his voice and feel the pace of my heart quicken, such was the joy of working with him. He was amongst a handful of the best detectives I ever worked with. I always felt our combined efforts ensured a professional and complete investigation.

Dick decided he wanted to put the items I had found on the

Police Five TV programme on the Independent Television network, ITV. It was a weekly five-minute show where the police appealed for witnesses to crimes in the London area.

This presented me with a problem. The opening and display of these items on TV would jeopardise any fragile evidence, such as fibres, which they might contain. It would be very difficult to supervise the viewing of such items and still maintain their evidential integrity. A defence lawyer would rightly ask some difficult questions if any evidence was later presented. Although I had undertaken an examination of the gloves, keys (car and Yale) and the jacket, I was mindful that further examination and comparison for fibres on the recovered gloves and jacket with clothing from a suspect at a later date might prove an evidential link.

Dick's problem was much more immediate. He didn't want to lose the media attention and the opportunity to find a witness with events fresh in their minds, and without such a witness we were unlikely to ever get to the laboratory comparison stage. Therefore I took the step of once again opening the exhibit bags and recovering what I could for future examination. This was a compromise as a laboratory search would be much more detailed but would take time we didn't have.

The items were opened for the recording of the show the following day and viewed on TV within a few days.

Nothing much happened but Dick got lots of calls. The gloves were identified as those issued to members of the British Army and referred to as 'Northern Ireland Gloves' by those in the know. The numbers '588' in the gloves, it was suggested, referred to the last few numbers of a soldier's warrant number. Dick had a bit to go on there.

No witnesses came forward to immediately identify the 'Manto' jacket and the trail ran a bit cold over the later months. But Dick never gave up.

One afternoon a few months later, Dick informed me that he was going to arrest two young men in connection with the robbery. I dug out my report and made a note of the things we should look for to connect a suspect with the robbery. I knew Dick would have retained my thoughts and advice on this from the original investigation, but I wanted to be thorough.

The Yale key might fit one of the suspects' front door locks. If it did we should photograph the door in its position before seizing the door, complete with flat number and lock in place. This was to prevent any defence lawyer suggesting that we had switched the lock; I was beginning to get wise about such allegations.

I also suggested that we should take dental impressions from the suspects. I had a few forensic dentist contacts and I made the necessary calls to get one on standby for the day of the arrest and search.

So a few mornings later we converged at Romford Police Station shortly after five am for a briefing with local officers.

Two teams set out, one to each of the addresses of the two suspects. I went to one, armed with the key. Shortly after the occupants, politely and without fuss, opened the door to the first address, the premises were secured by armed officers and I removed the Yale key from its bag and, in Dick's presence, tried it in the lock. The barrel turned with reassuring ease. It fitted. Cinderella, you will go to the ball, I thought.

In the coming hours the door was photographed removed and then replaced, free of charge, courtesy of the Metropolitan Police. In the next months the significance of the key and lock would be investigated to identify the number of combinations and the probability of one particular key fitting an individual lock. For the moment it was, of course, promising that the key opened the door.

Back at the police station it was time to take the dental impressions. First, we had to seek the consent of the suspects and also get the authority of a police superintendent. The former was remarkably easy. The suspects had been dealt with courteously but the request took them by surprise. One detective remarked that they probably expected the police to knock their teeth out and were relieved we only wanted to take impressions.

My call to the London Hospital Medical School a few days earlier had intended to instruct Bernard Sims, the renowned forensic odontologist. Such was the emerging demand for this science (mainly in the area of disaster victim identification), that he designed and delivered a course in Forensic Dentistry. So it was one of his graduates, Luigi Ciapperelli, who came on this occasion.

Luigi looked at the Curtis key and confirmed that it was a bite mark and he set about obtaining the dental impressions from the two suspects. Enquiries which Dick later made revealed that of the two men arrested, Saul and Fowler, only Fowler held a driving licence. Not that having a driving licence had anything to do with it – many people drive cars without licences. The fact was that Saul couldn't drive. We made a point of not telling Ciapperelli this as it was irrelevant to his examination and we wanted his opinion based solely on the marks evidence and not clouded by other issues.

In the weeks that followed I had meetings with Luigi about the bite marks. I also took him to meet Pam Hamer, a forensic chemist at the Metropolitan Police Forensic Science Laboratory, and discussed with them both the bite mark and striation evidence. Luigi had already made some examination of the dental impressions taken from Saul and Fowler. Pam Hamer was interested in the striations but the marks were very small. Any meaningful comparison would have to consider the angle and direction of the marks, if this evidence was to be useful and a potential match found. In the end it was clear that Luigi thought there was enough detail in the spatial arrangement of the marks on the key itself for a meaningful comparison to be made. He had noticed something I had not. Although there were striations emerging from the marks, there were indentations relating to the spatial arrangements and shapes of the tip of the teeth which could help identify the donor.

A few weeks later I got a call from Luigi. Having completed his work and undertaken quality checks with his colleagues at the London Hospital regarding his methodology, he was sure that only the teeth of Fowler could have made the marks on the key. His statement arrived. It appears that the dentistry (that is the spatial shape and arrangement of our teeth) is unique and there was enough information within the mark to match the specific dentistry of Fowler.

That was good news for the investigation but more was to follow. Dick had come across Saul when he was investigating the source of the gloves I had found in the alleyway. They were indeed military issue and the number did refer to the last three digits of a soldier's warrant number. When Dick traced all soldiers whose warrant numbers ended in 588 he got a tidy list. None of them, however, could he implicate in the robbery. But one of these soldiers had had his gloves stolen. This seemed to be going nowhere until Saul's name came to his attention and Dick realised that Saul had been discharged from the Army and had served in the same regiment as the soldier who had lost his gloves.

When I had heard the name 'Saul', as we were briefed by Dick at Romford Police Station on the morning of his arrest, his name seemed familiar to me, but I couldn't remember why. It wasn't until some weeks later that I suspected that I had dealt with him before and found time to do something about it. I pulled out all my reports and flicked through them all.

There it was. Many, many months before, Saul had been arrested by another detective in the office, also for an armed robbery offence. It wasn't a promising investigation. The officer in that case had come to me late, the offence was already old. He had arrested the suspect and seized his clothing. There was one big problem. The getaway car had been recovered, but it had not been initially linked to this robbery and had been restored to the owners many miles away in the heart of Essex. The family had been using the car for a week.

Once again, listening to the saying 'if you don't look you won't find', I agreed with the officer to drive to Essex. I contacted the owner of the car and arranged to examine it at their house. The examination wasn't very fruitful. But I did recover some fibres and some finger marks. All the finger marks were later found to belong to the owner and family members. Given the seriousness of the offence I also prepared a laboratory submission with all these details. Submitting the seized clothing of Saul (who I had not seen) and the fibres I had recovered from the cars, I was not surprised when the scientist stated that the fibres of the clothing were too common for any meaningful comparison. The items were collected and, with no evidence in the case, the clothing was returned to the suspect and any prospect of charges dropped.

When I looked closely at the laboratory submission I noticed that a 'blue jacket' had been taken from Saul on that first occasion but it had been returned to him when the case was dropped. I thought the unthinkable. What were the chances of the denim 'Manto' jacket which I had recovered from the alleyway being the 'blue jacket' previously taken from Saul and returned to him before this latest robbery occurred.

Having worked as a member of the scientific staff at the Forensic Science Laboratory for three years I knew that whoever had examined the jacket taken from Saul would have some specific notes about it and this would include any labels. I excitedly called the laboratory and was put through to Dr De Souza, a forensic biologist. When I explained my enquiry and asked if she could identify the jacket from its labels she went to get the file and called me back within a few minutes. I was particularly interested to know if the jacket had a manufacturer's label bearing the name 'Manto'. There was silence as she read her notes and then she said, 'Yes, it is a Manto jacket.' I could hardly confine my excitement. I then asked if I brought a jacket which I suspected of being the same one, could she identify it from her description, the labels and her notes. From my own training at the laboratory I knew that was likely to be so. What she then said stunned me. 'I can do better than that.' She went on. 'I cut and removed a small square control sample from under the arm and it is retained on the file.' If I had the jacket, the small square would physically fit back in the hole which was made.

I ran around the Flying Squad office like a headless chicken. I spoke to the officer in the Saul case and probably made no sense whatever to him.

Contacting the property officer at the office, I quickly booked out the Manto jacket in its sealed bag and went straight to the laboratory. I don't remember the journey but when I arrived I was taken to a small examination room. A crowd of scientists from the biology section had heard the story and assembled at a suitable distance. Dr De Souza opened the bag on a carefully prepared bench. Removing the small square control sample from a plastic bag attached to the file, she lifted the arm of the jacket and offered it up to a small hole. It fitted perfectly. There was wild excitement and applause.

I was pleased but Dick was ecstatic. The jacket could be directly linked to Saul. It is strange that I didn't notice the hole under the sleeve when I first inspected it, but even if I had it wouldn't have meant anything to me. The jacket had been paraded on TV to identify its owner, but we had the answer. It was only because I was a common factor in both cases and kept accurate and comprehensive notes that the link was made.

At the trial, the fact that the jacket had been seized in another investigation was carefully introduced so as not to prejudice the case against Saul. We referred to the jacket being seized on another occasion. The evidence that the jacket discarded at the alley belonged to Saul and the key in the pocket fitted his front door was successfully introduced.

The fun wasn't over yet. The introduction of the bite-mark evidence against Fowler met with interest in the first few days of the trial. I had suggested to Dick that he might want to speak to the defence and see if they intended to examine the marks independently. We were pretty confident about the evidence and didn't want the usual scrum and confusion on the first day of the trial as often occurs if the defence team realises that there is some scientific evidence they should get checked out independently. If the evidence was sound, and we believed it to be so, it would withstand the rigorous testing by the defence. The best interest of justice and the trial process would be preserved.

Predictably, on the first day of the trial we were informed that the defence were organising their own examination. I was happy to facilitate the examinations and Luigi Ciapperelli gave his full support. The forensic dentistry field is still a small one and Luigi knew the expert instructed by the defence.

The trial was held at Court Number 19 at the Central Criminal Court, Old Bailey in the City of London. It is the smallest court in the building and I understand it was converted from an office to provide an additional court. By comparison to the other courtrooms it's a cupboard and is sometimes referred to as such.

The close proximity of witness, presiding judge, counsel, jurors and defendant make it a very cosy environment. Not that cosy is a word that anyone would want to associate with a criminal trial.

I gave my evidence and was allowed to sit in court and hear the evidence of Luigi. Forensic dentistry evidence is pretty rare in criminal cases and I was interested in seeing how this was delivered, to learn how it was presented and received. I also wanted to know if we could improve how such evidence was presented so that the jurors had the right information on which to make their decision. This was not to improperly influence their decision but to ensure that it was firmly presented in a fair and ethical way.

Luigi gave a very studied and balanced view of the marks and the impressions he had taken from Saul and Fowler. He explained the development of teeth as we get older and referred to the specific dentistry of both defendants. With the aid of charts and diagrams he showed the spatial arrangement of Saul's and Fowler's teeth. He could quickly exclude Saul from making the marks. Referring to the shape of the marks of the individual teeth and their spatial arrangement, he stated that it was his conclusion that Fowler, and only Fowler, could have made these marks.

From the beginning of Luigi's evidence it was apparent that the defence were not going to call their own witness. This is their prerogative and can be for any number of reasons. One, and perhaps the most common, is that the defence expert agrees with the prosecution expert. Another is that, rather than counter the evidence in person, the defence expert remains in court whilst the prosecution expert gives their evidence. In this way the defence expert can advise defence counsel on questions to ask to test the evidence and the witness's approach.

During Luigi's evidence the defence expert sat beside Fowler, explaining the evidence. By a series of movements using Luigi's dental models the defence expert explained what it meant. A quizzical look came over Fowler's face and I could see that he was asking his own expert what he thought. To this his own defence expert indicated that he too thought Fowler had made the mark. Suddenly Fowler lunged at his own expert and started wrestling with him. All hell seemed to break loose for a moment and the court was cleared. Calm was restored. The judge ordered a break; I mentioned to Dick what I had observed. What Dick did next was something I will never forget, and it was a lesson for me. Dick spoke to the prosecution counsel.

After the break Luigi concluded his evidence, this time the defence expert was sitting next to counsel, most definitely out of Fowler's reach.

To the surprise of almost everyone in the court, the prosecution counsel asked for the next witness to be called. He called the defence expert! It is very unusual for a lawyer to call a witness whose evidence is not known and without a written report or statement. This could cause damage to his case. The defence were not calling their witness; his presence in court whilst Luigi had given his evidence had indicated that. The scuffle with the defendant indicated more still and so it looked like the prosecution were on to a sure thing.

Sure enough, the evidence of the defence expert was quickly given, he agreed with the methodology of the prosecution and the identification which had been made. The defence expert also concluded that Fowler, and Fowler alone, had made the marks on the key.

Afterwards, Dick reminded me that there is no possession in a witness. The truth is the truth after all. If a defence expert knows it and it is to the prosecution's advantage and they know about it, then the witness can be called.

At the conclusion of the trial, both men were convicted of armed robbery. Dick and I were both commended by the Commissioner. But I wore a smile of satisfaction for some time, not because two men were detained at Her Majesty's pleasure, which is a sadness and reality of human life, but because I was trained to do a job and I was working as a member of a professional team.

10. Eleven Fibres

The elderly lady was terrified, she could not see her attacker, but she could see the large knife and hear his violent shouts.

On an unremarkable morning, the peace of a local community was broken by a terrifying act of violence. A man walked into a bank in Debden High Street, grabbed an elderly woman from behind and held a long-bladed knife to her throat.

He hurled threats at the bank staff who, in response, handed over £4,000. This was an unusually high amount because, contrary to common belief, banks, especially small local branches, don't hold much cash.

The man was masked so no one got a really good look at his face, and his tracksuit hid his otherwise stocky build.

The robber left the bank, and his terrified victim, and ran off down the high street and into a wooded park area. Police officers were quick to respond and the wood was sealed off. The police helicopter arrived quickly overhead but there was no sign of the suspect.

Then, out of the far end of the wood, a jogger emerged. Dressed in running shorts and T-shirt he was sweaty and out of breath. All very normal perhaps, but not in the circumstances which had shattered the day's peace. He was approached by the officers who were protecting the wide cordon and searching the wood. They were not happy with his account and he was arrested.

Debden is a community on the border of London and the

Essex countryside. Its high street provides for the sprawling leafy community. It had its own station, part of the London Underground network, and a quick link into the heart of the metropolis. The term underground station is a bit of a misnomer, the station and track are elevated high above the ground and passengers travel many miles into London before the tunnel disappears beneath the surface. It's a quiet place and not used to such acts of violence and certainly not in broad daylight.

Having heard the call on Channel 7, the Met's main HQ crime radio channel. I made my way quickly to the scene. It would be possible that the local SOCO would get there before me but my interest heightened when I heard that a suspect had been arrested.

Although the remit of the Flying Squad was to investigate all armed robberies at banks, building societies, Post Offices and security vehicles, it was always the local officers who arrived first. Each Squad office had a large area to cover, so it would be the local uniformed officers and perhaps detectives who would take the first steps, but the Squad would take over as soon as it could.

For my part, I could not be in two places at the same time. I was the only SOCO at the north-east London branch office so, in many cases, my divisional colleagues would attend if I was already committed elsewhere. Where the robbery scene may have been dealt with by the local SOCO, I always dealt with any vehicle recovered myself. This was for two reasons. Firstly, because it could be dealt with at a more leisurely pace later. Secondly, vehicles are a great source of evidence and intelligence about the robbery and those who have committed these offences.

Although I may be beaten to the scene by the local SOCO, any slight delay in my response would allow time for me to hear if any suspect had been arrested. Prisoners were a priority for the Squad. Any suspect arrested was a bonus not to be missed.

I quickly got to the scene and reviewed what had taken

place. There was little to do at the bank itself, the suspect had been gloved as well as masked, but the public door to the bank would still need examination. If the suspect who had been arrested was the offender, his description had changed from that of a masked, gloved, tracksuited man carrying a knife and a bag containing £4,000, to that of a jogger in a pair of shorts, training shoes and a T-shirt.

I anticipated that a search of the woods would reveal, if we had the right man, a pile of clothing including the mask and the money and knife. By now the description of the mask was that of a dark woolly balaclava. My interest intensified further. So I decided that the suspect should receive my attention. I called on a colleague to examine the bank whilst I went to the local police station where the suspect was being held.

By the time I arrived I got news that a dog handler with his canine assistant had indeed found such a pile. Clothing, money, knife, mask, gloves, it was all there. I gave instructions on how the find should be recovered and a local detective made his way to deal with it. There wasn't another SOCO available, and officers were trained to deal with such matters. They had been doing so long before the arrival of SOCOs, even if the science was moving on. It was covered.

For the moment I wanted to do one thing and one thing only. Comb the hair of the suspect. Everything else could wait a little longer.

When I arrived at Loughton Police Station, tensions were high. The suspect was still protesting his innocence.

I quickly identified myself to the custody officer, the officer in charge of the prisoner area. There were only local officers there; I had yet to be joined by colleagues from the Squad. A group of uniformed police officers involved in the arrest were also in the charge room. I informed the custody officer that it would very important to obtain a combing of the hair of the suspect and the reasons behind this. We would have to deal with the situation carefully because the suspect had to be informed of his rights in such matters. I didn't want the suspect to use any lull in the process to try and remove any traces of evidence once he knew what my intention was.

The custody officer's role is one of the two most demanding roles within the police service. The other one is the role of senior investigating officer, to which I refer elsewhere. The custody officer's role is governed by the Police and Criminal Evidence Act (1984) and its later amendments. Their role is to manage the detention of persons in police custody. They are not part of the investigation but ensure that the prisoner and their detention are properly managed.

Taking the custody officer to one side, I reminded him, just in case he needed it, of the particular parts within the Act which covered the taking of non-intimate samples.

The Act and the Code of Practice, a small book, was my constant companion. I had highlighted the parts referring to the sampling of a suspect for ease of reference and so I could quickly remind custody officers, inspectors and superintendents of the reasons and authorities required. I found that these busy professionals appreciated the targeted reference as they had many things to consider and an accurate prompt always met a welcome response.

In this case a man had been arrested for armed robbery, which was a Serious Arrestable Offence under the Act. I wanted an immediate head-hair combing. This was non-intimate sample as defined by the Act. It was from the exterior of the body and not from an intimate area. The reason I wanted to take this sample was because I believed that if the suspect was the offender and had worn the mask which had now been recovered, there was a strong chance that it would contain fibres from the mask. It would indicate recent contact, and it could indicate recent wearing.

For this to happen the suspect would have to agree in writing by signing a consent record and we would need the authority of an officer of the rank of inspector. This too was required by the Act. This was to ensure that we were not idly wasting our time and breaching the suspect's rights. The inspector would have to be convinced that the taking of the non-intimate sample would potentially prove or disprove the suspect's involvement in the offence. I was happy to advise so. Indeed I was pretty sure that if the mask was woolly as described and, given the prompt arrest and competent sampling, if he were the offender fibres would be found. If there were no fibres, that would be a pretty firm indication that the suspect was not involved. It was quite simple. Other more lengthy examinations might indeed follow, such as comparison of clothing, examination of the knife and money for fingerprints, but they would only conclude the same.

The examination of the suspect's hair for fibres originating from the mask were, in my opinion and emerging experience, a focused and powerful evidential indicator.

We had to go through the process of first asking for the consent of the suspect himself. However, if the suspect refused we had another card up our sleeves. As this was a Serious Arrestable Offence, a police superintendent could authorise the sample to be taken without the suspect's written consent. Any force required would have to be applied by police officers and, as a civilian, I would have to be excluded from the sampling as this could constitute an assault for which only police officers were authorised.

There was, however, a difficult problem. Once put to the suspect, he would know our intentions and the potential evidence we were seeking. I prepared myself to take the sample as soon as we had the appropriate consent and authority. When the custody sergeant went into the cell to ask for the written consent I waited outside. Not surprisingly the suspect refused to consent. What he wasn't expecting was that I had arranged for two officers to sit with him, in order to prevent him trying to wash his hair in the toilet bowl in his cell. However unpleasant that sounds it would not be the first time a suspect has tried to conceal their guilt in such a way. I wasn't going to give him that opportunity.

The police superintendent in charge of the station arrived quickly and the request made to him to take the samples without the written consent of the suspect. The superintendent was a large Scottish man with a booming voice. To my surprise he needed a little persuading. Either my explanation or his faith in the science did little to convince him. It was true, the taking of a sample by force, if that were needed, would be messy, extremely difficult and probably futile. If the suspect would allow the sample to be taken without a struggle, then I would be best placed and trained to take it. It would just be that he did not consent in writing. With the super's authority, that would be allowed within the rules of the Police and Criminal Evidence Act (PACE).

However, the superintendent was still uncertain whether the potential to find evidence which would 'prove or disprove' the suspect's involvement was there. In the end I put it as simply as I could. The mask by all accounts was woolly; if the suspect had worn the mask, in my experience there would be fibres in his hair from the mask; if he had not, none would be found. The super was convinced and granted the authority.

Now came the really difficult part of taking the sample. There was every chance that the suspect would struggle and the taking of the sample would be compromised. He was a well-built man. The suspect would be warned in such a case where he refused and no sample was taken that the refusal would be referred to in court and could imply his guilt in the matter. This is because the taking of the sample allows the opportunity to eliminate his involvement.

I briefed a police officer to take the sample. Although I intended to be present, I would not be allowed to help with the act of sampling because of the risk of an accusation of assault. If it came to an out and out fight, I would advise the officers that the sampling should be stopped as 'bad science' and I would make my notes and update the custody record accordingly.

The superintendent handled the matter perfectly. He went into the suspect's cell with the custody officer, closely followed by six burly officers. I waited at the door. The superintendent advised the suspect of his rights and that he had authorised the taking of the sample by force if necessary. He explained that this was allowed within the Police and Criminal Evidence Act. He then gave the suspect a blunt choice. Pointing to the six officers he said, 'You can choose. Either these six officers will take the sample or,' and then pointing to me at the rear, 'this short bald civilian gentleman shall. It's your choice.' The suspect glanced along the row of burly policemen and then looked at me. Without a word, and probably fearing a beating, he raised his finger and pointed it to me.

I then quickly set about my task. Opening a hair-combing kit, I quickly put on a pair of gloves and I unfolded a sheet of white paper from within. In one hand, I held the sheet under the man's head, asking him to nod forward, and with the other hand I drew the comb (containing a moistened lint pad in its teeth) through the man's hair. Backwards and forwards for a few minutes, I combed his hair over the paper. I finished by putting the seeded comb into the sheet and folding the paper around it. I placed it inside an exhibit bag and sealed and labelled it immediately. It was done. There was no struggle. But all the officers stayed just the same.

The suspect was to later refuse any further examination. We would have liked blood, saliva, urine and head-hair samples but that was not to be.

I held back the examination of the cash, but arranged for the knife to be examined for finger marks at the laboratory. They had a greater range of techniques which I did not have in the field. I also held back on linking the clothing found in the wood to the shorts and T-shirt the suspect was wearing when he was arrested. Finding the stolen money with the knife and woolly hat had associated that find with the robbery scene. I wanted to link the suspect to the woolly hat and by association with the robbery.

So my first and what turned out to be my main submission of material to the lab was simply the woolly mask and the hair combing.

A few weeks later I got a call from the laboratory. The hair-combing sample contained eleven dark fibres, each of which matched and were indistinguishable from those found in the woolly mask.

The subsequent trial lasted less than two days. The hair sampling played a major part in the evidence and at the end of the trial the suspect was found guilty and sentenced to eleven years in prison. I gave my evidence without event. It was accepted. The prosecution counsel remarked to me afterwards that eleven fibres had been found in the offender's hair, and he had received eleven years. 'What would have happened if you had recovered more?' he wondered.

11. Operation Young

Clarkie emerged from the mist; he was dressed head to foot in blue and wore a bullet-proof vest. The baseball cap with the chequered band on his head indicated that he was one of the boys in blue. Radios and other gadgets were pinned to him just as anyone watching a good police drama would expect.

He was in his element. It was the result of at least a year's hard work by the detectives at the Barnes branch office of the Flying Squad. Allan Clarke was their SOCO, a hard-working and totally effective professional, who I was pleased and honoured to be associated with.

The Barnes Flying Squad office was the smallest and least busy of the four branch offices. Its patch of south-west London had its fair share of robberies and armed robbers, but it lacked the gritty volume of east London where I was based. The Barnes team was ribbed by some of the other offices because it was so much quieter than some of its neighbours. But the officers there were just as professional and dedicated and effective in their work. Clarkie personified that.

The arrest which heralded my arrival outside the scene cordon was the culmination of investigation and surveillance under the codename Operation Young.

Not that the gestation period had gone unnoticed by the other offices, which regularly arrested 'on the pavement' many armed robbers in a similar period. One office had sent a birthday card to Barnes, another an MOT certificate (required by a car at three years of age) to draw attention to the length of their endeavours.

And 'on the pavement' was the classic way to do it. It clearly describes the arrest of the suspect as they approach their victim, the bank, building society or security guard transferring a bag of cash to one of these premises. It is the classic arrest of 'conspiracy to rob' and still the hardest to prove. Without the luxury of arresting suspects immediately after they have committed an offence, Flying Squad officers would arrest them going in, and so the intent of the suspect had to be proved. Its benefits were obvious, bank employees and members of the public were not put at risk. The downside is that the suspect would put try to put forward a defence which would negate the fifteen years of imprisonment they could expect for armed robbery, and present some other explanation, even if they were masked and carrying a gun. The arrest on the pavement was inherently dangerous for the Squad officers, many of whom were not armed. Yes, there were armed officers present, but not all the officers were routinely armed. Their bravery was only matched by what to onlookers would appear as stupidity. But brave they were. That bravery was not without a very professional purpose. It is very dangerous for an armed police officer to have direct physical contact with someone they are trying to arrest. Apart from the danger of a weapon being discharged at close quarters, the suspect may try to disarm the arresting officer, making the situation even more dangerous. From a scientific evidence point of view it is very unhelpful if the arresting officer is armed as they could contaminate the suspect with residues if they have fired shots or are contaminated with firearms discharge residues (FDRs). So it is normal for armed officers to control the arrest whilst unarmed officers lay hands on the suspect to effect an arrest.

Tonight the alleged robbers had been caught. It was alleged that, during the arrest, the suspect had fired shots at the arresting officers.

As Clarkie briefed me and my two Flying Squad SOCO

colleagues who had raced from the three corners of London to help Barnes in its hour of need, a priority emerged to examine the detained suspect who had allegedly fired the shots for FDRs. FDRs are the small particles which emerge from the chamber of a weapon when it is fired and form a cloud. They fall on the back of the hand and sometimes on the face if a weapon is held closer for firing. They are delicate and fall off the hands and face within a few hours. They can remain a little longer in facial or head hair and longer in pockets of clothing. The residues are specific to firearms discharge as they contain three elements, which in combination are only found in the percussion cap of ammunition and in the residues from their discharge. I volunteered to go to the police station where the suspect in question was being held.

When I arrived at the police station the suspect was still being booked into the custody area. He was still clothed, which was good because I wanted to examine him for residues before his clothing was removed. This was to ensure that there was no disturbance of any material which was directly on his exposed skin areas.

Once again I considered PACE. Under the Act, the swabbing of exposed external areas of a suspect could be undertaken with the consent of a suspect and with the authority of a police inspector, where it was believed that evidence could be found to prove or disprove the involvement in a criminal offence. As explained before, in a serious case, such as this, even if the suspect refused or did not consent in writing, the external samples could still be taken with the authority of a superintendent.

To say that the suspect was happy for me to take the samples may be stretching the view. Anyone arrested in an offence such as conspiracy to rob and discharging a firearm at arresting officers is unlikely to be at their best. With the appropriate authorities, and in the absence of any force being needed, I could undertake the examination, which I did. Had it come to a struggle, though, I would have to advise that the swabbing was unpractical in such a situation. This is because any force used could not be controlled and there would be a risk of poor and possibly contaminated sampling and, of course, injury. Again, as I've said before, in that case my notes and the custody record would show the refusal. This in itself could be presented in evidence and a prosecution lawyer use a clause in the Act to suggests that a refusal hid the complicity of the suspect. The examination had the ability to disprove as well as prove involvement.

Having examined many suspects for FDRs in the past, I was very familiar with the procedure. The Metropolitan Police Forensic Science Laboratory provided a special swabbing kit for the purpose. The kit was made under specific conditions to ensure that its contents were free from contamination before it was released for use. Its batch and history were monitored. When used, the procedure started with the operator (such as me) obtaining control samples from the room in which the examination was taking place and also from my own hands. Again this was to check and ensure that there was no contamination from the sampling process.

Only once this was done would I then put on a pair of gloves from within the kit and swab, with small sticky pre-labelled tabs, the fingers, back of hands and the face of the suspect. I would then comb the hair of the suspect for residues, using a comb with lint-filled moistened teeth designed for the purpose. The combing was also suitable for fibres and glass examination should that also be required later.

Having completed each swabbing, the items were placed back in the sample tubes, an examination information sheet filled in and all the items, including the sheet, placed in the single bag provided for the purpose which I labelled and sealed. It was marked my Exhibit PFM/1. It was the only exhibit I personally took. I ensured it was entered on the suspect's custody record and placed with the property seized from him.

Having completed my examination and notes, I left the arresting detective officer present to recover the suspect's clothing.

It was over a year later that I was called to give evidence at the trial of the suspect and his co-defendants at the Central Criminal Court at the Old Bailey in the City of London.

I probably sat outside the court for a couple of hours, but by then I was an old hand, and, like other expert witnesses, I was only called to the court once my turn was imminent.

The case was obviously being fiercely contested by the defence team. This was evident from the fact that no detectives were allowed in court, with the exception of the exhibits officers in the case (a detective constable from the Barnes office), who was needed to find exhibits when they were called for. The absence of the officer in the case (the leading investigator) was bound to hamper the progress of the case from an investigation point from view but indicated mistrust of the police by the defence.

The court usher called my name and I entered the courtroom, it was one of the newer larger rooms. The witness box was a few paces inside the door with the judge immediately to my left and the jury further left still. A row of lead barristers, one prosecutor and one for each of the defendants, sat in line, with a similar row of junior counsel behind. Then behind them were all the defendants (including the one I had examined) flanked by prison officers.

The fact that I had only taken one exhibit, the swabs for suspected FDRs, during the examination of the suspect did not necessarily mean that my time in the witness box was to be quick, straightforward and painless.

However, it was – so much so that I have little memory of it. I explained what I had done and I identified my exhibit PFM/1 when it was presented to me. What I do remember is the cross-examination by the lead counsel representing the defendant I had examined. He, I was later to find out, was the son of a leading politician and member of the House of Lords.

Defence counsel's opening remarks to me were unusual. He

stated that there were no allegations about my conduct during the investigation. This rather took me aback. That's very kind of you, I thought. He went on to say that his client had never fired a weapon and that he wanted me to explain how I had sealed the item before I passed it on. From bitter experience in other cases over the last two or so years I then knew I was in for a day or so in the witness box, arguing about when I had sealed the item, whether it had been interfered with and even if it was still in the same bag.

I seized the moment.

I had already had the opportunity to look at the exhibit when presenting my evidence in chief. Before identifying it to the court, I had ensured that it bore all the hallmarks of my original exhibit: the exhibit number, signature, signature seal, date, time, place, suspect's name and my report number. They were all there. There was no doubt that this was my original exhibit. I had also noticed the single opening and resealing with the signature and name of Dr Geoff Warman of the Metropolitan Police Forensic Science Laboratory. I had many dealings with Geoff and his colleagues, where he was a senior scientist and expert in FDRs. It was apparent to me (although not my evidence) that Geoff had examined the item at the laboratory before resealing it at the end of his examination.

As counsel spoke, I interrupted him and asked His Lordship if I could once again look at my exhibit PFM/1.

It is dangerous to appear clever when giving evidence, but experience and certainly exposure to the way of the courtroom can give you some confidence. I had no wish to stand in the witness box for a day whilst counsel wove a web of doubt about the origin and integrity of my exhibit, because I was sure of certain facts.

Holding the item in front of me I explained that the item bore the name of the suspect, my exhibit number and signature, the date and time it was sealed and also my signature seal. I observed that it contained one opening for which I could not account but also that I noticed the seal and signature across that opening of Dr Warman, who, if asked, might be able to throw light on that subject. I went on to state that when the item left my possession it was sealed and had it been received in any condition other than sealed I would expect the scientist who was asked to examine it to reject it for fear of contamination.

I closed with the statement that if, as counsel was suggesting, someone had interfered with the item after I took the swabs, contaminating or planting FDRs, it would have had to have taken place before I sealed the item at 16.47 as recorded on the item and in my notes on the day in question. I would have had to have been a party to any act of contamination or planting and I was not.

Shocked by my words, counsel said, 'And that is your answer?' 'It is, My Lord,' I replied. Counsel sat down with a stunned slump.

His Lordship thanked me and I was released from giving further evidence. The court rose for lunch and I walked out of court pretty pleased that I had avoided a prolonged time in the witness box. I was pursued from the court by DC Regan, a real-life namesake of that fictional Flying Squad detective, who was the exhibits officer in the case and the only officer allowed in the court. He had witnessed the whole (but I was pleased to say short) episode and he gleefully and vigorously shook my hand.

I made my way back to the office. 'Sorted,' I could hear the fictional Jack Regan say.

12. Turning the Key

The lifeless body of Stephen Reynolds was found at 30 Victoria Buildings, lying in a pool of blood. He had been shot through the head. There were no witnesses to the event and he would have remained undiscovered for much longer had the anonymous call not been made to the emergency services.

The post-mortem examination revealed that he had been drinking and that he had been killed by a single bullet as he lay in bed.

The investigation into his murder was being led by the local detective chief inspector at Bethnal Green Police Station. Most murders at the time were transferred to the Major Investigation Team at Division Headquarters, but such was their workload that they could not take this case, although it clearly fell into their category: difficult to solve cases. The DCI had only a small team drawn from the CID office. Their enquiries revealed that Stephen had a criminal record. Mainly petty crimes in his youth but now in his early twenties he had graduated to armed robbery. He had a conviction for driving a getaway car. He was a wheelman.

Keith Verrals received the call at the Flying Squad office. The DCI wanted to know if we had anything on Reynolds or had any interest in him. We hadn't, but the circumstances interested Keith and so he asked me to go with him to the incident room at Bethnal Green to have a look at the case.

Keith was a thorough and meticulous detective. A detective

constable then, tall and generally a quiet man, he didn't fit the image of flamboyant, confident lads that typified many of his Flying Squad peers, but he towered above many in his ability, commitment, hard work and success.

Whenever a call came in to a robbery in progress somewhere in north-east London he would be prepared to respond. He and his sergeant, Steve Waller, were a cool but committed team. Getting involved was their lifeblood. No only for solving the immediate crime but gathering intelligence and a database of knowledge about the ever-changing profile of the robberies on our patch and who was committing them.

Keith and I arrived at Bethnal Green, an old Victorian-built police station in London's East End. The building had long outlived its usefulness with its winding corridors and tiny staircases which would be worthy of a theme park maze. Trudging around the building with bags and armfuls of exhibits was a nightmare.

The CID office was a new addition to the building, a large-scale refurbished loft conversion. Quite airy, once you had found your way all the way to the top of the building.

We sat in on a briefing. There were no more than six or seven of us, including Keith and me. I was a little appalled at the size of the investigation team, given the amount of work needed to solve the crime.

The circumstances of the crime were a little unusual. Stephen was a single man, with a criminal history, living alone, well known in local pubs, in fact very well known. He liked a drink. Unemployed, and on state benefit, his only interests were drinking and cars. His pride and joy was a slightly old but special edition Ford. It was a lad's car. His flat was on the second floor of a block of flats built nearly a hundred years before, the front door opening on to the exposed walkway.

We listened to what was known about the case. There was no apparent motive but, of course, there was that strange call to the emergency services alerting them to the scene. Who was the caller? Were they the last person to see him alive? Were they his killer? The call transcript was short, the voice was male. The original phone call was made from a pay phone a few miles away.

Keith had an intuition about this guy and so we decided to have a closer look. I knew with Keith we were not wasting our time. If you don't look you don't find. We decided to visit the scene and then we would look through all the items recovered during the investigations. First of all we reviewed the scene photographs so that we could relate the scene as it was now, some days later, to the day his body was found.

There had been no forced entry, so either the front door was open, or his killer had been let in by Stephen or had a key. The flat was relatively tidy, as tidy as you could expect a flat occupied by single man living in such circumstances to be. There was no sign of any struggle.

Stephen's Ford was parked outside the block of flats where he lived. Locked and secure.

Looking through the exhibits register and inspecting the sealed items through their bags revealed a few interesting thoughts.

Stephen's front door key was amongst the items recovered from the scene, but no key to his car. Checks revealed that no Ford car key was found. Those who knew him had already told investigators that his car was his prized possession and he wouldn't let anyone else drive it. What had been found in his flat was a key to another car. A key to a Volkswagen, and the key was very new. There was no car in the immediate vicinity of the scene which the key fitted and none of his friends or neighbours had seen him with a VW.

This made my and Keith's ears immediately prick up. We had an interest in VW cars. For the past two months we had seen a series of armed robberies on Post Office security vans. In fact there were two series, which we had thought were one, until a clear pattern emerged which allowed us to separate them.

Both series were attacks by masked men armed with an assortment of handguns and shotguns on Post Office security vans as they delivered or picked up cash at small Post Offices dotted around the East End.

The first team used Ford Sierra cars; all stolen and displaying false number plates so as not to appear stolen. It was only as the series developed that I realised that the plates to each successive recovered car had been reattached with identical-looking screws. The original plastic screws had been discarded in favour of metal screws that I recovered on each car. I had examined most, if not all, of the stolen cars over the past weeks and there was no doubt in my mind that they were linked by this trait of this team.

The second team, also targeting Post Office vans at the same time and in the same geographic area, used VW cars. They also false-plated their getaway cars to hide their true identity. This time the new number plates were each attached with three strips of double-sided rubber tape. Once again, I had examined most or all of the cars at length and a distinct pattern had emerged.

It was only when the two series were compared side by side that we could clearly differentiate between the two teams. The determining factors were the cars they used, Ford Sierra or VW Golf, and how they reattached the false plates, metal screws or tape.

So the knowledge that Stephen was a suspected wheelman and finding a VW key with no apparent accompanying car really caught our attention.

What made it more interesting still was that there had been two armed robberies on Post Office security vans in the week preceding Stephen's death. The last was only a few days before his body was found.

Keith was a little unsure what to do with the VW key and where it could take us. I had some hope that there was intelligence locked literally in the key's manufacture. I was struck by how new and unused it looked. We made enquiries at a local

VW car dealer and found that the key was a new sort fitted to that year's models. Things moved quickly from there on. A call to VW revealed that there were a thousand or so combinations for each key. The new models were only a few months old. So we managed to get a full list of every car which had that key number fitted. It was a pretty long list. Finally, Keith ran the index numbers of each vehicle through the police computer. We hit the jackpot. One and only one VW with that key number was reported as stolen. It had not been recovered and there was every likelihood that it was sitting somewhere bearing the false plates of another vehicle, hiding its true identity.

The Vehicle Identification Number was circulated as this was the best way to identify a vehicle's true identity. An extensive search failed to find the car, but Keith and I were ready once it was found to see if it bore false plates, attached by rubber tape and if the key fitted.

The robbery series on Post Office security vans using VW getaway cars stopped with Stephen's death. Our information helped the murder squad detectives. It appeared that Stephen had been shot by the leader of the gang when he failed to meet them early one morning for another planned robbery. The leader went to Stephen's flat; finding him drunk and unable to drive, his anger exploded and he coolly shot Stephen. It was the killer who had called the police. Although he planned to use the VW car, he took the wrong key, he took the key to Stephen's own car.

It was a year later that I received a call that the VW had been found. I went to examine it with a colleague, Keith couldn't come but he waited on the end of the phone to hear the outcome.

Sure enough the plates were false and attached with strips of double-sided tape. And the key sweetly opened the door and started the engine.

We also managed to solve the other robbery series involving the Ford Sierra cars. Once the robbers had been identified and arrested, a search of one of their premises revealed, amongst other important items such as guns, a box of screws matching those I had found on each of the previously examined getaway cars. The scientist at the lab could only comment that they were of the same size and type, and were from the same manufacturer. I gave evidence at the trial regarding the somewhat unusual manner in which the original plates and plastic screws had been replaced by false plates and that visually indistinguishable metal screws were found on each Ford Sierra in the series of robberies on Post Office security vans. Although not specific or necessarily strong enough evidence to link the suspect to the crime, it had some evidential value when considered with other evidence. More importantly, it linked the scenes together by method and thereby strengthened the case.

13. Corroborating the Supergrass

Villains don't like 'grasses'. It is a dangerous and lonely occupation within the criminal world. Usually, a police informant or 'grass' is someone on the periphery of a criminal gang, but it is someone who knows what has gone on and sometimes, more usefully, what is about to happen.

Investigating serious and organised crime is a difficult task, so if someone is on the inside and is willing to help the police the offer will rarely be turned down. Some grasses may actually be part of the criminal gang. So their participation must be carefully handled, with full consent given, clear guidelines followed and with painstaking management by their police handlers and senior police commanders. Such a grass is classed as a participating informant. They must not encourage or be part of the planning of the crime in any way or they would be rightly accused of provocation, egging the crime on, a crime which would not happen if they weren't involved. They are encouraged to frustrate the crime, leaving the main participants to be arrested for less substantial offences, such as conspiracy.

Occasionally, when a team of criminals is arrested for a serious offence such as armed robbery, one of them might opt to roll over, turn Queen's evidence and be a grass, not only in the case for which they have been arrested but for others the gang has committed. There must be no incentive or promises to the individual, other than that the judge will be told of their help in the investigation. A prison sentence, albeit a shorter one, will be served in separate prison facilities. With safeguards in place such an individual may be given 'resident informant' or 'supergrass' status. Then the work of the police really begins.

The supergrass system had, however, fallen into serious disrepute in the 1970s. The system had been completely discarded in armed robbery investigations. A number of high-profile cases had collapsed when the evidence of the supergrass was discredited. They were often accused of giving the police what they wanted to hear. Easily contested by strong defence counsel and without independent corroboration, the use of supergrasses served no use. But that was about to change. There was a new tool and I, like many others, was trained to use it. The crime scene and forensic science evidence was to make or break this case.

The first offence which the Flying Squad investigated, one which was to become part of a large series, occurred in the spring of 1985. Early one morning, three armed men arrived at the crematorium in Enfield, north London. They took the staff hostage and waited for a security van to arrive. The van was due to drop off a small amount of wages but, unknown to the gang, the delivery time had been changed that morning. The gang waited but, once the expected time passed, they left the staff tied up and departed empty-handed. A device had been strapped to one of the hostages. It was found to be a viable device and, although no explosive substance was present, it could have caused some injury.

Two weeks later, Hertfordshire Police were called to the premises of Cross and Herbert in Hoddeston. Members of staff had been tied up and held hostage by two men, again when a security van was due to arrive. The van's crew sensed something was wrong as the area was unusually quiet and aborted the drop. So once again the gang left empty-handed.

Three weeks later, the Flying Squad investigated an attempted armed robbery at a business premises in Brimsdown, Enfield. Three men took the staff hostage whilst they expected a security van to arrive. It didn't, so they left.

Two months later, the premises of Imperial Cold Storage in Tottenham took the gang's attention. Two men armed with a handgun and a shotgun took members of staff hostage. A security van arrived and one guard made a drop but he was quickly attacked and an explosive device was strapped to him with threats that if he didn't comply it would be detonated. He was made to go back to the van. His colleagues were overpowered.

By this time other workers were arriving for work and a shot was fired. A manager too arrived and he was overpowered and another shot was fired. The gang escaped in the manager's car with a large quantity of cash.

The Flying Squad linked these scenes together because descriptions and other factors matched and, quite simply, large-scale robberies are not that common. The gang had left a number of items behind, but not a single finger mark. Most interesting to Detective Constable Kevin Shapland, who was investigating the crimes, was the explosive device which they had left strapped to the terrified guard at Imperial Cold Storage.

Kevin arranged for the offence to be publicised on the BBC *Crimewatch* programme. This was a now monthly opportunity for police to appeal to a large TV audience for any information members of the public might have regarding serious crime investigations. It was popular prime TV viewing and it had resulted in many successes. Apart from members of the public calling in, police and prison officers from around the country would watch in and have information which the police network had failed to communicate. This is not a criticism but a reality with the sheer volume of information which circulates in the police service. The programme has also resulted in the prompt arrest of suspects whose descriptions or photographs have been so accurate that the suspects themselves walked into a police station to give themselves up.

The device was shown on the programme but the response was lukewarm at best, but then something happened which can only be described as luck. Luck is something which sometime happens and Kevin could be said to be luckier than most detectives. The saying 'you make you own luck' has elements of truth. Kevin's sheer productivity led to things which meant nothing on their own suddenly falling into place.

A young boy living in Broxbourne, Hertfordshire had been watching TV one night and slotted in a video to watch a film he had recorded some weeks before. The video had recorded part of the *Crimewatch* programme which was broadcast before the film. The boy saw Kevin's appeal and, more importantly, recognised the device. The boy was, like many teenage boys, a bit of a geek, a bit of a hoarder. A few weeks before, the boy had been looking through a plastic bag left out by a neighbour for that morning's refuse collection in the road where he lived. In it he found a circuit board which looked remarkably like the one which Kevin had shown. The boy also found a mask and a wig. The boy kept the pieces and was particularly inquisitive about the device, but having studied it and played with the mask he later threw all the pieces away.

The boy called the local police, who contacted Kevin. Although the boy had thrown away the device he had found he was able to draw it. Kevin was convinced that this was a firm lead and no coincidence. So he made enquiries about the occupant of Emerald, the house outside which the boy had found the items. The house had recently changed hands. The previous owner ran an electrical business, but enquiries led nowhere, and it was pretty clear that he had nothing whatsoever to do with the robberies. Kevin's attention moved to the new occupants. David and Rita Croke moved to Emerald from rented accommodation in Enfield where they had lived for many years. David apparently had no regular job and Kevin ascertained that he had a couple of very minor criminal conviction many years before. The house was in Rita's name, but had been bought outright for cash.

Kevin was working on other investigations and other lines of enquiry. But he made more discreet enquiries about the Emerald lead and would pass by the house at regular intervals and note the registration numbers of cars parked on the drive or nearby.

It was then that another offence took place. In December 1985 Joe Symes, who worked as a guard at the Armaguard security depot in Harlow, Essex, returned home late one evening. Opening the door he found his wife and daughter being held hostage in their own home by two armed and masked men. It was apparent the men knew a lot about Joe and his family and where he worked. They strapped a device to him and told him that they would detonate it if he didn't do exactly as they said.

Joe and his family were kept hostage overnight. His wife and child were allowed to go to sleep but Joe was quizzed. Joe was a custodian, so he held one of the sets of keys to the premises, but two sets were needed to gain full access to the company vault. Another custodian needed to be overpowered. Very early the following morning Joe was made to drive back to his place of work. As other workers, including a second custodian, arrived for work they were attacked. This gave the gang full access to the vault and allowed them to strip it of a large quantity of cash. The employees were locked in a room and it was a few hours before the alarm was raised. Joe's wife and child were found unharmed, but tied up at the family home. They were terrified and had suffered a long ordeal. The robbery was the largest in Essex Police's history and news quickly filtered through to the Flying Squad office. Essex set up a major incident room headed by a detective superintendent.

The device was disrupted by the Army Ordnance Corps. But when later reconstructed it was found to be a dummy. It was found to contain nothing more than wires and lights, which nevertheless had a terrifying effect on the victims.

Kevin made immediate contact with the Essex investigation team. He was seconded to the investigation there for a short while. There was a concern that the *Crimewatch* programme may have led to a copycat team trying their luck. It was a serious concern which needed to be borne in mind.

Further observations were made of the coming and goings at Emerald. One day there was particular activity at the premises. Surveillance photographs showed the presence of a car that was registered to the wife of a man also very well known amongst detective for his past criminal activity. There was also a photograph of a tall slim man. When the photograph was passed around the Flying Squad office, Phil Burrows, a detective sergeant, immediately recognised him. The man was Don Barrett. He was a former supergrass and a division one armed robber. The investigation was given an official operation title and Operation Standard was born.

Donald Walter Barrett was a career criminal, with a string of convictions for violence and armed robbery going back over thirty years. Now approaching fifty, he was a tall handsome man, but masked and holding a shotgun he would frighten the hell out of any law-abiding member of the public who would have the misfortune to meet him.

Barrett had been a supergrass in the 1970s. He had been caught 'bang to rights' at an armed robbery by the Flying Squad. He had turned supergrass against his criminal colleagues, which resulted in a string of lengthy convictions for them. His reward was a lighter, but still considerable, sentence. In his early days he had been at the wrong end of a supergrass's evidence. Bertie Smalls, the very first supergrass, had informed on him.

Once out of prison Barrett went back to his old ways. He was known as a grass amongst the top divisions of robbers, but Croke, with no convictions or apparent experience in armed robbery, decided to work with him. I'm not sure if he knew of Barrett's past or his craft as a ruthless robber was sufficient to make him attractive to work with. Equally, Croke may have believed that Barrett wouldn't or couldn't be a supergrass again and that made him more attractive. Whatever the reason, Croke did work with Barrett. Barrett knew how the police worked, maybe Croke thought this would be useful. If he did, he would be wrong.

Other players were noted coming and going at Emerald. Barrett and Croke travelled down to Battersea in London, followed by a police surveillance team. Barrett and Croke paid particular attention to Shield Security, a security company premises on an industrial estate. A car was noticed there which had also been seen outside Emerald. It belonged to a young man called Al Turner who worked at the security company.

A full surveillance operation was mounted over the coming weeks. It was pretty clear that Shield Security was to receive the gang's attention and Turner was the inside man. For this reason the company could not be contacted directly by the detectives for fear that anyone close to the management might be involved or unwittingly let out to Turner or any other crooked employee that the police were on to them.

One night there was late-night activity at Emerald with Barrett and Croke both present. In the early hours of the following morning, Turner drove to work at the depot, followed by Barrett and Croke in a blue Ford Escort van.

The full police team were called in and were briefed at Lambeth Police Support HQ. From there I was called to slip quietly into a rear entrance of Battersea Police Station with Kevin and a few other officers. This station was at the entrance to the industrial estate where Shield was located. It was normally only open during daylight hours to serve the local business community. The building remained in darkness throughout the night, hiding its cargo of detectives, including Kevin Shapland, who kept 'eyeball' or observation from a darkened first-floor office window.

Turner waited for a colleague to arrive. Barrett and Croke were parked up nearby. Then, rather unexpectedly, Turner came out of the building carrying a small but very heavy box, followed by his colleague. They got into a white security van and drove off, followed closely by Barrett and Croke in the blue van.

It was decision time for the police commander. Peter Gwynne, the detective chief superintendent, immediately gave the order for the surveillance team to split. Half would stay at the industrial estate, whilst half would follow the vehicle at a discreet distance. The police helicopter was used to track the vehicles as they made their way north across London, eventually picking up the M1 motorway.

All the time the blue Escort van remained close behind the security van. Moving north caused problems for the trailing surveillance officers and detectives. They were armed and they needed to inform each police force area they entered that they were there.

Finally, the security van pulled into the service area at Newport Pagnall, near Milton Keynes in Buckinghamshire. Turner went and got two cups of coffee and returned to the vehicle, pursued closely on foot by Barrett and Croke, who by this stage was wearing a poorly fitting wig. The white van quickly left the service area and it was seen that Croke was driving it, followed by Barrett, on his own in the blue van. That was enough. Within half a mile of the service area the signal to 'attack' was given. To give the 'attack' is the pinnacle of a Flying Squad detective's career and normally reserved for the senior officer on the ground. I have observed it many times and it still fills me with emotion and pride to have witnessed such brave action by police officers. It is when the tables are turned and the criminals who think they are in control suddenly realise they are not. Out of the very woodwork, normal-looking members of the public emerge, in unison, show their true colours and pounce on the gang as they literally go 'across the pavement'. Well, the pavement this time was the M1, the major motorway running through England. Listening on the radio back in Battersea, I heard the words 'Attack, attack, attack'. Not then a religious man I still said a prayer, for the safety of those going into action. The next few minutes were an anxious wait until the news of the arrests was conveyed with the welcome information that they had been effected without injury.

Flying Squad vehicles had forced the white and blue vans to stop. The Squad officers emerged from their cars, surrounded the vans, and with sheer overwhelming numbers and fire power quickly took control, but not before Croke and Barrett had tried to make a run for it. Turner and his colleague were both found tied up and lying face down in the back of the white security van.

Barrett took it like the seasoned professional robber he was. Croke not quite so. It was his first arrest in such circumstances, his world had been turned upside down and he hadn't seen it coming.

Both men were in possession of loaded handguns, ammunition, radio scanners (for monitoring police radio frequencies, unsuccessfully on this occasion). Croke was wearing the wig and Barrett a balaclava mask. A knife was taken off Croke.

Turner and his colleague were released from their bonds and to his surprise, Turner was promptly arrested. The content of the box was examined and revealed a quantity of gold bullion bars valued at a quarter of a million pounds.

The motorway was closed for half an hour as the suspects were taken away and the vehicles recovered. I was already on my way and within an hour I had arrived at Milton Keynes Police Station.

At the police station, Barrett realised his predicament. He would die in prison, either from old age or from an attack by another inmate. He quickly offered to turn grass. At first the suggestion may have been laughed at, but it soon received more serious consideration. The rest of the team were obviously not going to help the detectives. So his offer was carefully considered. After a few days' discussion at the highest levels within the force, it was accepted. Barrett became the first man in British legal history to be a supergrass for the second time.

I knew I was working with competent and talented detectives, I knew my job and I was sure we would be able to determine if Barrett was telling the truth or not. We had to find strong independent corroboration which would satisfy the most testing defence examination. It would take many months of meticulous work by a diverse team of professionals, but the truth was out there. We would have to review many old scenes, some going back years. It would involve undertaking new examinations of suspects, their homes and workplaces to find incriminating evidence. This was the nature of using crime scene and forensic science evidence to corroborate the supergrass.

The fact that Barrett had been caught was testament to the fact that there is no such thing as a perfect crime. Even he, who had spent a lifetime committing crime, getting caught and informing, had made mistakes. Some of the obvious thoughts probably went through his mind as he stood on the windy hard shoulder of the M1. Evidence would convict him if he chose to keep tight lipped about his involvement. And not only for the offence for which he had been arrested, but for others too. His attractiveness to the team was his awareness of new forensic techniques and the things he had learned as a career criminal and a grass, and these all proved to be useless. He simply created more and different types of evidence.

The investigator who pursued him for two years was Kevin Shapland. Kevin was a prolific detective. Prematurely grey with a full head of hair and in his early thirties, he maintained a string of informants. This kept the Flying Squad north-east London office busy on its own. No mean feat when the office at the time contained fifty detectives, many amongst the élite of their profession. Kevin was a detective constable, the lowest detective rank, but his abilities outshone many of much higher rank. Kevin wasn't interested in promotion; he never took the necessary exam to make sergeant. It was his choice. He didn't want it and didn't need it. The rank of detective sergeant of the Flying Squad was a career milestone for most. As detective constable he would be the junior, the bag carrier to his sergeant. But such was Kevin's reputation that his sergeant rightly acknowledged who was senior. Kevin was the only detective constable to be widely known to have a detective sergeant as his bag carrier.

There was no detective task that he couldn't turn his talents to. He often led the investigation with only the cursory eye of a senior officer. His talent and maturity always shone through. On the occasions when the investigation wasn't his, he would always volunteer to help, just as one of the guys, taking statements, interviewing suspects or handling the exhibits register. To each he would give total professionalism.

Kevin is simply the best detective I have ever worked with, and there have been many contenders.

So Barrett's arrest may have seemed a foregone conclusion. Nonetheless, it is remarkable since it came out of a situation that in the early days seemed to hold little prospect.

The suspects were held 'incommunicado', which means they were briefly denied any contact with the outside world, including legal representation, whilst searches and other arrests were made. This was to prevent other suspects finding out what had happened and escaping or trying to destroy evidence. I say trying to because the very action of destroying evidence often produces more. I will not elaborate! So the arrests at Newport Pagnall triggered a series of arrests and searches. Rita Croke was confronted by a detective as she walked to the front of Emerald with a black plastic refuse bag. She must have already known or suspected something was up, because the bag contained a pistol, shotgun cartridges, hats and clothing. She was arrested and brought to Milton Keynes also.

Things were hectic at Milton Keynes Police Station. This was the biggest thing to happen there in a long time. The first thing I did on arriving was to introduce myself to the local SOCOs, of which there were four. I briefed them as to what had happened and asked for their assistance, which I was pledged, with the exception of one who appeared uninterested. He could not be shaken from reading a newspaper, sat in his chair, even when the Metropolitan Police helicopter, the only one in the country at that time, landed directly outside his window. I wouldn't have minded but it didn't even appear a decent newspaper. I realised I wasn't going to get any help from him, and, quite frankly, I didn't want it. Coming in from the Met, and particularly from the Flying Squad, often had an adverse affect on provincial officers. Many Met, and perhaps some Flying Squad, officers tried to lord it over their provincial colleagues. The Met was generally good, and the Squad special, simply because of the volume and level of crime it had to investigate. Many provincial officers were every bit as skilled and committed. This was something I tried to recognise and communicate as soon as I went into a police station outside London. I often needed help and the best way to get it was to recognise the worth of others. Swooping in unannounced at provincial police forces was the nature of the job, and my approach normally ensured absolute assistance. I was fortunate to witness some excellent commitment and professionalism amongst the new colleagues I encountered.

Operation Standard now had a number of urgent priorities. The vehicles would require supervised removal to the police station and the prisoners would need to be examined. I briefed the local SOCOs and divided up the work.

I was present when Barrett was examined. This took place before any interview. A police surgeon was called to take blood samples and he arrived promptly. As well as preparing bags and containers for the samples we would take, I had scanned the room for sharp objects. I had had a scare a few years before. In a similar situation, a suspect had noticed a kitchen knife left by a member of the custody staff after an inappropriate meal. The suspect made a move to grab the knife to aid his escape but was thwarted by a quick-thinking police officer. Barrett was brought into the examination room by a police custody officer and stood with his back to the examination couch. I was busy, carefully writing down the doctor's extremely long and unusual name when I heard the doctor say, 'What samples do you want?' Still concentrating on writing the doctor's name, I gathered my thoughts. Before I could speak, I heard Barrett's gravely voice confidently reply, 'Oh the usual, blood, urine, saliva, hair samples.' Instead of addressing his question to Kevin, the doctor had asked Barrett. When I looked up I realised why he had made the mistake. Barrett was dressed in a smart shirt and tie. Kevin was dressed in blue jeans and T-shirt. Given Barrett's smart appearance the doctor had assumed that he was the detective and Kevin was the man in custody. Stunned for a moment, I intervened and told the doctor the error of his ways. Barrett had seized and capitalised on the moment even though he could not possibly profit from such an action. Once I had pointed out the mistake to the flustered doctor, we all laughed at the humour of the situation. It demonstrated Barrett's calm and cheekiness in the most serious of situations for him. It underlined to me the fact that although Barrett was in custody and going nowhere, he was nevertheless still extremely alert and a very formidable adversary.

The examination was thorough and conducted in an atmosphere of cooperation by Barrett. He consented to all the samples, although he could have refused some. Blood and saliva samples were taken for grouping (DNA technology had yet to be used in forensic science at that time), blood and urine for drugs and alcohol, to determine the physical state of the suspect. Hair combings and hair samples were taken for hair and fibre examinations. All of Barrett's outer clothing was taken.

The episode in the examination room was an insight into Barrett's considerable knowledge, and it was pretty accurate. He had gone through every criminal academy on offer. Although his knowledge was good he had made mistakes, not least being caught. He had left clues which would link him to previous offences that we were investigating.

It was over the next few hours that Barrett surveyed his situation. He was, after all, a former supergrass and his time in prison, which was likely to be lengthy, would be more unpleasant (if that were possible) and dangerous. He would be segregated from the main prison population with the sex offenders, but his life could be in danger and he knew it.

Croke appeared to be the mastermind, but he was by, comparison, of relative good character previously. So, if anyone was expected to roll over, it would be him. In any event it was Barrett who quickly offered to turn informant, to the surprise of Kevin Shapland and Detective Sergeant Dick Kirby. If Kevin was the best detective I have ever worked with, Dick was a strong contender for the runner-up slot. Dick was a cunning and shrewd craftsman. It was he who paved the way for Barrett to be accepted as a supergrass for the second time. This was no mean feat and involved taking a 'without prejudice' statement, which Barrett was told would never have seen the light of day again if the Director of Public Prosecutions had rejected his offer to inform.

The statement was accepted and Barrett knew that the court would learn of his cooperation and he could fall on their mercy.

The investigation in hand was not about mercy for Barrett, but rather truth. There was a lot of work for me to do. Not least the completion of the vehicle examination and the collation of all the exhibits which had been recovered. I elected to stay in Milton Keynes for a few days rather than spend a couple of hours driving each day in the heavy traffic back to London. I was put up in a pleasant guest room on one of the upper floors of the police station. The station was new and had three major incident suites which were put at our disposal. The scenes of crime suite boasted a group of spacious rooms, including office, examination room and photographic studio. It occurred to me that they were expecting a lot of trouble in the future. The facilities made the job much easier.

We already suspected the team of involvement in at least four offences. Barrett quickly told us of another seven offences, making a total of eleven major armed robberies.

Within a few days, Barrett was taken to the secret and secure location in east London which would be his home for over a year until the trial a long way in the future. The investigation team would also be based there.

The issue of corroboration came up almost immediately. An initial statement was taken from Barrett outlining the extent of the gang's activity. A meeting was called by Detective Inspector Ken Grange, who had been given the overall responsibility for the investigation. Present were a team of about eight officers, myself and a typist. The team would remain together until the trial, although I still had to undertake my normal duties back at the main office on other investigations.

Dick advised that a detailed separate statement be taken from Barrett for each offence. Corroboration was a key issue from the very beginning. The disrepute into which the supergrass system had fallen was the result of previous supergrasses making up stories to please their interrogators. That could not happen here. It was at that point that someone suggested that Barrett should tell us where we could find forensic and other evidence. It may have been that some of the detectives present were giving Barrett credit for his forensic knowledge or awareness. The incident in the examination room at Milton Keynes was fresh in their minds. I was deeply unhappy with this approach. He would be leading us and that was not good as far as I was concerned. I felt it wasn't just about corroborating the offences themselves. I thought it was important to corroborate as much as possible of what Barrett told us, however trivial. This would ensure that the whole of Barrett's story was accurate. This was accepted and it would be my role primarily to look at the detailed statements, seek corroboration from whatever had been recovered in the previous investigations and undertake or arrange further examinations if they were necessary. The eleven offences covered six police force areas going back four years. Around £1.4 million had been stolen and a lot of innocent victims assaulted and terrorised in the process.

A long and detailed statement was obtained for each offence. One of the investigation team was designated to ensure that all the case papers and exhibits were obtained from the police force concerned.

Detective Constable Ray Bennett was given the job of exhibits officer, the task of controlling all the exhibits. Apart from the original exhibit numbers, an additional identification serial number was added to indicate in which offence the item was recovered. This would ensure that where numbers were similar or duplicated, they would be easily referred to and understood.

The integrity of the items was paramount. Without this any further examinations would be impossible. So the condition in which each item was received and how it was packaged, labelled and sealed was examined.

In only one case did the items reach us in an unsealed condition and without clear documentation, which meant that we could not undertake further comparison. The integrity of the items had been breached possibly by ongoing inspection by the original investigators after the first laboratory examinations. I could not tell if we even had the original items as they were not sealed, even though they matched the documented descriptions. Someone had decided that the sealing, labelling and integrity of the items were no longer an issue. They were wrong. The items had not been destroyed as at the conclusion of an investigation. The fact that we found them in a police property store showed that the case had not been closed. This was a shame but equally a fact. It is not uncommon for the integrity of items to be neglected after a long period of time, once it is felt that the detailed forensic examinations have been completed. The fact is that they are really never complete and items should be sealed and accompanied by a complete record of their opening and examination until the time they are destroyed.

The examination of Emerald could have taken months and could have been without a clear purpose. So a strategy was adopted which meant that there would be a comprehensive search but the scene would be left as intact as possible. This meant that return visits could be made as more information from Barrett came to light. Police would remain in control of the premises for some weeks as it was technically a continuing search.

Emerald was a bungalow with a big garden and an exterior garage. A large quantity of material was recovered in the search. Each piece was described, documented, labelled and sealed whilst its potential was evaluated.

Once all the initial searches had been completed, the core group of the team sat down with the exhibit registers for each offence and search. The group included the senior investigator, his deputy, other detectives, the exhibits officer and me. Every statement had to be read and understood to identify potential areas of evidence and corroboration. Every single item of the many hundreds we had collected together was considered in turn. Each item was evaluated. I asked the question, 'What could this item be examined for to prove or disprove the allegations made?' The answers ranged from finding the offenders' finger marks on a surface, to which they did not have legitimate access, to establishing that wires cut at the crime scene were cut by a pair of wire-cutters found at a suspect's address. Often items would require a sequence of examinations, such as the wire-cutters for cutting marks, paint and fingerprints. So from scene, suspect, vehicle or suspect's address the contribution of every item to the case was considered. This was a mammoth task. It meant that nothing was missed. Every piece of intelligence and evidence could be recovered from all the items based on what we knew and what we suspected. Even at this relatively early stage we recognised that whatever answers we received from the laboratory examinations, there was likelihood that they would promote further questions. That was our hope and it is what investigation is all about.

Some questions were independent of the supergrass's insight. They were things we would have done routinely. In the search of Emerald a quantity of cutting implements, including wire-cutters, were recovered. Detailed examination of one of many revealed that it had been used to cut the perimeter fence wire at the Armaguard scene in Essex. The wig which Croke had been wearing at the time of his arrest contained fibres from a mask which had been dropped at Armaguard. A pot of adhesive recovered from Emerald was of identical composition to that used on the Armaguard 'bomb' device. A piece of cloth torn from a garment, complete with stitching of a different colour, found at Emerald matched a piece left inside the device recovered at the Cross and Herbert scene. The battery cover to the scanning device found at Armaguard fitted a scanner with a missing battery cover found at Emerald.

This evidence alone would have built a strong enough case against the gang for the Cross and Herbert and the Armaguard robberies. But there were other offences. This time Barrett would play his part.

About a month into the investigation a full picture of the allegations being made by Barrett was clear. Other suspects were implicated and areas for search identified. A detailed plan was drawn up of those who needed to be arrested and interviewed and where premises needed to be search for evidence. Extensive briefings were prepared and officers from all four Flying Squad branch offices around London called in to assist. Over a hundred and fifty officers converged on the north-east branch office at four am on the day of the searches. The five Squad SOCOs were there. Over twenty-four premises were to be searched simultaneously at six am. The briefings completed, the teams set out. The SOCOs were sent to the priority searches but were available to assist in any others should the need arise. By the end of that day hundreds of sealed items were deposited at the branch office. It would take me almost a year to work through and assess the entire potential evidence and arrange specialist examination at a forensic science laboratory.

Items for fingerprint examination I would examine or submit to the Metropolitan Police Fingerprint Laboratory. Many of the armed robberies we were now reinvestigating had been examined at a range of forensic science laboratories. Predominantly, the Metropolitan Police Forensic Science Laboratory and the Home Office Forensic Science Laboratory in Huntingdon had received items from the original investigations. At least two of the cases had been examined by a particular senior scientist, Kevan Dunnicliff, at the Huntingdon laboratory. Kevan was a quiet, bespectacled, studious individual. In his presence there was no doubt that this precise man was an expert in his field. I knew the sheer volume of work I was giving him would be demanding on his time. In discussion with him it was clear he understood the nature of the corroborative task we were undertaking. There was pressure on me to submit the cases to the Metropolitan Police Forensic Science Laboratory. It was geographically nearer to the new investigation team and our usual laboratory, but from an investigative point of view that was irrelevant. Most had been submitted to other Home Office forensic science laboratories and, more importantly, Armaguard had been sent to Kevan at Huntingdon. So it was my decision that all the items would be submitted there as Kevan had the most prior experience in the case. Nobody challenged this from within the investigation or in my professional chain of command. I arranged for Kevan to act as the lead scientist. As a forensic chemist he would have the main bulk of the work, particularly with the devices and components we had recovered. He would also call on the expert services of Mike Harris (a forensic biologist) and John Burns (a ballistics expert). The purpose of the examinations was made clear, establishing a link between suspect and scene or scene and scene. Kevan could coordinate this so that the best and most effective method of achieving our goals, if indeed there were links, could be made. The very nature of the task meant that there was a lot of cross-referencing and it would take time and resources. We all wanted to work as efficiently as possible. I made many trips to the laboratory to ensure Kevan, his team and the investigators back in London were kept up to date. The communication worked well and, although it took time, the case continued to build.

Sometimes we got answers we were not expecting. An interesting line of enquiry had us all confused for a while. At the Armaguard scene a white Honda van had been seen by two of the witnesses. In an unprompted statement from Barrett he told of how he went with Croke to a lock-up private garage where a van had been stored for over a year before the robbery. He also stated that Croke had accidentally pulled the garage door over the van, causing the door to slam against the front of the vehicle. Croke had driven the van across to France on his way to Malta for a holiday, directly after the successful Armaguard robbery. The van had broken down en route, and he abandoned it and bought another car to complete his journey.

Barrett had only visited the garage where the van was stored once. After some research it was found and I went there to undertake an examination. Enquiries locally revealed that it had been unused for some time. Opening the garage door it was found to be empty, apart from a pair of roof bars on the floor against the rear wall.

I carefully examined the door of the garage with a good lamp. There, on a cross-member on the inside surface, I saw a flake of firmly fixed and embedded paint. It had remained stuck there; even Barrett wasn't to know that. Measuring and recording it, I carefully removed the paint, placing it in a small sample container. I also took a control sample of the paint on the garage door so that this could be eliminated.

I then turned my attention to the roof bars on the garage

floor. Barrett hadn't mentioned them at all. He may never have seen or noticed them. What was striking from the start was that the fixings were set to fit a very small vehicle. Magnifying glass in hand, I carefully looked at the rusted grip end. I could see very small pieces of paint embedded there too. I could not see any real colour as the surface I was looking at was probably an undercoat. To remove them would be very difficult and potentially disastrous. So, having measured the gauge of the roof bar setting, I covered the grips with small plastic bags and taped along the shaft to secure and protect the grip ends.

The dimensions at which the bars were set were the exact size to fit a Honda van of the type described. It was of a particularly narrow width as the van was really quite small. Kevan made a detailed microscopic examination of the grip ends of the bars which revealed fragments of vehicle paint. The layer structure (primer, undercoat and top-coat) was that of a Honda van and model of the period. But the top coat was yellow. This was not the manufacturer's original finish and indicated that the vehicle from which it came had been resprayed. The witnesses had clearly described the small Honda van as white.

This paint found on the garage door too was from a white Honda van which had been resprayed yellow. This was significant information and corroborated Barrett but not the witnesses at Armaguard who had seen a white Honda van. Barrett had described it as yellow and he had seen it hit the garage door. The remnants of the van were found in France. Although it had been scrapped, someone had cut the rear off and turned it into a trailer. It was definitely yellow and paint samples were obtained to confirm the layer structure. The two witnesses from the Armaguard scene were re-interviewed and it was revealed exactly when they had seen the van. They had both seen the van before dusk, under sodium street lighting. When this was reconstructed it was clear that if anyone didn't already know the colour of the van it would appear white under the street lighting there.

This was significant to me and a testament to the corroboration process we had undertaken. Barrett told investigators what he had seen. The Armaguard witnesses too, but although their view was truthful, the sodium street lighting had deceived them. The paint and roof bars corrected this view. Barrett didn't even know about the roof bars and that corroborated his evidence and linked it to a Honda van, the type, if not the colour seen at the crime scene. Barrett was telling the police the truth. The corroboration process was working.

Barrett gave a statement regarding a robbery which occurred in Greenwich, south London, committed by him, Croke and other gang members. A security van was attacked in the street. Croke had tried to shoot through the armour-plated glass first with some home-made armour-piercing bullets and then with a builder's nail gun. Both failed but left the screen badly damaged. This offence would never have been linked to the gang if Barrett hadn't informed the investigators. There was nothing to link them description-wise or in the method of attack and it was lost in the recorded investigation detail. So it was never linked before Barrett brought it to our attention. Barrett said that Croke had experimented by making steel-headed ammunition and had accidentally discharged one in his garage. A return visit to Emerald was undertaken and the damage found, revealing yet more evidence.

Examination of the items from the Greenwich scene revealed another piece of cloth. It was found in the getaway car and was complete with a seam and stitching. It matched up with the two pieces of cloth found at Cross and Herbert and Emerald. There was a three-way connection. All these pieces of cloth had originated from the same garment.

Barrett went on to tell investigators where the industrial nail gun could be found. It was at the home address of another suspect. A search was undertaken and a Hilti builder's nail gun was recovered. Examination of the mechanism revealed fragments of glass which matched the laminated armoured screen of the security vehicle which had been attacked.

The holiday which Croke took in Malta with his wife was also to be significant. Barrett had joined them there. One evening, after a good meal with plenty of drink, David Croke decided to buy a boat and name it *Armag*, after the premises which they had robbed. It was a bit of bravado on his part and he saw the idea through. A few days later (no doubt having sobered up) this didn't seem such a good idea so it was over-painted with plain white paint. Barrett told us where the boat could be found. I knew that if we could find the boat we could use light sources to see through the upper paint layers to reveal the name underneath. Kevin Shapland arranged a trip to Malta on which I would accompany him. In the end it was Detective Inspector Ken Grange and Kevin Shapland who went. If the boat was found I would be called for. The boat was found, but senior officers at Scotland Yard felt that they had spent enough on this trip so the two detectives would have to do their best without me. I was disappointed and I spent a day on the phone to the Malta Police Laboratory which probably cost more than a trip would have. Under my direction they indeed revealed the name *Armag* from the lower paint surface of the boat. This was photographed. Kevin Shapland, ever the professional, took a statement that the word 'Armag' meant nothing in the local language.

In another twist, Barrett admitted to a bullion robbery that he and Croke had undertaken in the west of England. The amount reported stolen was under £100,000. But Barrett and Croke had actually stolen three times that amount. It was revealed that the company they robbed, at gunpoint, had been in fact recycling gold bullion from another major armed robbery. They had stolen already stolen gold! A dust coat found in the garage at Emerald had been examined for firearms residues in con-nection with Croke's alleged manufacture and discharging of weapons there. Fragments of bullion-quality gold were found in the pockets during this examination.

Although no finger marks matching the suspects had been found at any of the scenes, fingerprint evidence was to play an important role. Croke and others had opened bank accounts in false names. Their fingerprints were found on documents, which enabled a direct link between them and the accounts and deposits after each successful robbery to be made.

Even robbers have to use banks if they want to legitimise their ill gotten gains. In the major bullion robbery which preceded Croke and Barrett's robbery in the west of England, many other suspects drew attention to themselves in a variety of ways. One very large but not too bright individual was given the task of taking a quantity of laundered cash to deposit at a small bank in a village outside London. He towered well over six and a half feet tall and was almost as wide. He had to wait for the bank to open; its hours were limited to just a few and only on two days a week. The presence of such a stranger drew attention in the quiet village. When the bank finally opened he went inside to be greeted by the small, elderly bank cashier. Placing £3,000 in cash on the counter with details of the account into which it was to be paid, he turned smartly and was about to leave. He was stopped by the cashier who in a firm motherly voice told him to wait. Being the polite man he was in the company of such a matriarchal figure he stood still. He waited whilst she counted the cash. But there was a problem. There was £3,100 and not the £3,000 that had been written on the slip for him. 'What shall I do with the extra £100?' the lady asked. He was struck dumb. He had no instructions for this eventuality, it was outside his brief. So he thought for a while and then calmly said to the elderly lady, 'Have a drink!' turned and left. The episode was enough to draw attention to the money-laundering process taking place in small amounts around the country.

The case built against Croke and the other defendants, aided by Barrett's testimony and the corroboration was accumulating.

There was no silver bullet. Such is the nature of corroboration; there was lots of simple but significant independent scientific evidence which showed he was telling the truth in the small and large things.

As time went on, I was drawn back to other duties at the main office and I had to organise my time, undertaking examinations and then planning submissions to the laboratory. Trips to the lab allowed me to keep up to date with developments and ensure clear communication between investigators and laboratory. As information and result became available, they would be communicated and reviewed to see if yet more work was needed.

Once the statements were back from Kevan and the many scientists who had undertaken an array of examinations, they were each reviewed by the detectives and me to see if they led anywhere else. The integrity, history and examinations of every item were cross-referenced and the items prepared for easy accessibility at court. The whole process took over a year.

Lawyers advised that the trial would last at least four months. The police and prosecutors were ready. At one stage, in an attempt to get off a charge of armed robbery of the van at Newport Pagnall, Croke tried to claim that not only Al Turner but the other guard was also in on the crime. This would mean that, instead of robbery, they had committed a theft made to look like a robbery. The evidence, however, said something else.

The night before the trial was due to begin Kevin Shapland was informed that Croke was going to change his plea to guilty. The substantial amount of overwhelming independent crime scene and forensic science evidence had forced Croke and the other defendants to admit their offences. This was a massive success for the investigative team, detectives, crime scene investigators and forensic scientist alike. The following morning I joined the detectives in court to see Barrett, Croke and the other defendants in the dock at the Central Criminal Court, the

Old Bailey in London. Barrett was separate from the others and protected by prison officers.

His Honour Judge Michael Coombe, the presiding judge, gave credit to Croke for pleading guilty and thus saving the court valuable time, which would have resulted in his conviction in the face of overwhelming evidence had he not pleaded guilty. His victims had been terrified, he had taken families hostage, threatened them with explosive devices and discharged guns in the commission of his violent crimes. He was sentenced to twenty-three years' imprisonment. There were gasps in the courtroom. Had he not pleaded guilty he could have expected a sentence of over thirty years from His Honour.

Barrett too was a dangerous and evil man but he was given credit for his assistance to the police since his arrest. He was sentenced to sixteen years' imprisonment. Other defendants were given lesser but still significant terms of imprisonment.

Members of the investigation were commended by the trial judge when he was passed a hurriedly completed list. Kevin Shapland, Ken Grange and Dick Kirby were later commended by the Commissioner, and I by the Deputy Assistant Commissioner of the Metropolitan Police. I ensured that letters of thanks were sent to Kevan and his team for their incredible effort and professionalism.

This supergrass investigation had been thorough and transparent. For the guilty there was nowhere to hide, for there is nowhere to hide.

14. Bad News and Very Bad News

In 1989, the first promotion board, for scenes of crime officer (Grade 1) held since my joining the department was announced. It had been a long period since the last promotion board and there were lots of candidates but thankfully quite a few vacancies. The nine years had allowed me to hone my skills, culminating in a successful four-year tour on the Flying Squad, no mean feat. I was confident that I had a good chance. That didn't stop the butterflies in my stomach as I walked down Regency Street in London in October of that year to the interview. I calmed my nerves by whistling 'The Dambusters March' written by Eric Coates for the 1955 film. As I did so I began to march in step and I found myself being joined in my imagination by the solid professionals who I had worked with. Kevin Shapland, Dick Kirby, Norman Craig and many, many more until there was a veritable crowd of support. I'm not sure how the interview went. One of the panel, Dave Ince, was one of my bosses. A week or so later, on the day the results were announced, I got a message to phone him. I was busy with a robbery investigation. So when I phoned him a few hours later I apologised and explained the reason for my delay. 'You SOCO Ones are all the same,' he said. I had made it and it felt very good. The promotion meant that I would leave the Squad and I was posted to Kings Cross to be the manager of the eleven SOCOs in a wedge of London from there right out to Cheshunt and the Essex and Hertfordshire border.

My role at that time was seen as a supervisor, a senior professional, although I hated the thought of being just a supervisor. I wasn't impressed by some who seemed to drive around checking books and registers without offering professional development to those in their charge. So I wanted to get involved and lead. I wanted to be like Norman Craig and build on what he had taught me. I had been warned by one senior manager that I would have trouble delegating as I prefer to do the job myself. I didn't find that to be true, though. I didn't mind delegating. The problem with the busy workloads my team had was to find someone to delegate to. That, I was to realise, was what becoming a manager was all about. I hope I didn't 'lord it' over my team. I soon realised that my job was to make their job easier, not harder. I wanted to reward the hard work whist encouraging those who needed development. Equally I realised that the first-line supervisor was a key part of the organisation. Many organisations fail because they get this part wrong. They mess up the planning and communication.

A case I got heavily involved in was that of Gemma. Gemma had been nursing a sick child. The young mother had not slept, sick herself with worry, she had sat in a chair next to her child's bed in the emergency room at North Middlesex Hospital. The emergency room had experienced a busy night. It provided a service to a large part of north London. There is nothing routine about a London hospital emergency room at night, other than the volume of people. The nursing staff have to deal with all aspects of human beings at their most vulnerable. The injured, the drunk, the seriously ill and their worried relatives all are there.

In the early hours of the morning, the child was admitted to the children's ward and was out of danger and resting peacefully. At six am Gemma decided to go home, have a shower and rest for a few hours before returning to the hospital.

She walked out of the hospital, crossed the road and decided to take the direct route home on foot. This meant entering the public park and gardens, the gates of which had just opened.

Walking purposefully through the gates it was only a few paces later that she was grabbed from behind and a hand was pulled over his mouth. The man was much stronger than her and although she struggled she could not get free. She was dragged into a public toilet block and into the furthest cubicle. There she was subjected to vaginal rape. She only saw brief and restricted glimpses of her attacker's face. She did notice a logo on an article of his clothing, a dark-coloured sweater. It was over very quickly. Her attacker warned her not to look at him and not to scream. Otherwise he would return. He left as quickly as he had appeared. She sat on the toilet seat and, in her own words, she discharged what the rapist had ejaculated into her into the toilet bowl.

I had started duty at Kings Cross Police Station at nine am. The morning ring-around the area identified the number of burglaries requiring examination at each station and the staff available. More importantly, it identified one serious crime. A quick look at the resources told me that the staff on duty were already overstretched and it would be difficult to write someone, let alone two, off for at least a day. It was down to me and so I set off to Edmonton.

The local detective chief inspector was on the case as the officer in charge. The toilet block had been sealed off and I advised and made sure that Gemma was being examined by a forensic medical examiner. She was being counselled by an experienced and trained female officer. It would be some time before a full statement was available, but at a suitable break the story of what had happened was relayed to me by the female officer.

I was immediately struck by the fact that Gemma had not flushed the toilet before she left to seek help after her ordeal. The first officers at the scene had identified that the toilet block had been cleaned and the floors washed before the park gates were opened shortly before six am. To the credit of the officers, no one, not even the first officers, had entered the block at all. A great job of scene preservation.

A sense of urgency struck me. Two potentially useful areas of evidence immediately became apparent. If I could find any, only the shoe marks of the offender and the victim would be on the toilet block floor. Secondly, and more importantly, there was a chance that the discharged semen was still in the toilet bowl and that could help identify the offender.

The year was 1990 and DNA evidence was being used in only the most serious crime cases. The technique was still in its infancy in crime investigation, but its power as an investigative tool was already recognised.

Within an hour or so, the victim examination covered and with a brief indication of what the victim thought had happened, I arrived at the scene.

The toilet block was of red-brick construction at least fifty years old. It sat immediately inside and to the left of the gates to the park. The main road was only yards away with the North Middlesex Hospital on the other side of the busy North Circular Road.

The park was well maintained and the toilet block well cared for, shown by the fact that it had been cleaned that very morning before the park opened.

A police officer stood guard at the gate and the area was cordoned off with police incident tape.

The paths were regular and covered with tarmac and the grass and flowerbeds were soft with residue of the morning dew. A large pyracantha (firethorn) bush was in flower and extended along the path to the right of the door and entrance of the ladies' toilet where the rape had taken place.

The external paths and flowerbeds would require search and examination, but that would have to come later. There was a greater priority. I was concerned about recovering any remaining semen and the genetic material it contained from the toilet.

I was unsure about any degradation or dilution which might occur.

I made a focused examination of the path leading to the toilet block door before peering inside.

The floor was stone tiled and dry. It appeared clean and free from any dust, as you would expect, having just been cleaned. The door faced a wall turning right into a short passage. To the far right was a bank of four toilet cubicles, each with a private door. The victim had described that it was the furthest cubicle from the door, the one on the far left, into which she had been dragged.

I had a dilemma. Normally, I would carefully examine the floor for shoe marks, or at least clear a narrow path to the furthest cubicle. But I was unsure if I had time to do that. If there was semen in the toilet bowl I was unsure how it might degrade or dilute. So I decided to clear a path as quickly as possible within eighteen inches of the wall on the left side. I thought that with the floor having been cleaned and with only two known occupants since (the offender and the victim), this area was least likely to contain shoe marks. I cleared the path with oblique lighting, held close to the floor in front of me. I didn't find any shoe marks and I was very soon at the cubicle door. Again securing the door back so I didn't disturb anything for a later complete examination, I cleared the floor area inside the cubicle. Then, looking inside, I could see a column of opaque white fluid stretching from the top surface of the water in the bowl to the bottom. Using a teat pipette I drew the fluid up and secured it in a glass evidence bottle.

It was my intention to quickly freeze it and get it to the laboratory, but when I returned to the Edmonton Police Station to do just that, I received an update from the detective chief inspector.

A suspect had been arrested. A young man had been making a nuisance of himself the night before within the very emergency department of the hospital where Gemma had been nursing her sick daughter. He had demanded to be admitted, but there was nothing physically wrong with him and, although a nuisance, he went away after police were called. His description was very similar to the somewhat thin description Gemma had given of the man who raped her. Events quickly developed.

Having recovered what I thought was going to be important evidence, I called the Forensic Science Laboratory. DNA at that time was only being used in the most serious cases, mainly murder, but I managed to persuade the lab to quickly look at the material I had recovered and a sample of blood (if we could get one) from the suspect. Under the Police and Criminal Evidence Act we only had forty-eight hours from the time of arrest to charge or release any suspect.

The suspect was examined in the early afternoon, his clothes seized and a number of samples taken from him, most importantly a blood sample for grouping and profiling. A police motorcyclist took the material which I had recovered from the scene, swabs from the victim and blood samples from the suspect to the lab. It was expected there and they quickly undertook the task of examining it.

I returned to the scene and completed an examination of the toilet block, the floor and walls of the cubicle and then a search of the outside bushes and flowerbeds. The latter in case the offender had been hiding there before the offence. I even took a sample of the flowering pyracantha bush as I thought it would make an interesting contact trace item should the offender have brushed against it.

The extensive examination of the toilet block went on past the late afternoon and into the evening. It revealed some finger marks, but it was a public area and although this particular area was a female domain, I wasn't too hopeful of identification. I developed a couple of partial shoe marks on the tiled floor of the block. It appeared that the floor had dried before the offender dragged the victim inside. Wet marks may have been more easily left and although I looked for marks in dust, I found none.

Officers searched the suspect's address and a full statement was being obtained from the victim. It had been a traumatic day for her and she still had a sick child in hospital. The female police officers were trying to help her through this trauma, whilst giving her the best opportunity to identify who had attacked her.

It had been a long day for the investigators, but any thought of that was put aside, with a professional eye on what we had to do and feelings of compassion for Gemma.

I returned to Edmonton the following morning, evaluating any updates in the context of my examination and planning a more detailed follow-up laboratory submission.

The laboratory indicated that the DNA analysis would take longer than the forty-eight hours we had to charge or release the suspect. They did say that they would undertake a simple blood grouping of the scene material and the blood samples from the suspect and the victim. This would be useful in linking the suspect to the scene if he was the offender.

The second laboratory submission would include the clothing taken from the victim, which would be examined for semen, fibres and hair and also clothing from the suspect for fibres and hair. Blood and urine samples would be examined for alcohol to help complete a picture of the events of the offence and of those involved or suspected.

An identification parade was arranged by the officers where Gemma would be invited to try and identify the man who had attacked her from a line of similar-looking men, drawn at random from the local population. It was held in the afternoon of that second day and Gemma identified a man by saying, 'I think it's number four.' It was our detained suspect but it wasn't the strongest of identifications.

I called the lab a couple of times to see if there was any progress, but there was none. They knew we were under pressure.

By late afternoon a review of the case considered the description of the offender, the actions of the suspect and the fact that he broadly fitted that description and the fact that Gemma had picked him out of the line-up, albeit with reluctance. The detectives decided that they had enough evidence to charge him with the offence of rape and remand him into custody.

A short while before the suspect was going to be charged, I called the lab to see if they had any information. They promised an update within the hour. It was apparent in the voice of the scientist they had something but they were checking their findings.

I was in the charge room of the police station at six pm. The suspect's hands were still black with the remains of fingerprint ink. His fingerprints had been taken, as is normal, just before he was to be charged with the offence of rape. In the air was the smell of petroleum spirit, which had been used to wash the main bulk of the printer's ink off the suspect's hands. The phone rang on the charge room desk. It was for me. It was the scientist. 'It is not him,' said the voice on the other end of the phone.

I was silent and listened further.

'I have two pieces of bad news for you,' she said. 'OK,' I said. She went on. The first was that whilst the lab was undertaking the longer DNA examination, they had completed the blood screening. They could completely eliminate the suspect as the donor of the semen by blood grouping. The crime scene samples contained a mixture of two blood groups. One matched the victim, the other did not and could not match our suspect. Whoever the offender was, it wasn't the man currently in custody. There was further bad news to follow. They had identified semen mixed with vaginal material in the sample from the toilet bowl and also the vaginal swabs taken from the victim. When they examined the sample taken from the bowl they confirmed it was seminal fluid but contained no sperm heads. It is the sperm head which contains the material which could be identified at that time by DNA. In the absence of sperm heads DNA identification was not possible. This was confirmed in the examination of the vaginal swabs.

So there was double bad news for the investigators. The offender wasn't our suspect and we wouldn't be able to tell who it was from the DNA.

I indicated to the custody sergeant to wait for a moment before continuing with the charge. I pulled the detective chief inspector to one side and gave him the very bad news. 'What do you mean?' he said with incredulity. He didn't believe me; he didn't want to believe me. It had been a long couple of days and a lot of hard work had gone into where we were.

We both went up to the CID office to discuss the matter further. The double bad news was difficult to handle and I was more than the messenger, I had orchestrated the urgent laboratory examination. Without this evidence the suspect could have been charged and, for all I know, convicted, on the remaining evidence.

But the fact was simple, on the simple test of blood grouping alone, the suspect could be eliminated as the donor of the semen which I had recovered from the bowl of the fourth cubicle of the ladies' toilet in the park the day before. A review of that very statement confirmed that the semen in the bowl originated from the offender and as such the suspect could be safely eliminated from the enquiry.

Still not convinced and clutching to any hope that the suspect in the charge room was the right man, the detective chief inspector took me to see the head of the CID on the Division, whose office was two floors above. I had known Detective Chief Superintendent Bill Peters for a number of years. A tall elegant man, it was he who had to show some wisdom in the matter. The facts were explained to him. I was firm; I carefully quoted the words of the scientist as carefully as I had written them down.

The implication that the much publicised and new DNA

evidence was unlikely to be useful in this case through impotency drew some questioned looks. 'He is firing blanks,' I explained. All the guys immediately understood.

The evidence was clear and Bill Peters' decision was quick and to the point. The suspect was to be released immediately and his property returned to him. He was innocent and he had been eliminated.

It was a disappointment. Painful though that was to the investigation team, it was the truth and justice had been done.

The bags containing the suspect's clothing were opened and the items returned to him. He left a free and innocent man.

The collection and identification of forensic evidence is a building process, each positive comparison or identification strengthening the case, depending on the strength of the evidence type. It is all based on context and, most importantly, probability. Occasionally a piece of simple evidence with a relatively small statistical probability to imply guilt can more powerfully eliminate a suspect from an enquiry. It is one of forensic science's most powerful tools, the ability to exclude, to eliminate.

I wondered what would have happened to the suspect if he had matched the blood group of the offender. He would have been charged that night, that was plain, only to be eliminated, I would hope, by another grouping system which the laboratory routinely used in parallel with the ABO grouping system.

We now had to pick ourselves up and start again. At the end of a second long day I joined the DCI and his team for a drink at the local pub. I didn't feel as if I was the most popular guy in the bar. The detectives were all disappointed, but not that the suspect had gone free. He was clearly innocent and the officers perhaps reluctantly had to accept that.

The next few days were difficult and revealed no further suspects. It appeared to be a complete-stranger rape. No finger marks were identified and the information that could be put on to databases – shoe marks, blood groups – was done.

We explored the potential reasons for the impotency of the offender in the hope that this might focus our search. The offender, whoever he was, was impotent through natural causes or perhaps through use of certain drugs. A body builder, who used anabolic steroids perhaps, was one suggestion. That line of enquiry didn't lead anywhere useful.

The trail went cold and with no suspect the other original scene material and the clothing of the victim was placed in storage in their sealed exhibit bags.

About two years, later one of the detectives from the investigation had to go and arrest a local man for an unrelated indecent assault offence. Whilst at the man's home the officer noticed an article of clothing which he recalled was similar to one briefly seen and mentioned in Gemma's statement. It had the logo which Gemma had described.

The detective seized the sweater and contacted a colleague and submitted it and Gemma's outer clothing, which was still in the original sealed bags, to the laboratory. This time the lab found fibres on the outer surface of Gemma's clothing which matched the sweater.

The pace of the first few days of the investigation, with its highs and very low lows had given way to a long period of waiting. The discipline and professionalism paid off in time. A young woman had been raped, a young man cleared of the offence by a simple blood test, when some evidence may have convicted him. Then, after a long passage of time, a sound piece of observation by an alert detective meant that the right offender was found and his involvement proven.

Any excitement about bringing the offender to justice had long gone. It was good to know that we and Gemma knew that he had been caught. My lasting thought was for the effect that the crime had taken on that young woman's life. To us it was a job. Yes, we had compassion and commitment to the victim, but it was still a job. I hope Gemma came to terms with her ordeal and lived a normal and full life.

15. Coffee on the Carpet

'Have you got a blood bottle?'

I had only called into the SOCO office at Edmonton Police Station that Monday lunchtime for a brief visit. As I was sitting at the desk, a detective poked his head through the door and asked.

'What is it for?' I replied.

'I have just spoken to the lab about a man who claimed he had been drugged by his former wife who then abducted their daughter,' he said.

I think we can do better that just a blood bottle, I thought.

Poisoning cases are pretty rare and I didn't want to miss the chance of investigating one, particularly where there were great evidential opportunities.

The victim, a man in his thirties, reported that his ex-wife had arrived with a friend unexpectedly on Saturday morning at the family home. The family were Italian but had been living in north London and had a young daughter.

The relationship was pleasant, even though the father had retained custody of the child once her mother returned to Italy. So when his ex-wife turned up she was welcomed into the house.

They chatted politely and she had offered to make some coffee. On taking a sip it was so strong and hot that it burned his lips and he dropped the cup on to the carpet. It made a stain but it was quickly cleaned up using a carpet-cleaning solution.

Another cup quickly turned up, this time he managed to drink it and that was about the last thing he remembered. He awoke late on Sunday night. He was very sick but he managed to call an ambulance. He was taken to the local hospital where he had remained overnight. Police officers were made aware of his allegation in the early hours of Monday morning, but thought there was little physically they could do. They were junior in service, inexperienced and were not aware of what to do. They hadn't asked for advice either. The officer who had approached me for the bottle had picked up the case on the Monday morning. He spoke to someone at the lab who suggested that he should get a blood sample.

I was pretty upset with our collective response so far. There was plenty we could do but we now had to act fast.

A quick call to the hospital ensured that they would collect any and every drop of urine that the victim could or would pass. Also a check to trace, recover and preserve any urine or blood samples which the hospital themselves had taken for their use. It would also be very useful to us.

I quickly went to the hospital with the detective, who was much happier now that someone seemed to know what they were doing. We managed to get a large urine sample and track down the samples the hospital had indeed taken.

Urine is a very important sample in poisoning cases which have occurred over the preceding few days. The bladder is the waste bucket of the body and many substances or their by-products stay there until the bladder is emptied. Blood is also very important but drugs and other substances can quickly metabolise and pass through into the urine.

With the detective we confirmed the victim's story. He was still feeling the effects of whatever he had received, but there were no lasting effects and the hospital wanted to release him. So, taking that opportunity, the detective and I took him back to his house, the scene of the crime.

The house was a large detached house set back off a quiet

tree-lined avenue. It was very leafy, giving an air of quiet sub-urban tranquillity.

The house was very tidy and that became a problem, because it was apparent that the victim's house cleaner had visited the house that very morning, ignorant of her employer's illness, and had cleaned the house.

The man showed me around the house. I was particularly interested in the staining on the carpet. If the second cup contained some poison, the first one probably had too and that had been spilled. The clean-up operation had been good. The light-coloured carpet bore only a wet patch. There was little sign of the strong coffee which the victim said he had dropped.

A quick search of the kitchen revealed that all the cups had been washed up and put away. There were no wrappers in the kitchen bin, which contained a new bag. A search of the bin outside the house revealed that even that had been emptied that very morning by the local refuse collectors. I wasn't having much luck.

But I had one more trick up my sleeve.

Returning to the lounge I announced to the victim and the detective that I wanted to lift the carpet and see what was underneath the stained area.

The lounge was very well furnished and the carpet fitted wall to wall. It took quite a while to move the furniture to an area so that the carpet could be raised.

Slowly rolling back the carpet revealed a rubber underlay. The detective had been concerned about the disturbance I was causing but his expression changed as, directly below the wet patch, a round and distinct dark-brown shape appeared in the foam underlay.

With permission I quickly cut out a large square around the whole stain and placed it in a large glass jar. If there was any poison, it would still be in the stain.

The detective was impressed.

The hospital had already undertaken some tests of the blood sample they had taken. The Poisons Unit identified a common tranquilliser, valium, in a high enough dose to ensure a deep sleep for our victim, which indeed he had received.

Submitting the urine and foam underlay samples to the Forensic Science Laboratory, it was a few weeks before their results were available.

Their results were all the more interesting. Using the carpet sample they had managed to extract the poison from the foam. It was indeed a tranquilliser and very similar to valium but not identical. Indeed they had not seen it before. Having researched further, they manage to conclude that, although it was from the same group of drugs as valium, it was a variation only available in Italy.

Warrants were issued with Interpol for the arrest of the victims ex-wife and her friend.

A few months later the detective in the case went to Italy and asked me to accompany him. He wanted to arrest the woman and also search for the source of the drug which was only available on prescription in Italy. By that time I had moved on and was working at the laboratory. A request for me to go with the detective was turned down. The head of SO3 Branch would not allow me to go, so it fell to a colleague to make the trip.

By all accounts the expected trip to foreign lands wasn't all it should have been. The part of Italy where they visited was in a remote country area in Sicily, and the woman's family were well connected with the underworld. Even the local police were not very friendly to the visitors from the UK. My colleagues spent most of their time in their hotel rooms.

The matter was later settled without the criminal charges being pursued. We had gone a long way from simply supplying a glass bottle to the detective.

16. Diploma

I was in a boxing ring and getting hit by blows from which I could not protect myself. That was how it felt. One of the consequences of working on the Flying Squad for a year or so was the steady stream of court appearances at the Central Criminal Court. I was examining in the region of ten prisoners, arrested by the Squad for armed robbery, every month. That inevitably meant that I could guarantee at least one and probably two or three calls a month to give evidence.

Armed robbery trials are generally heavily contested and attract the hardest-hitting defence barristers to defend their clients from such serious charges.

Taking a case to trial should mean that the investigation has shown there is a case to answer. My work was about establishing the truth, the facts, and leaving the justice bit up to the court.

Invariably, the defence team had done their homework. That was obviously true of the prosecution team too. Barristers can, however, be called away or delayed by other cases. This affects both defence and prosecution and undoes a lot of preparation work. From my perspective lots of hard work went into case preparation and briefing prosecution counsel. It involved getting clear dialogue with them so that they fully understood the case and the work we had done. So when there was a change of counsel the work had to be repeated. In the biggest of cases, where counsel were extensively briefed, a change of court date may be arranged. In smaller cases a replacement counsel could be appointed and brought up to speed at relatively short notice, sometimes only a day before, or even on the first day of the trial itself. On at least one occasion such a prosecution barrister was to ask (in their re-examination) seemingly irrelevant question, clearly because they had not read the case papers, rather than emphasising the evidence in chief. Occasionally whilst giving evidence I would realise that the barrister was placing some emphasis on a weak area of evidence when there was something much stronger available. It is the duty of a witness to answer the questions they are asked, however irrelevant they may seem. On only one occasion have I felt compelled to clarify a point which (from my viewpoint) had been misrepresented by the line of questioning. This may be seen by counsel as interfering, after all they are managing the line of questioning. The witness, particularly the expert witness, has a duty not to leave misleading evidence unaddressed.

The court process is a trial and an examination of evidence. Although employed by the police, it was my duty as a professional to remain impartial and only seek the truth (although giving evidence is a test for the witness too). It is important that evidence is tested so that inaccurate or incomplete evidence is not accepted as fact by the court. I welcomed a rigorous defence examination. Later in my time on the Flying Squad when a trial date was approaching and no defence examination of the exhibits had been requested, I would prompt the officer in the case to call the defence and remind them. It usually saved a lot of running around during the trial and, I felt, served the judicial process better. Later in my career I would observe that where miscarriages of justice occurred, the defence had not been vigorous, they had not tested the evidence and had not asked the questions which they should have. So although cross-examination may be stressful it is important for a witness's evidence to be thoroughly tested.

Preparation for me involved ensuring I was familiar with my original notes, any submissions I had made to the laboratory and my statements. In giving evidence I would be allowed to refer to my notes but not my statement, once I had asked the presiding judge for permission to do so. I would be asked by the judge when the notes were made. My reply would be 'at the time of my examination' as this was always so. What was less pleasant was the questioning of my qualification to give evidence, and my impartiality and allegations of blind loyalty to my police colleagues rather than the truth. Loyalty to the court and to the truth is a little harder to demonstrate.

As a witness most often called by the prosecution it would be the prosecution barrister who would be the first to question me in court. In this way the evidence in chief which counsel would wish to draw out, is given. Then the defence barrister for each defendant (and there could be many) had a chance in turn to cross-examine me. That could be a gruelling experience. Even if my evidence only concerned one defendant, the other defendant's counsel would use the opportunity to explore the evidence, or lack of it, relating to their client.

On one occasion I was called over to the Finchley Flying Squad office. Their surveillance team had been keeping tabs on a couple of men who they thought were about to commit an armed robbery. Much to their dismay they lost them after they left their flat, only to find out that a bank had been robbed. All they could do was listen to the robbery as it unfolded on the police radio. But the men returned to their flat. They weren't carrying anything, but the officers were convinced they were involved. A decision was made to enter the flat, arrest them and search for evidence.

By the time I arrived at the office my colleague was dealing with the scene. When the men were arrested, one had just had a shower and was drying himself off and the other was literally getting out of the shower.

The getaway car, the stolen money, masks and guns had yet

to be found. But I thought that they may be found together, even at a much later date, depending on where they were hidden. So I suggested that we should get an immediate hair-combing sample from the men in the hope that, if they were responsible, the fibres in the combing would match the masks. This would be great evidence of association if in fact the masks and other items were found in the car.

The fact that both men had showered did not deter me in suggesting the sampling because there had been some published research in the *Journal of the Forensic Science Society* suggesting that fibres could persist in head hair for days and even after washing.

I went immediately to the police station where the men were being held. A police surgeon was called to take blood samples for grouping and alcohol and drugs examination, pretty standard but not as critical in my mind as the hair combing. In any event the suspects refused to give the blood samples at that time, as was their right, but they agreed to give hair samples, possibly because they knew they could be taken by force if necessary. I used the opportunity to ask the police surgeon to take the hair combing from one suspect whilst I did the other. This would prevent any possibility of contamination and was good practice. He had not taken a hair combing before, so I briefed him and showed him how to take the sample. I had asked for, and got, the authority from a senior police officer to take the samples. The police surgeon seemed pretty happy. So I set about examining my man. I took my time. Overlooked by a detective, I opened the hair combing kits and put on a pair of gloves. I spread out a sheet of paper and then got the suspect to stand over the sheet whilst I combed his hair backwards and forwards with the seeded comb. I placed the comb in the sheet before folding it over to retain all the collected debris. Placing it in a bag and sealing it, I completed my notes. A pretty simple procedure, undertaken with integrity and discipline, I knew it could be a critical piece of evidence. I checked on the doctor's progress with the other suspect. He had already left and the detective who had been with him showed me the exhibit he had taken. I wasn't too impressed with the condition of the item; I could see it through the plastic bag. The detective's words worried me. Apparently the doctor hadn't taken too kindly to being briefed by a civilian scenes of crime officer, even an informed one. He had taken the combing with one sweep of the hair and some muttered comments before handing the sealed item to the detective and leaving. I suppose I should have been grateful for the fact that he had sealed the item.

I felt there was little I could do. We had had our chance and I would have to await the laboratory examination. With that in mind I arranged for the combings to go straight to the lab. I wanted them out of our possession and in the possession of the lab to prevent any allegations of deliberate contamination or planting of evidence. The lab had to be persuaded to take the items as it was a new case and there were no items to compare them with. I was getting wise to allegations of planting and thought this an ideal opportunity to bury that one in this case, as the masks, stolen money, weapons and getaway car had yet to be found. The lab understood my somewhat unusual submission and accepted the items later the same day.

Sure enough, the getaway vehicle was found, along with the masks and some remnants of the stolen money. A footwear mark was found at the bank where the robbery had occurred and that was compared with shoes found at the suspects' address. However, it was the hair combing which was to be critical to the case.

When the scientist examined the hair combing I had taken they found a large number of fibres which matched one of the masks. Examination of the combing taken by the doctor from the second suspect showed no fibres found. I was disappointed but this had seemed inevitable given the observation of the detective who witnessed the sample being taken.

Nevertheless my evidence would connect the mask and other items with the suspects who were arrested together after they returned to their flat.

I expected there to be a fight at court, but I didn't expect what actually turned out. My evidence in chief went pretty well. After all, it was a pretty simple operation. I described how I took the sample. Then came the allegation. It was that I had planted the evidence and was part of a Flying Squad conspiracy to frame two innocent men. It was suggested that I had not properly sealed the item or switched bags so that evidence could be planted by me or my Flying Squad colleagues. Meanwhile, the sample taken properly from the other suspect, by the 'good doctor' was negative, implying I was lying and both men were innocent. The doctor was qualified and a pillar of the professional medical community; I had no such protection. The final nail in the coffin of my integrity or credibility as a witness was voiced with damning style. 'Mr Millen, you are employed by the Metropolitan Police, you are paid by them, you work closely with these detectives, you probably have a beer with them from time to time.' I mentally nodded. 'You will say exactly what they tell you to say.' I was done for and so was the case. The evidence linking the men (together by association) with the masks and stolen goods was strong, but that did not matter. I'm not sure how the other evidence went but the suspects were acquitted. The allegations made against me, although untrue, nevertheless damaged the integrity of the case.

It was a bruising experience, and I realised more than ever that I needed a professional shield, one by which I could demonstrate my integrity and professionalism.

I had been a member of the Forensic Science Society for a few years. The Society was at that time a learned body whose aim was to promote the application of forensic science. Its membership was made up of scientists, academics, medics, lawyers, police and crime scene personnel. It held three scientific conferences each year and I for one had benefited immensely from the interaction with other professionals at such meetings. Not only were the presentations stimulating and informative, but the interaction over dinner and in the bar provided me with a great intellectual resource and a network of professional contacts I hold to this day.

The crime scene had been seen by many scientist and laboratory directors as purely a 'technician' exercise; the important and sexy stuff was all done in the lab. That attitude started to change in the 1980s. As forensic science developed so did the crime scene examination part. It was quickly realised by many who had not seen it before that if the scene is dealt with badly there is little the scientist can do to resurrect the case. The presence of many crime scene people at the Society's meetings encouraged the development, exactly as the aims of the Society wished.

The Society had realised that many practitioners came from the classical scientific areas of biology and chemistry, but there were no vocational qualifications in specialised areas of forensic science. Dr Ray Williams was the President of the Society in the mid 1980s. He had retired as the Director of the Metropolitan Police Forensic Science Laboratory. He was one of the 'good and great' of the civil service and forensic science world. He had not been an ardent supporter of the crime scene case whilst director, but I felt that during his presidency he realised its importance and became one of its greatest champions. Having stepped down as president after a two-year term, Dr Williams stayed on the council as Chair of the Professional Awards Committee. He was going to implement a series of professional awards in the forensic science areas of documents and of fire investigation where there were no formal qualifications. Alongside Dr Williams on the committee was Dr Brian Caddy, who acted as secretary. In the years to come Brian was to see this process through and be elected to the presidency of the Society itself. Brian was an academic and senior lecturer in Forensic Science at the University of Strathclyde, rising to professor before his retirement at the beginning of the new century.

One morning in 1988 whilst on the Flying Squad, I got a call from my boss, Mark Godfree, who had called in at the neighbouring Leyton Police Station. There was a letter for me there which had been improperly addressed. I asked him to open the letter and read the contents to me. The contents made me dash to the car and drive to read the letter in person.

It seemed that I must have had a conversation with someone at a Society meeting about the need for a professional qualification in crime scene. There was reference to previous letters, which I had not received. The upshot was that the Society intended to set up a diploma in crime scene examination and I was invited to join the committee. Then came the shock. The first meeting of the committee was going to be held that very day at two pm at the Home Office Forensic Science Laboratory in Birmingham. It was already ten am. I didn't hesitate. I could not miss the opportunity and I wanted to be there at the very beginning. I spoke to my boss. I'm not sure if it was a request or a statement, but within a few minutes I was on my way to Birmingham. I arrived with just fifteen minute to spare.

The Birmingham laboratory was hidden away in an industrial area of the inner city. From outside you would have no idea what went on behind the grey 1950s building. Parking was a nightmare and the amount of broken windscreen glass on the streets indicated that crime went right up to the doorway.

I entered the building to a different world. I was expected and was shown to the meeting room on the first floor. The others were already present. I immediately recognised Bob Wayment, a SOCO 1 from the Met who I quickly realised had put my name forward. Dr Williams was there and Dr Caddy and I addressed them formally. I remember being in awe of them and it took many months before I could call either by their first names. Eddy Marchant, a chief superintendent from Durham Constabulary, was there with Chris Jordison, an inspector at the Scientific Aids School at Durham. Durham Constabulary had a long history of support for the Society.

The meeting was very fruitful and we quickly set about defining the need and establishing a process for recognising professional standards in crime scene. Bob Wayment was appointed the Secretary to the Crime Scene Examination Diploma Committee, as it was then known. Within the year Bob decided to join the police force proper so I jumped at the chance and took over. My enthusiasm for the project was obvious and with the encouragement of Drs Williams and Caddy and support of the others I knew this was going to work. In the months that followed there was one change which I insisted upon. It was a change in name for the diploma. Crime Scene Examination wasn't good enough and didn't reflect the integration within the investigative process which was emerging. The science which I was practising and which I believed had a greater need and benefit went beyond pure examination. It reflected the review and analysis of the answers which the science gave within the overall investigation. There was a gap, or at least the danger of one, between the police detective and the forensic scientist. I considered that this may have been organisational, an outcome of the environment in which I worked, but the more I looked the more I realised that this was not just about job roles, this was about investigation practice. I put a case for the diploma to be in Crime Scene Investigation. It was a little-known and unused term at that time. That was to change in the following years, as our imagination and that of the general public, fuelled by television, was to engage.

The diploma was founded to test and encourage the development of crime scene investigators. The process was developed to involve examinations in theory and practical application. There was also an interview for the candidate in front of a panel of examiners of which one was a crime scene specialist.

The other two members of the panel were from other areas of the Society and could be a forensic scientist or an academic. This was to ensure the roundness of the applicant. It is difficult to test ethics but throughout the process the candidate would have to face difficult questions and dilemmas, the answers to which would demonstrate their professionalism and impartiality. This was not only about what evidence they would find but equally, if not more importantly, how they would look, and what the answers meant and what they would do with them.

The diploma had strength because it was awarded independent of employment. This was not in-house accreditation but an award by the Society and its varied membership within the sciences and professions. A key challenge for me was to ensure that any aspects of practice specific to one or only a few organisations were not accepted to the disadvantage of other candidates. Many organisations develop practice to meet their own needs, but this is organisational plumbing and not reflected in other places undertaking the same work. So there was a need to strip off practice and perhaps procedures and look at the basics of integrity, sound practice and underpinning knowledge and values. This became even more important when the diploma received interest from the Society's overseas membership. The legal environment in which the candidate worked would vary. Although aspects of law could not be specifically tested, the candidate needed to demonstrate that they understood the legal framework in which they worked and the implications to the evidence which they sought and presented.

One of the questions students on the Scene of Crime course at Hendon in mid 1980 were asked in the examination was, 'What is the phone number of the Fire Investigation Unit?' as if this was an underpinning principle of forensic science. So no questions like that would be relevant to an international vocational qualification such as the diploma. Likewise I recall in a test on the course I took in 1980 a question asking me to list the eleven people who should be present at an exhumation. There was nothing about their role, the answer required was just a list. So I just began to list those whom I could remember: the coroner (to witness and supervise the investigation); the senior investigating officer (who investigates on behalf of the coroner); the cemetery superintendent (to identify the correct grave plot); the original undertaker (to identify the coffin); a photographer (to photograph the process); a scenes of crime officer (to take soil samples around and underneath the coffin, particularly in poisoning cases); a pathologist (and if possible the original pathologist who would undertake the further post-mortem examination). Having named seven, I was by this time drying up so I suggested four gravediggers. You can never have too many gravediggers at an exhumation, I suggested. Well my tutor was not impressed with this, although it brought howls of laughter from my classmates. He thought I was being flippant. I suggested that if I had been flippant I would have included the deceased as one of the eleven. What I learned from this was that testing investigators wasn't about empty lists but about purpose and principle and how they could be achieved and recognised. So it is the role of the people present that is important, rather than just their presence, which ensures that all the investigative requirements are met. If by chance one person is missing, I would want to know who can undertake that role and keep the investigation on track.

It would take three years for the work of the committee to be complete. The first examination for the Diploma in Crime Scene Investigation was held in 1990. The diploma was to become well established and is now held by successful candidates around the world. I was proud to notice that within two years we would have successful candidates on four continents.

In the UK the need for accreditation of crime scene personnel grew and other awards and diplomas followed. Namely these were the University of Durham Diploma in Scientific Support Skills, National Vocational Qualifications and then a host of university undergraduate and postgraduate degrees. More recently, accreditation of those in the UK practising in the forensic sciences has been possible through the Council for the Registration of Forensic Practitioners. The Forensic Science Society is now a professional body and offers membership and fellowship to suitably qualified members. As a practitioner and later manager I welcomed and supported the movement to independent accreditation. It was something that my bosses back in my days in the Met could not understand and would not support.

Back then, my involvement in the diploma was met with a frosty reception by the Head of SO3 Branch at New Scotland Yard. He ruled over a branch made up of fingerprint, crime scene and photographic officers. He was a fingerprint officer and at that time the branch was embroiled in a painful battle which would require the need for all SOCOs to be trained for a five-year period to become fingerprint experts like their fingerprint officer colleagues. The two groups would be brought together as one and renamed identification officers. To me it was a clear example of not listening to the needs of those working within the field. Instead, it felt to me and my SOCO colleagues that our noses were being rubbed in the dirt and that fingerprint officers were better. Fingerprint identification is an important police science, albeit one operated outside the main forensic science community and by many who would not then have considered themselves or be considered by others as scientists. Therein lay the problem. It was probably from insecurity that the head of SO3 Branch and his close advisers (who were greater in number within the branch) felt the need to subsume the crime scene into the fingerprint field.

As a fledgling manager it struck me as an incredible waste of time, money and resources. Every SOCO (and there were over 200 of us) would each be trained for five years so that we could present the marks we found at court. That would be over 1,000 man years. In reality the existing 150 or so fingerprint experts already identified marks submitted to the branch by SOCOs and a smaller number of experts were needed to present the evidence at court. I had no problem with receiving training in better ways to develop and evaluate marks at the scene, that would increase quality, but full expertise was not needed. I had already realised that well-motivated and active SOCOs were better at finding finger marks because they did it every day. They constantly improved their skills. The identification officer programme ran for ten years before the truth came out and the Met once again recruited directly and specifically officers who were SOCOs in all but name and who did not need to undergo fingerprint expertise training before they were let loose on crime scene. The training was reduced from over four years to a matter of months.

I was not a supporter of the identification officer programme and was never to join. However, having worked as a professional for over ten years and felt the beating in court from having no external accreditation of my skills, I thought that was where the need lay. Professional development and external accreditation, that is what was required.

My elation at being invited to join the Society's diploma committee was soon dampened. It was obvious from the outset that the Head of SO3 Branch did not approve of external accreditation. If anyone was to accredit Met personnel it was going to be him. He missed the point completely. It was the independent part, with participation of scientists, lawyers, academics, police and independent experts, which gave it its strength. The dinosaurs at the top of SO3 could not see that. They were stuck in the authoritarian era of post-war Scotland Yard and their only concession to the fact that this was no longer the 1950s was that they had stopped wearing hats.

Within a year, I was using ten days of my precious annual leave to attend the meetings up and down the country to prepare the award. It was a strain but, either through bloody-mindedness or stupidity, I continued.

Diploma

To aid my preparation for the first examinations I went to Tottenham Court Road in London and purchased, at the personal expense of £500, an Amstrad word processor. The lack of support from my employer made me a little bitter but I was determined to see this through. Looking back I realise that this helped my career and my approach to it. I had always suffered from one small disadvantage. My handwriting had always been atrocious. My brain worked faster than I could write and it wasn't until I began to type that many realised I couldn't spell either. But I improved and this marked the beginning of a time where I could express myself and communicate in writing with others as I ascended the professional tree.

After three years' work (and many days of leave!) we were ready to offer the first diploma examinations. No support from the Met meant that no examinations were held there. On a late summer's day in 1990 simultaneous examinations were held in Harrogate and Surrey in the UK and in Hong Kong and Australia. I completed a night duty at New Scotland Yard and then drove down to Reigate Police in Surrey where two Surrey and one Met officer took the diploma. Surrey Police provided the room and I supervised the examination.

A short time later I once again officially wrote to the head of SO3 Branch. I could now demonstrate that the diploma was a reality. It was also a first. It was the first diploma of its kind in the world and it had attracted international interest.

I was called to see the head of SO3 Branch and met him in his grand office at New Scotland Yard in London. He would not entertain the idea and his opposition was clear. In the privacy of his office he gave me a stark warning. Either I would cease my work on the diploma or my career and any hope of progress would end there and then. I was taken aback by the comment, but I was too fired up, too committed. I looked him straight in the eye and with a little nervousness but with conviction said I would continue, ending with the words, 'history will say who was right'.

A few weeks later the registry file from New Scotland Yard landed on my desk at Kings Cross with the official rejection, but obviously without the threat.

I minuted the file with the words, 'In the absence of your support I thank you for your time.' One of my managers up the food chain, himself a fingerprint officer, later gleefully congratulated me on my bold putdown.

Fate provided me with a lifeboat, although I wasn't to know that when I had spoken to the head of SO3 Branch. Surrey Police had advertised for a scientific support manager to head a new department. I had originally applied but I had been sifted out before the interviews. However, no one was appointed. All those interviewed were forensic laboratory scientists who were not entirely committed to developing the new scientific support department there. One candidate was offered the job. He was from another smaller force and although he had no forensic science or crime scene background he was a manager of the scientific support department there. He negotiated a better salary back in his own force and didn't take up the Surrey offer. Within two months Surrey Police re-advertised the post. They had clarified what they wanted. I phoned to see if they would reconsider me.

Throughout my time as an investigator and particularly during the work preparing the diploma, I had pondered at length on the role and purpose of crime scene investigation and where it sat within the overall process of criminal investigation. Often I would lie awake at night, unable to sleep, thinking about how we could do things much better. The planning and order which I developed in my subconsciousness led me to seek the role of manager and not just supervisor. I wanted desperately to get involved with the planning, development and implementation of a better system of delivering forensic science to the police and courts. Surrey was going to be my chance.

Five candidates were interviewed, made up of crime scene personnel seeking promotion like myself. One candidate was the soon-to-retire detective inspector from the Laboratory Liaison section at the Metropolitan Police Forensic Science Laboratory. He had over thirty years' experience and he was the favourite as far as I was concerned. I hoped that I offered the future as well as just a safe present.

I was interviewed by two detective superintendents, John Milner and Pat Crossan, at Surrey Police Headquarters in Guildford. The head of personnel completed the three-person panel. John Milner was the chairperson and he played things pretty straight. As I walked into his office where the interview took place I had an overcoat draped over my arm and I was carrying a briefcase. John took my coat and carefully hung it in his wardrobe. Pat Crossan was more inquisitorial and prodded me with some subjects which were controversial. He wanted me to open up and on one subject I disagreed with him and gave my reasons for doing so. I quickly realised he liked the competition and wanted a strong character. My solid operational background and time on the Flying Squad stood me in good stead. My managerial background was relatively modest, but my work and drive developing the Society's diploma showed that I was progressive in my field. Surrey had hosted a site for the diploma examinations the year before when two of its SOCOs took the examination. It had been John Milner who had supported his staff. By luck, on the very morning of the interview, an article which I had written, was published in *The Police Review*. It was called 'Setting Standards' and I made sure to mention it in the interview.

The interview went well and the following morning I received a call from John Milner offering me the job. I shook as I took the call at my desk at the Met Police Laboratory. It was a good two-grade promotion for me. My Met Police SOCO colleagues looked on in anticipation. Given the battle we had had, and my personal battle with the then head of SO3 Branch, I was a bit of a hero. So for a second time I found that I was a second choice, but that didn't bother me. I didn't hold that against Surrey either! I knew I was right for the job and I was determined to do it well. I negotiated a good salary, much better than the one the first successful candidate had done. He was later to lose his job back at his old force within a couple of years when he didn't make the mark.

I was to enjoy working for John Milner. He was to be my immediate line manager. The post I was filling had previously been held by a detective chief inspector. Surrey, like most forces, realised that a permanent professional was needed. A major review within the UK forces recommended the appointment of scientific support managers to bring the sections together under one manager. Although it was good career development for DCIs seeking promotion to head the crime scene, fingerprint and photographic sections for a short while, it did nothing to develop the sections themselves. One strange situation was that as I was a civilian manager of the new department, I was to be the direct line manager to a detective inspector (who was head of the fingerprint section) and a detective sergeant and many constables within the crime scene team. Ray Elvy was the detective inspector. He was the consummate professional and both he and I had to work at this new relationship for it was the first time a civilian was managing a detective officer as senior as an inspector within the force.

John was pleased with my appointment and I was flattered when he regularly reminded officers at the senior detectives meetings that my appointment was an 'opportunity' for the force. This I took in its wider sense, meaning the new post which I occupied, but John's tone added a personal touch. I was only to work with John on one major investigation. That was because Pat Crossan headed the operational side of the HQ crime department. I was to support Pat Crossan in many major investigations and I enjoyed working with this talented, committed, utterly professional senior detective.

My commitment to develop myself and the colleagues who I worked with was to be given a chance. I left the Met with a little sadness and a lot of trepidation, but I felt that I was making the right move. It was going to be hard work and fun and at times painful, but it was the right thing to do. The development of the individual, or a profession, does not come without pain. I was about to step up to the plate.

17. Surrey Without a Fringe on Top

It wasn't a particularly welcoming start. I arrived at Surrey Police Headquarters early one April morning to begin my first day at work there. I had been nervous with expectant anticipation for the days leading up to it. This was a big move.

I was thirty-something, prematurely bald, and I had a background as a proven crime scene investigator and first-line supervisor. Now I was to manage. My role was to lead a complete unit. I had a vision of where I wanted to go with the department. There were opportunities in science and its application which few, if any, police force had even started to realise. I had some idea of where they were now, but I had to get the detail.

It seemed that I wasn't expected. I was shown to the canteen and sat there for a while. Ray Elvy eventually found me there. Both the detective superintendents had been called away.

The vacuum caused by having no DCI in the post for some time meant that the office I was due to have had been occupied by someone else. I quickly realised that I was literally going to have to start from scratch.

Ray showed me round and introduced me to the members of the HQ fingerprint and photographic staff. Many were puzzled that a civilian had been appointed and didn't seem as enthusiastic as I was. I was probably just another boss to them, and not even a police officer. I got a better reception from the scenes of crime personnel on division, many of whom I knew.

First things first. I had to find an office and a desk. Finding the office was relatively easy – there was a good-sized room in a converted police house at the end of a terrace of houses in the grounds of the Mount Browne site. Many of the houses had been converted to offices because of the lack of space. The desk literally came out of a skip. It was earmarked for the dump. It was large but it would do. I had worked out of the back of a car for four years on the Flying Squad and so any desk was a luxury. The estate manager ensured that the locks on the desk were changed and I quickly settled down to work. I would keep that desk for six years until a new laboratory facility building was built solely for scientific support.

At the end of my first day I went home with a massive headache. And it lasted for a few days as my brain computed the massive task I had undertaken. I wasn't to know it (there were few computers available) but I needed the human equivalent of a faster processor and a higher RAM!

Some good advice I had received early in my life was that when starting a new job it is best to keep your ears open and mouth closed. This I did. I met, visited and got to know as best I could all the members of what was to become the scientific support department. I also was introduced to the senior detective team and HQ crime staff as well as other people I would interact with.

I went to the head of personnel and drew out the personal files of all the scientific support staff and read them. I didn't want to prejudge, I would make my own mind up, but I felt it was important to do a little homework. Reading the files I quickly realised the talents, qualification and baggage. I was committed to give everyone a chance, and hoped it would be reciprocated.

Surrey had a sound and solid background in delivering

fingerprint and forensic evidence, and some present and former members of staff were well respected within the force and within the region. My arrival, timed like many in similar posts within the UK service, marked a time of change in technology and opportunity. It was a blank sheet of paper, an open door. Never before had the crime scene, fingerprint and photographic sections been managed by a single professional manager. There were lots of ideas which, until then, had fallen on stony ground. The development of the scenes of crime section had been hampered by the historical police rank structure. I had observed for a long time that talented police scenes of crime officers throughout the UK were put off applying for promotion as it usually meant leaving the department and returning to other police roles. There was little incentive to develop the person or the science. Civilianisation of the police roles brought a career structure which benefited the development of both and was well advanced in Surrey. Perhaps those in authority in Surrey were just waiting for someone who knew how to implement the required changes when I arrived. I had to nurture the sponsors and focus the sections and all the individuals within it.

Key players were the three senior SOCOs, Martin Gaule, Trevor Wykes and Mike Thomas (later replaced by John Armstrong), who each covered a geographical area, and the head of the fingerprint bureau, Ray Elvy, and the head of the photographic section, Ken Williams. With the SOCOs I was on home ground as I was one of them. Both Ray and Ken were professional but I felt a little wariness on both their parts. Ken was a strong and vocal character. Ray was quieter and played things closer to his chest.

Ken had been with Surrey for over thirty years. In fact he joined as a police cadet the year I was born, but later chose to go into the new photographic section in the early 1960s. Ken was a doer. He had a totally professional approach and was up for any new idea which would improve the way he and his team did their job. He was also demanding, but I didn't mind that.

To him I was a mere boy. But within a few weeks I had won him round. It was Ray who pointed it out to me. I took comfort from that because I felt I still had to prove myself to him. I don't know what clinched it with Ken. Perhaps he realised I was just as committed as him and, although I was a lot younger, perhaps he recognised that with me he could realise his ambitions for his section. Both he and I were pushing at the same open door as far as I was concerned. He was years ahead of many other forces, save for the Met, who had their own forensic science laboratory to call upon.

Within a month or so I had a pretty clear picture in my mind. Surrey was a good force. It was nothing like the Met, of course. It was much, much smaller but the people were committed. The scientific support personnel lacked management, leadership and direction. In relation to other forces they were doing OK. They were solid and reliable but nothing special, or nothing special about them had been recognised as such by the force and those around. That was in spite of the excellent work undertaken by Ray Elvy in the field of fingerprint computerisation and by Ken Williams in forensic photography. I wanted to change that. In my mind I started to map out what needed to happen.

First was to see what the force needed from scientific support. I quickly realised that the problems and lack of development had started over ten years before. It takes five years to train a fingerprint expert. So it is too late to wait for a vacancy to occur. For too long it had reacted to demands rather than predict them. Many of the issues which affected the department were historical. So I concluded that if those who went before me (if anyone actually had) had seen the opportunity they could have predicted and prevented them. My role, I decided, was to put the department on a firm footing and see long into the future, so that we were always ahead of the game. I didn't want whoever succeeded me to be in the same position.

Over the next months and year I developed a plan which supported the force and HQ crime plans. I used these as an opportunity to introduce practices and technology which would ensure that crime scene and forensic science played its part to the full in the deduction and reduction of crime. This would lead to the development of staff within the department and beyond. There were several aspects which would be addressed. They were based on the business plans needs and goals of the force. I would ensure that every member of the department would have three personal objectives as part of their annual development and goals. Two would directly support section goals for crime scene, fingerprint or photography. Each would in turn support scientific support, HQ crime department and ultimately force goals. Every member of the department could see that their personal objectives were directly supporting a force goal. The third personal objective was one for the individual. It too would have a direct link to the force goals but it was one which would ensure a personal goal or interest of the individual, such as study, a project or development, would matter. It was both a reward and a motivator.

Training of the first officers to attend the crime scene in scene preservation along with detective training in forensic science awareness was also important. This would ensure that the potential for forensic evidence was realised. Detectives would also spend time visiting the forensic science laboratory.

Even the most committed individual needs motivation and reward. The grading structure for each discipline within crime scene, fingerprint and photography were non-existent. There were workers and there was a manager. I had already realised the most important grades are those at the front line – they deliver the goods. Equally there was a need for managers but not all that many. However, it was important to distinguish between a new raw recruit and those with many years of experience and high skill levels. I wanted to achieve this without creating more managers. So I introduced a progression scheme. One existed in embryo within the fingerprint department. I also took the idea from the fluid grading scheme in operation within the government forensic science laboratory service. There, qualified staff could progress from scientific officer through higher scientific officer to senior scientific officer over a period of years, dependent on skills. A pay rise and a new title would greet each progression. All the staff remained operational and not necessarily managers. The goal within each discipline was to get to the senior grade.

So I developed the career guide scheme which existed for fingerprint officers and extended it so it also included crime scene and forensic photographers. They would all enter at grade 2, progress through grade 1 to a senior grade which was the expert grade. Above that would be a small number of managerial posts. Managers were needed but effective management was more important. Those in senior grades would be expected to, and be given the opportunity to, deputise for the manager in their absence.

Developments in technology and changes in legislation and practice also offered opportunities to detect more crime. The use of DNA technology has mushroomed since the first case in the UK in 1987. Techniques continued to become more sensitive, allowing even smaller stains of blood and other DNA-rich material to be examined and a profile obtained. That had its limitations because crime scene DNA is only of any use if there is a suspect profile to compare it against. In 1995 the law in England and Wales was changed to allow the sampling of most of the people who were charged, cautioned or reported for recordable offences. This covered most crime cases. It meant that a sample could be taken and searched against DNA found at unsolved crime scenes. The samples from suspects could be lawfully retained on a database provided the suspects were not acquitted of the offence for which they had been arrested. The National DNA Database (NDNAD) was born. The data remained the property of the police service. The database was administered by the Forensic Science Service, the UK's main forensic science laboratory provider. The technology for increasing the recovery of DNA from crime scenes increased and there is no reason to suggest that techniques will not improve further.

The development of high-intensity light sources and their use in sequence with chemical methods offered a greater ability to develop finger mark and forensic evidence at crime scenes and material removed from them. Surrey was well placed. Ken Williams was a pioneer within provincial police forces who developed simple and practical ways in which to apply these technologies.

For almost a hundred years fingerprint evidence had been given in court in England and Wales based on the sixteen-point standard. Marks were said to be identical with prints taken from a suspect where there were sixteen identical points in identical sequence. The points which experts use are the bifurcations and ridge endings found on the friction ridges of fingers, palms and feet. Simply put this is where a raised ridge splits or forks (bifurcates) or stops (ridge ends). Such characteristics are random and different in sequence between individuals. Sixteen points in identical sequence was enough for an expert to say the mark and prints are identical. Although that figure was sound it was not based on any statistical analysis or probability. It was only the exposure to other scientific disciplines that raised the issue of experts giving evidence when less than sixteen points were found. The opinion of the expert would take into account other factors which had always influenced the expert in reaching a conclusion. Up to then they were not referred to and not given in evidence. A change in the way in which fingerprint evidence was given in court would take place because it was sound science, but there were many fingerprint experts who disagreed and they were comfortable to stand behind a sixteen-point standard, even though it was historically and not science based.

Perhaps more significant was the ability of fingerprint officers to classify marks and prints, search and share them with other police forces. A national Automated Fingerprint Identification

System had been proposed by the UK Home Office in the mid 1980s, many years before. The major player was the Metropolitan Police but by 1992 there was no sight on the horizon of a national system. The main losers in this were the provincial forces such as Surrey who attracted criminals from major cities like London but had no way of sharing fingerprint intelligence through computers. For this reason, four forces got together and proposed a system of their own, led by John Hoddinot, the Chief Constable of Hampshire Constabulary and a career detective. Surrey was one of the four and Ray Elvy, the Surrey bureau head, played an active role. Within a year the four had grown to thirty-six out of forty-three forces, almost a national system. The Automated Fingerprint Retrieval (AFR) consortium was born and would run until the millennium when a Home Office national system would be finally introduced.

As I worked with Ray, this quiet man demonstrated a total and comprehensive commitment to his role as head of the Surrey bureau and to the development of a system which would talk fingerprints to other forces. He was an absolute rock, totally dependable and astonishingly hard working. On the sixteen-point standard we would differ. He did not want this to change. He was an expert practitioner and I had a duty to listen carefully and respect his view. I saw things from a view of the wider scientific community and the needs of the courts. The change process was a difficult one and although change was happening it was important not to leave anyone behind. Ray was another unsung hero, who quietly and with little fuss delivered much to the people of Surrey and far beyond.

Surrey had yet another important resource. Nick Sawyer, a senior scenes of crime officer, showed an exceptional interest in shoe-mark intelligence. Shoe marks have formed an important part of my work ever since I first investigated crime scenes. Marks and ways to catalogue and index them for intelligence purposes were not new then. What Nick Sawyer did was to use the available computer technology to improve the communication amongst those with an interest. He developed a computerised coding system based on a system used at the Metropolitan Police Laboratory for over fifteen years. The Surrey Shoefit system allowed for an alpha numeric code to be assigned to marks recovered from the scene and the footwear of persons passing through our custody centres. The code could be added to the computerised crime reports and the custody records of detained persons. It was a quick and reliable intelligence source which was based solely (please excuse the pun) on shoe-mark patterns. It was not an evidential system. Linked with the other intelligence on the system, connections could be made. Sometimes the mere mention of the link would help a person detained for one offence realise the game was up and admit to many more. For a firm evidential link, both marks and shoes would need to go to a forensic science laboratory. Shoefit provided an important missing link. The database was dynamic and simply updated by Nick for the whole force area. The shoe-mark patterns we found were not specific to Surrey, and so the database was just as important to other forces and some took it on. Some forces had yet to introduce computerised crime and custody record systems and so could not benefit form the fast intelligence link. There were other systems in use in other forces but they needed many hours of data input from SOCOs on a daily basis which was a demand on time and a duplication of resources. Shoefit was good because it was quick and very simple and it gave results. In the years since, other systems have developed and the graphics improved, but the basis is the same, it is all about the pattern of shoes. It hasn't changed since I operated my own shoe-mark index as a SOCO back at City Road in 1980.

The way forensic science was delivered to police forces was also changing. The crime scene teams were responsible for the investigation of the scene and the recording and recovery of forensic and fingerprint evidence. After an evaluation of the evidential material and the investigative needs of each case, items were submitted to outside forensic science laboratories for identification and comparison work. This ensured independent answers to important investigative questions. These services had to be paid for. The benefit was that any laboratory or expert qualified and competent to examine the material could be engaged to do so. So, instead of employing a small laboratory staff undertaking a narrow range of services, a full range of services could be engaged for the same costs by using independent laboratories. The main laboratory service was the former Home Office forensic science laboratories, the Forensic Science Service. But there were other laboratories and they have flourished since. All these laboratories now provide full ranges of service in direct competition. And that is good because it raises standards to ensure the needs of investigators are met.

Managing the budget for the use of forensic science laboratories was my responsibility as scientific support manager. I wanted to ensure that as little as possible got in the way of investigators on the ground making sound decisions in this matter. So rather than imposing decisions from Police HQ, I set out the criterion for using the laboratories and delegated the decisions to the local crime scene managers. It would be their role to ensure the criterion was met. It would also ensure sound communication between detectives and crime scene personnel. The criterion I developed was quite simple. If the submission of any item to the laboratory could meaningfully answer an investigator's question, which could not be answered by other means, then it should be submitted, irrespective of the cost. The last clause drew a raised eyebrow from the director of finance but I was firm on this and he really had no problem once I explained why it was necessary. Since we were paying the laboratory for each examination they made there were potential critics, in particular defence lawyers, who might suggest that we didn't fully investigate a case because it was too costly. So the criterion was ethical and responsible. The detail of the criterion explained that 'meaningfully answer' included identifying material, linking offences and people and eliminating suspects. A few years later when the Metropolitan Police were reviewing the use of their own laboratory (which resulted in it joining the Forensic Science Service) it quoted the criterion as an example of good practice.

Surrey County Council approved a plan to build a new scientific support centre which would bring the physical and human resources together. Although the main forensic laboratory work would continue to be undertaken in an outside laboratory, the front-end search, recovery, recording and intelligence responsibilities remained within the force. This would ensure that light sources and chemical treatments could be applied in sequence by a team of crime scene investigators, forensic photographers, fingerprint experts and any number of specific forensic scientists. The new centre in Surrey would include two separate examination rooms, complete with independent extraction to prevent contamination. Also present would be a hazard examination room for items heavily soiled with blood and body fluids. Not even forensic science laboratories had those facilities. It may be because, up to then, such stained items would not be examined because they were too unpleasant. New technologies meant that doing nothing was not a satisfactory answer. So Surrey would have a facility not only to deal safely with such items but to examine and recover all the forensic evidence which they contained. The room would be fitted with seamless stainless-steel worktops, which could be hosed down, and drying facilities for soiled items. There was even a separate entrance for staff (to prevent unpleasant materials coming through the main door) and shower facilities for staff working in the area so they could clean themselves up after. A full-height garage with vehicle lift, and a door which would ensure a total blackout, so that the light sources could be used, completed the examination and search facilities.

The combined opportunity of increased recovery of evidence through light sources and identification through fingerprint and DNA computerisation and practice meant that the next five years were going to be exciting. To put Surrey in a position where it would benefit from all these opportunities, a coordinated plan was needed. So in 1995 we put together the Bureau 2000 project to map out how each of these opportunities would be realised along with those which came along in the meantime. It would mean budgeting for extra equipment and staff and a phased implementation so that all the strings pulled and came together at the right time.

The Society's diploma went from strength to strength, with a healthy number of committed professional putting themselves forward as candidates. Many successful 'diplomats' would use the award as a springboard for their own careers, rising to management and senior management in forces in the UK and organisations overseas. Having obtained the permission of the chief constable, Surrey became the home of the practical examinations held over three long weekends in June between 1992 and 1999. The examinations brought together practitioners, scientists, academics and lawyers. One stalwart of the exam process was Dr Jim Thorpe, who regularly made the journey from the University of Strathclyde in Scotland to Surrey. He had succeeded Brian Caddy as the head of the Society's Professional Awards Committee in 1992. I served as a member of the Council of the Forensic Science Society from 1992–5, whilst continuing as Secretary of the Crime Scene Investigation Diploma and running the examination programme. As chair of the scientific meeting committee, I helped plan and deliver the three scientific conferences held each year. By 1996 I had been elected vice president of the Society. It was a time of great change. A series of miscarriages of justice had shaken the police and forensic science communities. There were calls for professional registration and the Society's role itself was being challenged. The Society had led the programme for vocational qualification and accreditation but more was needed. Some people stressed a need for a professional body for forensic scientists. Many of those who called for such a body had not bothered to join the Society or use it as a mechanism to develop things. I observed that they were more interested in looking after their own vested interests within organisations than developing the science and how it was delivered. Some might accuse me of the same, but I would suggest they were wrong. My determination to do the right thing probably got me into trouble more often than it helped my career. The proposed professional body would duplicate many of the development resources which the Society offered, namely vocational qualifications, a scientific journal and a scientific conference programme. What was needed was a process of registration of all forensic practitioners alongside all this. The Society was caught on the hop and at the first meeting of a government-charged committee headed by Lord Dainton the Society's efforts were virtually overlooked. A meeting of the Society's governing council was held within a week and my blood was up. Members of the council worked on a written response to Dainton's committee, whilst I prepared a presentation on behalf of the Society which I would personally deliver when the committee next met.

Professor Caddy, representing the University of Strathclyde but also a member of the Society's council, was there. Also present was Bob Lees, a distinguished Scottish procurator fiscal who was the society's president. I remember nervously waiting outside the committee room at the forbidding Royal Society of Chemistry to deliver the presentation in January 1997. I felt that the very future of the Society was at stake if a duplicate organisation was to undertake things that the Society did, and did well. If this were needed then it had to be for the right reason and of course the Society would see the greater good and support progressive change. But a firm account of the Society's activities and position was needed. Lord Dainton was a charming, decisive and focused pillar of the scientific establishment but he immediate put me at my ease. The presentation went well and I could see by the responses of Brian Caddy and Bob Lees that

I had done a good job. The committee was given the written response to support my presentation. Within a short time the committee had decided to address the need for accreditation and leave all the other aspects of education, development, publication and meeting to others, the Society being the strongest in these fields. The Council for the Registration of Forensic Practitioners would grow out of Dainton's recommendations. It does just that – accredits practitioners, scientists, investigators and experts alike active in the delivery of forensic science to the courts.

The Society also developed professional membership, becoming a professional body for qualified members, to complement its learned status. Ordinary membership remains open for those who do not qualify for professional membership as the Society wishes to develop all those interested parties.

For me, all these matters would take time to come together but they did. They began to in 1997 when Her Majesty's Inspector of Constabulary conducted a full review of Surrey Police. This is an important Home Office review of the competency and efficiency of police forces. I was interviewed at length and had to demonstrate to the inspectors all the current practices and work of the department. In the final report, HM inspectors singled out the department. Scientific support was commended in four separate areas and then given an overall commendation: 'Her Majesty's Inspectors were extremely impressed by the range and quality of initiatives being pursued by the scientific support section and commend it as a centre of excellence.'

Throughout many years in Surrey I was blessed to have the constant support and encouragement of a number of senior officers – Detective Chief Superintendent Len Rikard, Assistant Chief Constables Peter Hampson and Peter Fahy, Deputy Chief Constable Ian Beckett and Chief Constable David Williams. Len Rikard was the first businessman I ever met in the police service, but he was also a great leader and senior detective. He applied business models to policing in a way I had not seen before. Like me he was analytical and he used his skills to look at the causes of crime and apply resources in the right places. He taught me that detecting crime was but a tool in reducing crime with the final goal of trying to engineer it out altogether. Utopia may be an unrealistic goal, but at least we should try, and try we did. The reduction of crime was the goal of David Williams and Ian Beckett, who used detection to fuel a whole programme of reductions in crime and disorder, working with communities, social workers and even architects to reduce the opportunity for crime and the things which motivate it. These were new views in 1994 and Surrey was at the forefront. Peter Hampson saw the big picture and realised the use and value of the scientific detection of crime. His constant support and encouragement for my work and that of colleagues such as Ray Elvy were a source of strength. There was continuity as these men moved on. Ian Blair, the new chief constable appointed in 1997 would obviously support the new scientific technologies and their application. He recognised my personal efforts and challenges, and ensured that the force's investment was properly applied. I found him to be a man of vision, courage, honour and compassion. I would expect that of someone who went on to become Commissioner of the Metropolitan Police as he did.

The science and practice we would develop in these years would be applied to the challenging crimes which Surrey Police had to investigate.

18. The Body in Lime

The role of the SIO is amongst the hardest in the UK police service. The senior investigating officer is responsible for the sound, professional investigation of major crimes such as murder and bringing the guilty to court. That in itself is hard enough, but they also have to manage the resources of the investigation, in particular the cost. I always found this an incredibly difficult conflict of responsibilities with huge potential for allegations of corner cutting and failing to fully investigate.

It is the nature of policing in the UK that detectives develop and rise, some to lofty ranks, and there is a steady and constant turnover at the top. When you have been around for some time and move on you often hear that a former colleague, one you knew when they were young, is now the senior detective and running the show. Life at the top is short as retirement quickly approaches and allows for the promotion of those below. Such is the cycle. A lot of talent is lost.

It is easy to remember colleagues as they were in their youth, rather than see what they have learned and become in the intervening years. Many may think of me that way. But I like to think we are all wiser, more mature and, above all, more experienced.

Brian Woodfield, in 1993 a detective chief inspector with Surrey Police, was one such colleague who rose, rightly, to the top of his trade. I didn't know him as a young officer although I heard stories about him. Like all of us, Brian was from humble hard-working stock. His mentor at the time I knew him was Pat Crossan, a detective superintendent and very much from the same school. Both had a steely, determined approach. Brian appeared a little less caring than Pat. It often strikes me that there is a loftiness, an arrogance, in some officers, but it is really the air of authority which the police officer, and more importantly, the detective must display to get to the truth. With Pat Crossan and Brian Woodfield that shield hid a deeply compassionate and practical side. These men would do their job and ensure that everyone around did theirs.

Brian strongly led his investigations and there were times when I had to advise caution or restraint. He always listened, and then he made his mind up, after all it was his investigation, he was in charge. When a key piece of evidence was found during a scene investigation he would shout, 'Get it down the lab!' It became quite a catch phrase. He even let slip that once, in the middle of the night, he woke up shouting it out aloud, to the dismay of his wife. He was passionate about his work and I liked that.

It was, however, something else which Brian said which has stuck with me. He regularly used just two words, which are the finest I have heard any investigator use. They were polite and targeted. He would say, 'Show me.' He would use them in investigations and they became particularly important when reviewing the work or cases of others.

In late August 1993, I was on a visit to the police National Training Centre for Scientific Support to Crime Investigation (NTCSSCI) in Durham, when I got a call from the east Surrey division. It was from Danny Finnerty, who was the duty crime scene manager. Danny was from the other side of the county and had taken the first call to this incident. The body of a man, naked and covered in a white powder, had been found. Danny was a very talented and capable professional, but he was under pressure from the officer in the case, Detective Chief Inspector Brian Woodfield. I often thought that I must have worked with a more professional and demanding detective than him, but I would have trouble remembering when. Until I remembered Pat Crossan of course.

Brian was directing the investigation at the scene with Danny struggling to assert his professional knowledge on the management of the scene. The role of the crime scene manager was very much in its evolution at that time, and there was no way Brian Woodfield wasn't going to control every aspect of the case, especially the scene. I didn't want that situation to change. After all the buck stops with the SIO. But with a little delegation on his part, I knew that his lot would be easier and he would get the answers he wanted.

In later years, it was conceivable that highly motivated, dynamic and capable SIOs such as Brian Woodfield would be kept out of the scene for much, if not all, of the time it was being examined. It is not a situation I support. Whereas the scene can be photographed and videoed, the presence of the SIO is important for them to understand the dynamics and layout of the scene from a first-hand perspective.

Certainly the practice had improved from when detectives would go into the scene unprotected and then call for the scenes of crime personnel. By this time we had persuaded them to withhold the presence of any detective officer until a path had been cleared from the outer cordon to the body. Usually only one detective (the SIO) would enter at that time with the pathologist.

In all cases it is important for a medical practitioner, with the skills and authority to determine and confirm that the deceased is, in fact, dead, to attend. Confirming a time at which life is no longer present is a matter of coroner law. I never wasted a moment in allowing a doctor into the scene where this was in any doubt. In those cases I would ensure that the doctor was quickly briefed to certify death with as little disturbance as possible and dispatch them inside unimpeded. It would then be necessary to deal with any aspect of their contamination of the scene or vice versa. I felt that if I was not sure the victim was dead any delay could cause a seriously injured victim to die when they could have been saved. I would have felt responsible if a victim had died on the way to the hospital, and I would have been heavily criticised by the coroner. My view was not always readily accepted by those embryo crime scene managers who I taught much later at NTCSSCI Durham, but I remain convinced of it to this day.

Later still, the presence of any officer, specialist scientist, medical or other expert would be based on a need identified as the investigation and scene examination developed. The scene would be managed by a crime scene manager whose responsibility came from the SIO.

Back at this scene Danny had done an excellent job by ignoring the obvious route in and out of the scene, preferring instead to cut a new path through some undisturbed vegetation straight to the body. It allowed the obvious and likely route of the offender to be examined at a more steady and professional pace.

The decision about whether the incident looks like murder, an accident or suicide is not always easy and, in any event, requires investigation. The scene which confronted Danny Finnerty and Brian Woodfield was probably easy to judge but they took all the right steps. The body was that of a naked male lying in a clearing behind some bushes, ten yards from a country road. The body was covered in a fine white powder. It would be an understatement to say it looked suspicious. If it were a suicide it would be a bizarre one.

The police had been called to the scene by two men, working in a landfill site in Redhill. They had been working for a few days by the perimeter fence. On the day in question they had noticed a mound of white powder which had appeared on the other side of the fence. During a break they walked out of the gate, around to the country lane adjacent to the site. What they discovered there was the naked body of the deceased and the white powder covering him.

After securing a common approach path from the perimeter to the body, Iain West, a distinguished Home Office pathologist entered the scene with the SIO and CSM. The scene was extensively photographed. A sample of the powder was taken at Brian Woodfield's request and immediately dispatched to the Forensic Science Laboratory at Aldermaston. Iain suggested the powder was lime as it had been in one of his first cases some thirty years before. The powder was confirmed as lime within a day. Brian Woodfield also ordered that soil samples should be taken from around the body. If he had a reason for this he didn't explain it to Danny, who by then was doing as he was told. I later asked Danny Finnerty for what purpose they were taken, the reply being because the SIO had said so.

The post mortem revealed that the man had been stabbed. A tattoo on his body was recorded and circulated to police forces for comparison with missing persons reports. When an individual is reported missing by concerned relatives or friends it is normal to take a description which would include height, weight, hair, eye colour and any distinguishing features such as scars, birthmarks or tattoos. Other items such as the clothing they were wearing, along with any jewellery, may help their identification. The police record these details and circulate them to other stations and forces. Nowadays, obtaining a sample of potential DNA would be extremely useful. That would have to come from a hairbrush or wristband of a watch strap. That technology had yet to be invented in 1993. We had to rely on simpler methods to identify our victim but the tattoo gave us a great chance, provided that had been recorded somewhere. We were in luck. The victim was quickly identified as a man from south London who had been missing for four weeks.

Brian Woodfield rather cunningly and independently asked Iain West how long the victim had been dead. It was an interesting question to test the reliability of expert opinion and how that might appear in evidence. It was an open question so carefully delivered that the importance of the reply may have been overlooked by many, but not Brian. Iain's reply was five weeks. Brian of course already knew by that stage that the victim had only been missing for four weeks. We would have to look at what Iain based his opinion on.

I returned to Surrey and reviewed the scene investigation with Martin Gaule (the crime scene manager for the east Surrey division which included the Redhill area), who had accompanied me to Durham.

A key investigative question emerged. It was, 'How long has the deceased been there?' The importance of this was to narrow down the investigation to a shorter period of time than the four weeks between him going missing and the discovery of his body. It might indicate a shorter time frame for potential witnesses to the dumping of the body and indicate for how long he was kept (dead or alive) at another or other locations. Two other things had also been determined. The first was that he had been dead for most, if not all, of the four weeks and he had not been killed here.

Other matters were also determined in the first few days of the investigation. The body had been covered in fifty-four kilogrammes of industrial-quality lime, calcium hydroxide (with traces of calcium carbonate), the sort used as in the farming industry. The deceased had also lost weight, some five or six kilogrammes at least since he went missing. In fact it was later suggested that the lime had probably drawn water from his body (and carbon dioxide from the atmosphere to increase its mass), causing the deceased to lose weight after he was dead.

The problem remained. How could we determine how long the body had been at the scene? I suggested we might be able to determine how long the lime had been there by its effect on its surroundings. I assumed that the body and the lime were put there at the same time. It was a good assumption because although there had been a small amount of animal interest in the body, this was limited to an exposed area covered with only a thin layer of lime. Even this would have been bitter and unpleasant to the most determined fox looking for food. It remained an assumption, however, and so was documented as such as we pursued this line of enquiry. If that assumption proved to be wrong a later review would identify the error and allow further, more appropriate, investigations to be made. That was the purpose of recording the nature of the assumption.

We could also try entomology (the science of bugs and flies and the like). This can be used as a timeline by determining the age and development of bugs against known charts of rate of growth and temperature. Unfortunately, the lime not only deterred foxes but insects too. If it had been the intention of whoever dumped the body to use the lime to cause its rapid decay, it had quite the opposite effect. It prevented decomposition by deterring the natural course of nature and, in fact, preserved the body for us.

To confirm this and close it as a line of enquiry, I tried to contact the two leading experts in forensic entomology. It was August and they were both out of the country on holiday. I confirmed my approach by phone and followed it up with a statement to close that avenue when one had returned.

I reviewed the crime scene photos and began to think how we could determine the time presence of the lime. The first potential method was to determine the change in acidity of the soil, as lime is a strong alkali. I took advice from Pam Hamer, a forensic chemist and former colleague at the Metropolitan Police Forensic Science Laboratory. I had a huge amount of respect for Pam and knew she would understand what I was trying to do. It would require core samples to a depth of one or two metres and a record of the rainfall over the past four weeks. It might not work but it was worth a try. I found a company that took core soil samples and arranged for them to visit the scene where they took a dozen or so samples from the area where the body was found and control samples from the surrounding area. It only cost some tens of pounds for all the samples, taken under the supervision of a crime scene manager and team to ensure the correct documentation and integrity of the sampling.

As it happened we didn't have to use the soil samples, though it had been prudent to quickly secure them. In my conversation with Pam Hamer, I had asked about the effect of lime (an agricultural chemical) on the vegetation. Neither of us knew where to start but came to the conclusion that the National Botanical Gardens at Kew was a good start. So that was my next port of call. Two or three calls followed as each person passed me on to someone else. My fifth call was to a gentleman at the Ministry of Agriculture, Fisheries and Foods. He was a soil chemist although he preferred the title of agricultural engineer. The important thing was that his life's work and expert subject was the effect of chemicals on vegetation. Bingo. By absolute chance he was based in Guildford, our county town, but he could have been anywhere in the country as far as I was concerned, I had found someone who could help us.

I carefully briefed him as to my position and responsibility and the question I needed to answer. Could he determine how long the lime had been there given the conditions I had described? In briefing someone who is an expert in a particular field but not accustomed to the demands, requirements and niceties of the criminal justice system it is important to lay out some ground rules for his protection and our integrity. I didn't want him to stray off his subject and say things which he could not back up.

I did this by telling him the circumstances of the discovery of the body and the confidential nature of our enquiry. I gave him the results of the laboratory examination of the powder and its quantity. I informed him I could show him the scene photographs taken on the day the body was found and arrange for him to visit the scene which was by now a week old. I explained to him that I would like him to observe the photographs and interpret them for us if he could. How long had the lime had been there? If he could he would have to demonstrate on what basis he was making his observations and show any published scientific material which would support them. Wherever possible he should state what is fact and what is opinion based on his experience and expertise. I made notes of my briefing and arranged for Martin Gaule to take the scene photographs straight to him.

The reply and statement I got from Martin and our man was immediately encouraging. He described the four or so types of vegetation (grasses and ferns) surrounding the body and lime, each by their scientific name. He particularly noted one or two key types and suggested their documented growth rate. He then observed that the grasses on the edge of the lime were still depressed and suggested that the grasses had not regenerated and pushed through the lime in search of light. Based on this observation of the photograph and his knowledge it was his opinion that the lime had been there for no more than seven days.

This was a very good start. We had already whittled the time the body was dumped from four to one week. There was more to come.

Martin took our man to the scene with one of our forensic photographers. He surveyed the environment and confirmed the vegetation types. There were still some traces of the powder in the soil and grass. Now, based on this confirmation, and the regenerated growth that was now occurring at the scene, and on his observation and knowledge, it was his opinion that the lime had been there for no more than two days. This was a breakthrough.

It corroborated the observations of the two workmen, with some sound reproducible scientific evidence. It meant that investigators could target motorists who had travelled along the road in a two day period and who may have seen something suspicious. It meant that investigative time was not wasted trying to take statements from all the motorists who had driven that route in a four-week period. This line of enquiry had been useful and helped focus the investigation as it developed.

The overall investigation was soon transferred to the Metropolitan Police in London, based on rules agreed by chief police officers. It is governed by where the major part of the investigation lies. Although Surrey had the crime scene, it was in reality merely the dump site and that could have been anywhere. It was determined that the Met had the majority of the enquiries which had to be made based on the business and social affairs of the deceased.

I prepared a hand-over report for the SIO on all matters which the scientific support department had undertaken and then briefed my counterpart in London and the new SIO with Brian Woodfield.

Some years later, after lengthy extradition matters, a man stood trial for the murder. As for the lime and why the perpetrator(s) had used it, we never found out. It was probably a matter of a little knowledge being a dangerous thing. Lime had been used to cover bodies in plague pits in earlier centuries. Its purpose was to stop the spread of disease. Contrary to common belief it does not cause decomposition, but quite the opposite: it preserves the body by deterring the normal course of nature.

I also reflected on how we managed the investigation process. Did I use the scientific support staff to their best potential? These were still early days in the development of my management of the process and not just how we supported the investigation. Danny Finnerty had been the first crime scene manager to respond to the scene, but he was not a member of the local team. He dealt with the first few hours and in reality that seemed to be a good formula without having the local manager on call all the time. I was concerned that on my return to the county, I had asked Martin Gaule (the local CSM) to take over from Danny. I didn't want Danny to feel that he was being replaced for some negative reason, which was not the case. Danny had done an excellent job, but I had to plan. I would have to learn how to get the best out of people and there is not only a need for continuity but also perhaps local knowledge, not least knowing the facilities and resources immediately to hand. In the future, as far as possible I would use the local team to respond and see a case through. Outsiders, particularly those on call, would be the first responders, but the local team with their relationship with local officers and detectives, I decided, would be best placed and motivated to see a case of local interest through. Keeping the local team out only demoralised the team. When a big case broke I would use outside personnel to fill in behind the local team for the day-to-day work, whilst they handled the big case.

Whilst I was busy with the nuts and bolts of supporting the investigation with the scientific team there was one aspect of the case which presented a wonderful opportunity and I offer it as a final reflection. It often amuses me. It is the only case I know of where the offenders themselves helped preserve the scene for the police.

19. Crime Scene Manager

It is the major crime scene which brings together all the aspects of practice and resource. The start is often as not confused, very confused. There is emotion amongst the victims and witnesses and high activity amongst the first officers to respond. The priority is the preservation of life. It takes precedence over everything else. The next priority is detaining any offenders who are escaping from the scene. But preservation of life comes first.

As a crime scene investigator I often found myself picking up the pieces once the scene was secure and suspected offenders and injured victims had been taken away. The immediate goal was always to establish order, and to take control. Only then could a planned and balanced investigation take place. My role, however, evolved as the concept of crime scene investigation, and all its benefits, grew and was accepted and ultimately demanded by detectives. The progression was not only to manage my own actions, but those of other scene investigators and other police resources, even serving officers.

Crime scene management was a relatively new concept when I went to Surrey. One person with a crime scene, rather than a detective, background to control the investigation at the scene was a novelty. Of course there had been managers but they were often senior detectives and had no professional expertise in forensic investigation themselves. The model, where it existed up to then, used a detective, often in a laboratory liaison role, which I felt really wasn't part of the continuum or escalation process which I have previously described. The old system had served the police service well, with many fine exponents from whom I had learnt a lot, but there was a need to change, to develop. In reality, I had been practising the role now recognised as crime scene manager since my time on the Flying Squad. The bedrock for my skills was that of an apprentice examining and investigating thousands of minor and major crime scenes. As a crime scene manager it was my role to plan and implement a process so that all the information, intelligence and evidence was recovered and communicated at the earliest opportunity to the senior investigating officer. As a crime scene manager, I was the link between the scene, the laboratory and the SIO.

On my arrival at a major crime scene I often found the first officers had taken step to preserve it and establish a cordon. My first actions were to confirm that all steps to preserve life had taken place. Sometimes this was obvious, but could never be assumed. Someone with medical training had to confirm death. Until that was done it was best to assume that the victim was alive and get medical assistance there and into the scene without any delay or hindrance.

The initial cordon would be decided by those first officers but it would be my second action to check it. I would review this and would either agree or revise, and in many cases outwardly extend it. Wider is always best as it can be reduced later. It is difficult but not impossible to extend a cordon and if there is a sound reason the earlier that move is taken the better. I would ensure that a log of those entering and leaving the scene (and the relevant times) had been started. The cordon would normally be protected by police officers to ensure that only those with a need or role in the scene could enter it. That need would be determined solely by me once I had taken responsibility for the scene. I also needed to backtrack and list those who entered and left the scene from its discovery. It could be necessary to examine them and possibly recover their clothing and footwear to eliminate this from anything which could subsequently be found in the scene examination.

The initial activity always involved listening, assessing the nature of the allegation and what staff resources were available to deal with the numbers of scenes (people, places, vehicles, objects) that had already been identified. My job was to ensure that these areas were addressed in order of priority. Where scene investigators were not available, clear instructions to other police personnel on how to preserve the subject until a scene investigator was available were given and they could be instructed to deal with the situation.

The actual crime scene could often wait, as it was more likely that people, and sometimes vehicles, required more immediate action.

All suspects have rights. They have a basic right to medical attention. They have a right of human dignity. In law, dependent on the jurisdiction, they have a right to refuse to be examined. In some jurisdictions (such as England and Wales) the right of the suspect to be examined can be overruled to allow the recovery of clothing and the taking of some samples, by force if necessary. These are limited to external, non-intimate areas, where it is believed that the evidence recovered has the ability to eliminate or implicate the suspect. Changes in legislation in the UK have allowed such examinations to take place. They protect the rights of the individual and also the investigator who is acting within the law.

Many years ago, before such laws were implemented I dealt with one offence which tested my morality and integrity. During a bungled armed robbery, shots were fired at police officers who had arrived quickly at the scene. A suspect was arrested in a violent struggle with the unarmed officers. Both the suspect and officers received injuries and were taken to hospital. On hearing the details of what had happened, I called a colleague to deal with the scene of the robbery. He was some way away. I made my way immediately to the hospital to deal with the suspect and hopefully undertake some examination which would eliminate or implicate his involvement in the robbery, and in particularly the discharge of a firearm. Thankfully, the firing of guns in the commission of crime was relatively rare both then and now. The particular examination I had in mind was to swab the hands and face of the suspect to recover any gunshot residues. This would indicate his proximity to a gun when it was fired. The particles in question are delicate and are quickly lost from the skin but can be retained longer on hair, such as exposed beards, moustaches and head hair.

At that time there were no rules allowing the taking of samples by force. If the suspect refused that was the end of the matter. Any evidence which would implicate or eliminate them would just be lost. On arriving at the Emergency Room of the hospital and seeing the condition of the suspect and hearing the manner of his arrest, it was clear that this man was not going to consent to any police examination. I knew some of the medical staff from previous visits. I can't recall exactly what happened next but I take full responsibility for it. There was no way the suspect was going to allow anyone to swab his hands for evidence; a white coat was called for which I duly put on. I went into the cubicle and managed to swab one hand and was on the second before the suspect realised that this was not a normal medical procedure. Ducking a punch, I exited with what I had. It was underhand and I am neither proud nor ashamed, it just seemed the right thing to do. I was searching for the truth. I was prepared to recount my actions before a judge and take full responsibility if what I had done was deemed wrong in some aspect of the law. I was unsure whether I had broken the law. If I had I was ignorant (no defence, I know), but my goal was to seek the truth so that the court could decide. Nobody was going to get hurt (although the flailing right hand of the suspect once he realised what was going on could have injured me). The examination of the swab I had taken indicated that the suspect had been in close proximity to a gun when it was discharged. The suspect was found guilty of firing at the police officers. I was never called to give evidence, so never had to explain my actions. A few years later, after pressure from many of us, the law was changed to allow examinations such as the swabbing of external skin to take place even when the suspect refuses and even by force in the cases of serious crime such as shooting incidents.

Whether a suspect is in custody or not, some initial steps are naturally made at the scene whilst the initial confusion calms down. It helps establish order and control, so I would instruct a crime scene investigator or photographer to take external photographs of the scene.

I would begin to identify the type of search and the types of specialist who would be needed as information came to light. The very nature of investigation is that as the search takes place and other things are seen and found, further specialists may be needed. Good time management was always needed so that these specialists were called to enable them to get to the scene at a time when they were needed, otherwise there could be periods of delay with other specialists hanging around.

Part of my initial scene assessment needed to include any hazards or dangers which might affect the investigators and specialists who would go into the scene. I had to plan for this and included it in any briefing I gave. The right information and the right protective clothing and equipment are essential. Then there were the changeable conditions such as weather or lighting for the outside scene. You can't change the weather or nightfall but you can prioritise examinations and protect key areas within the scene as well as bring in additional lighting.

Having listened to all the information available and most importantly the needs of the SIO, I had to agree the examination and search plan. The SIO always wants as much information as early as possible. This becomes more important when someone has been arrested from the outset. The clock will be ticking and there may be limits on how long the suspect can be detained before release. Any investigation of a suspected murder scene is likely to take a number of days. In any event the SIO will want to interview the suspect and will want as much information from us at the earliest opportunity so they are in a position of strength, not ignorance. If the right person has been detained they will know more about the scene than anyone else. The SIO will want to redress this balance.

I was responsible for briefing all the investigators and specialists about the scene and their role. I was always open for discussion but it is necessary to determine clear areas of responsibility and terms of reference for each member of the team.

As I said earlier, examining a whole major crime scene often takes days, so it is necessary to break it down into manageable parts and prioritise. A body is always an early and obvious priority. So a common approach path (CAP) would be cleared from the edge of the cordon to the body. The route of the CAP, however, may not be the most obvious. If it is the route any offender is known or likely to have taken, then the area and the items within in it may take a long time to clear. So, often another route, from another door or window when the scene is a building, would need to be found. This would ensure that the CAP to the body is established quickly. In woodland areas, rather than take an obvious path, it is often possible to cut a new direct path through the undergrowth, bypassing areas which will take a long time to examine.

Once a CAP was established to the body, I would ensure that an inner cordon around the body itself was made. This was not always defined with police scene tape as you might see on TV, but it may include a smaller room or defined area around the body. With the body in sight I would review with the team what examination steps would need to take place to allow the body to be removed for a post-mortem (PM) examination without jeopardising any evidence. It was common to call a specialist if something unusual was noticed. There are always time pressures: the SIO needs to know how the victim died and this may only be determined at PM. However, some things cannot be rushed and it must take whatever time it needs. The temperature close to the body will be taken and recorded at regular intervals. This is because it affects the temperature of the body, and it may be important in determining the time of death later. At this stage a medical examiner or pathologist often enters the scene to see the body where it lies. It is their job to identify the time, cause and manner of death. So their examination often starts at the scene. The steps to enable removal of the body are determined and the need to record and recover any immediately obvious material assessed. The taping for fibres or the removal of some or all items of clothing can also take place, if they are likely to be contaminated (for example with blood) when the body is placed in a body bag.

An area around the body is prepared for removal, the body placed in a bag and removed to the edge of the outer cordon. A scene investigator or other officer needs to accompany the body to the mortuary for continuity and identification.

Depending on the time pressures of the investigation, members of the crime scene team may need to accompany the body and assist the pathologist with the post-mortem examination. There is always a need for continuity of intelligence from the scene to the post mortem so at the very least the scene manager or a crime scene investigator needs to be present. Information about the time, cause and manner of death affects the remaining examination of the crime scene. Where time pressures are high or the weather at the scene is deteriorating, additional scene investigators are called to deal with the post mortem. In these cases I would ensure that one of the original scene investigators continues with the scene whilst the PM takes place.

The outcome of the time, cause and manner of death is always a milestone in the investigation. At the very least it gives the SIO and those planning to interview any suspect some important information. The SIO would often call for a 'debrief' on the investigation to date and I would need to be there. I would have to relay key information but it is the individual investigators who have been to the scene and seen the evidence first hand who need to communicate this personally. If at all feasible I would ensure as many as possible were present at the debrief. Information from other lines of enquiry and from other witnesses is often relayed at these debriefs, some evidence from the scene may, once relayed, identify the need for further work.

Up to that point the events have usually and adequately filled a busy day. With a suspect in custody, any current examination at the scene would have to continue no matter what the time of day or night. The original scene investigators would need to be rested and, if possible, the scene would be closed down or a small team left to undertake essential work. Whenever possible, I would allow the team to rest and return at a suitable time the following day. Before I took any break I would ensure that the investigators and specialists needed for the following day were booked and briefed so that there would be no delay when work resumed.

The next day would always start with a review and a continuation of the examination plan. Recovery and search in a planned manner would give way to sequential and possibly destructive evidence recovery techniques. The use of light sources and chemical methods ensures that all potential areas for finger marks and other evidence are examined and the search exhausted. Forensic evidence search takes in wider areas, towards the edge of the cordon. This is often undertaken by police search team officers and police dogs where the area is large. The SIO and I would need to ensure that the purpose of the search be identified, documented and communicated to all the search team members.

Once the examination plan for the scene was completed and reviewed by the team members, the final review would be undertaken by the SIO and me. This is to ensure that the investigation this far is to the SIO's satisfaction and that nothing is missing. I would ask the SIO to sign for the completed scene and release it back to its owner. There is often a need to clean the scene of any blood, body fluids or hazardous materials used in the examination and this would now take place. In heavily contaminated scene this is best undertaken by contractors.

It is easy to get tired of the endless debriefs, but another will follow. This time it takes place where once again the available information from all the scenes, suspects, victims and vehicles is compared with any findings at the scene. The debriefings are long but are an important method of cross-reference. Each is an important milestone. The question 'What do we have?' must be asked.

A few days before Christmas we were confronted with a missing mother and child from a 'safe house'. The woman had been the subject of domestic violence and was removed completely from her home area to the safety of a rural location. The fact that she was missing was concern enough. What increased the concern was that when a social worker visited the safe house, she could not get entry and noticed through the window a scene of damage. Police arrived and forced an entry. The house had few items of furniture, but what little was there was damaged. This included most of the fittings in the kitchen and bathroom, which were all heavily damaged. It looked deliberate. Concern for the woman and child continued when small amounts of blood were noticed smeared on the walls and also a small piece of bloodstained bone. I put in place a full crime scene examination from the outset. A team undertook all the steps I have already described and no time was wasted. I called a forensic scientist to interpret the blood (origin and distribution) and a pathologist to give advice on the bone. The key priorities were to identify if the blood and bone were of human origin. If they were we had a potential murder scene and two missing people. This would need large resources and probably the need for an investigation team to work through the Christmas holiday. The investigation would need lots of resources and police time and the financial bill would be high.

Naturally, the cost was not important, but I hoped I could find a way of answering the question quickly so that if a full murder investigation was needed we would know by the following morning, Christmas Eve. The intense scene investigation continued late into the night before Christmas Eve. I arranged for the items to be examined overnight. It meant a trip of 150 miles to a specific laboratory by police motorcycle for the items and for the scientist to work through the night. Forensic science laboratories are not routinely open all night, so special arrangements had to be made. They promised an answer by nine am on Christmas Eve.

Early the next morning the SIO called for a briefing whilst we awaited the laboratory test results. It was during the meeting that I received the call from the lab. The blood was dog in origin and the bone was chicken with traces of dog saliva. Whatever our concerns, at least there was nothing to suggest that the woman and her child had been injured at the house. I carefully noted the exact words which the scientist relayed so that I could enter an immediate written report of the conversation into the enquiry system. This took the pressure off mounting an immediate full examination of the rest of the house which would have taken at least two days. The SIO listened to the news with great interest. Enquiries were continuing with officers near the original home of the woman. To my surprise the SIO then gave instructions for a full and immediate escalation of the scene investigation. It was as if the result we had meant nothing. After a few minutes I asked if we could take a break. In the interval I expressed my view that although there were concerns, a full scene investigation would not give any intelligence about the location of the missing persons. If they were found harmed or if a suspect was arrested we could immediately review and commence whatever examination was necessary. I agreed to put in place a contingency plan. He agreed to this and back in the briefing this was relayed. The scene would be protected but for the moment any further examination would be delayed. It was a pragmatic decision based on reviewing the answers we had received and what they were telling us.

Within a few hours, both the woman and her child had been found unharmed. The damage had simply been caused by her when she decided to vacate the house, which said something about her character which we hadn't known. She had been in no danger on this occasion from her violent partner. The scene investigation had quickly answered the most important of questions and had helped the proper and efficient use of our resources. Our action and the concern everyone had shown her was right and proper, but she didn't appreciate it. We were not to know the outcome until we had investigated it and I'm sure we would do it all again if faced with a similar case.

In another case the body of an elderly man was found in his first-floor bedsit flat. There was no forced entry but he had a large bloody head wound. There were traces of blood found throughout the flat. The post mortem revealed that a blow to the head had contributed to his death, but there was nothing to suggest that anyone else was involved. There was suspicion that some money was missing from the flat, but that was never proven, and any strange neighbour would have quickly entered any SIO's sights as a potential suspect. The flat was extensively examined and re-examined over a period of three weeks. The medical history of the deceased revealed some dementia. A full review with SIO, scene investigators, forensic scientist and pathologist concluded that the death was accidental and not suspicious. The head wound was the result of a fall, which did not bleed immediately, but bled slowly and profusely over a period of time as he moved around the flat. There were no signs of violence, struggle, theft or other persons present at the time or following the injury. All the files and collected material were retained should any further information come to light. The coroner subsequently recorded an accidental death.

Reviews can record the fact that no crime has taken place, even if some acquaintances of the deceased have acted in a suspicious way. This may be a distraction but must not become a miscarriage of justice. I fear in some instances that is often the case. Reviews need to ask firm questions and not allow investigations to drift into untested assumptions.

If a suspect is in custody, a targeted and priority submission of items to the crime lab needs to take place. The purpose of this is to quickly answer key questions. Whose blood is on the suspect's clothing? Is it the victim's? Has there been a sexual assault? Can we identify whose DNA is on the victim? Is this the murder weapon? Does it contains the victim's blood? Are there any fingermarks on it? Whose fingermarks are they?

A more detailed consideration of every piece of recovered material is also needed to consider what potential evidence they contain and how it should be further examined. This discussion usually involved the SIO or their deputy or other senior member of their team sitting down with me and a scene investigator and going through each item one by one. Any required further examinations and their priority were recorded so that they could be addressed in order.

Each answer should prompt a question: What does the answer mean? What other questions does it throw up? The questioning only stops when each line of enquiry has been exhausted within the priorities of the overall investigation.

Aspects of the crime scene investigations do not stop when an individual is charged. Preparation has to be made to prepare the exhibits which are going to be called to court. On some occasions the prosecution and defence may agree a list which they will want to see during the court process. In any event, there has to be discipline in ensuring that all the exhibits are accounted for and have a full record of their recovery and where they have been. There needs to be statements from all the scientists or specialists who have examined them and a clear record of their continuity. That is so that they can be accounted for at any moment of their history. It is imperative that their integrity is maintained and that this is recorded.

I recall arriving at the Central Criminal Court in London for what was expected to be a lengthy trial. The care and discipline with which the case was prepared and managed clearly impressed both the prosecutor and defence legal teams. When each item was called for and a request to open the sealed item made, I was on hand to ensure that this viewing by lawyers and jurors was recorded. At the end of the viewing, the item was resealed and I made additional notes in the exhibit register. Within a few days the defence team must have realised the extent of evidence against the defendant and he changed his plea to that of guilty.

In another case the integrity and continuity of the exhibits was vigorously tested by defence lawyers. This was so detailed that I took the step of resealing the items once they had been examined in the presence of the defence lawyer and insisted on his signature on the reseal since he, and he alone, had handled the item in open court. He felt duty bound to agree since his line of attack was on just who had handled the item. He was now one of the very few who had. The trial was later stopped because the jury had received information which they should not have had and the presiding judge realised that a fair trial was no longer possible. The re-trial was interesting. The thorough inspection of the integrity and continuity of the exhibits was once again questioned but it seemed to peter out when it came the specific and important item which now bore the defence lawyer's signature. He must have forgotten or not realised the significance. 'And whose signatures are on this seal?' he asked. 'Well, one is mine and the other is yours, sir,' I replied. My notes could account for the time and place the item had been opened and resealed. The judge intervened to explain to the jury that the item had been opened at an earlier court proceeding, but the defence lawyer seemed to lose interest in challenging the integrity of the exhibits after that.

All this amounts to a hard, hard, slog which is never the view on those popular TV programmes. There is, however, more to come.

In the UK it is common practice in unsolved murder or other serious cases for the investigation to be reviewed by another senior investigator. This normally takes place at twenty-eight days. It is intended to give the case a fresh and independent view. The review is not to catch the original team out, though it may do that. Rather it challenges and tests the investigation, any assumptions and major lines of enquiry, investigative priorities and of course the forensic and scene investigations. The reviewing senior investigator may bring a small team, including a crime scene manager, to assist in the task.

I have been involved in cases which have been reviewed and I have reviewed others. In one review of a lengthy ongoing investigation the review team picked up a line of enquiry in which we were still waiting for a result. It involved the searching of finger marks found at the scene with our surrounding forces. We were part of a computerised fingerprint system, networked with thirty-four other forces, but some of our immediately neighbouring forces were not. So we had to send them copies of the marks and requested a search against their databases. When you are asking a colleague for a favour it is perhaps a little strange to check up that they have done it and to the standard you would expect. The review prompted us to check their search and speed up their reply. It resulted in identification. It also highlighted the need for a complete network solution.

In a case which I reviewed, a long investigation into the murder of a man had not resulted in any arrests for the crime. The body of the man had been found in a burnt-out car near the M25 motorway. Pat Crossan, the original senior investigating officer, was convinced that the man had been murdered at a certain house premises. Pat had ensured that Martin Gaule, the crime scene manager, examined every detail of the kitchen floor for signs of blood. Martin's thorough investigation determined that there was no blood on the floor and that there had been no clean up – even the dirt found in crevices (which one might expect) was still present. Pat Crossan had moved on and his deputy, DCI John Beavis, had kept a hold on the case. He asked me to review it and I made a few recommendations. In the review we determined that one of the suspects had a commercial garage premises. At about the time of the murder he had painted a large part of the garage floor red. Perhaps by fortune, at about the time of my review he vacated the premises. The investigators did not want it to get out that they were interested in the premises, but we wanted to examine it and look under the paint. So we came up with the novel idea of actually renting the premises, under the guise of a new business venture. It also meant that we didn't need a search warrant. This may be the first time the police actually rented a potential crime scene. The examination would need the scene investigators to work at night, as we would need a blackout to fully utilise the high-intensity light sources (HILS). This would be our first, non-destructive, examination, before any attempt was made to remove the paint. If the neighbours in the adjacent business premises were suspicious of our activity they didn't mention it. There were some conversations, but the scene investigators made it clear we were just starting up a business. Our strange hours, kept after all the others had gone home, meant that we could work inside in the dark without suspicion. Any visit meant that we had to dress down. I remember the detective inspector giving me a good look over as I turned up in a scruffy pair of jeans and T-shirt, not my usual suited attire. Once inside the premises full crime scene standards were maintained. Martin Gaule, a crime scene manager, SOCO John Dowswell and Ken Williams the head of forensic photography worked at the premises for a number of nights. We called a forensic scientist to assist and give advice at the search scene as the examination continued. Blood was found but it did not match the victim, it matched one of the suspects. This information was useful because it tied up with other blood found at other premises and helped complete a picture. The review of the case did result in a conviction. I put forward Martin Gaule, John Dowswell and Ken Williams for commendations from the Chief Constable, which they duly received, and a letter of thanks to the forensic science laboratory for the expert support of their scientist.

The review process is extremely important and valuable if it is carried out in a professional and diplomatic manner. It tests assumptions and will always assist the investigation and its ultimate detection.

So even when court proceedings are completed and no matter what the outcome (a not guilty or guilty verdict) all the items should be resealed and notes made in an exhibit register or report. This is because of the possibility of appeals and potential investigation later. The integrity and continuity of all exhibits needs to be maintained until they are destroyed or returned to an owner. That too is the final record in the exhibit register. Although these actions, like many others, may be undertaken by other police personnel, it was my responsibility to ensure that the right advice was given and practice adopted to ensure the integrity of the scientific investigation of the crime. That was my role as a crime scene manager and I took it seriously.

20. Gone for a Walk

At 9.15 am one Sunday morning in January, a few days into the New Year, William Ross reported his wife missing. Anna Ross had gone for a walk at four am in the morning to clear a head cold. She had not returned. He had driven around the area and phoned friends but he could not find her.

Bill and Anna lived with their infant daughter in a smart new house on the outskirts of Farnham, Surrey. When police officers attended the Ross home, Bill gave them a description of his wife including the stud earrings and matching necklace she was wearing. She suffered from the eating disorder bulimia and she would vomit after eating. He also describes how she had suffered abuse as a child and that she was 'vulnerable'. When some questions were asked about the clothing she was wearing when she left the house, it appeared that it was only her nightdress. All her coats were still in the house. The outside temperature was below zero and there was a heavy frost.

Searches were made of the local hospitals, and an appeal was broadcast on local radio. The neighbouring police force, Hampshire, was contacted as the house was within a mile of the constabulary border.

House to house enquiries were made and one neighbour stated that he saw Bill cleaning his Mini and Anna's Vauxhall at eight am that morning. That was shortly before he had called the police.

Bill was taken to the local police station while officers continued to search the surrounding area. Bill's mother came to look after her granddaughter.

At 4.18 pm a call was received by Hampshire Police. The naked and burnt body of a female had been found in a local beauty spot, the Abbots Wood Enclosure, in Alice Holt Forest. It was a mile of so from the Ross house.

Hampshire officers quickly attended the scene and took control. It was getting dark and it was still very cold and frosty. It had been cold and frosty all day.

The body was found outside a toilet block just off a car park. It was in full view. Perhaps the cold weather had deterred the dog owners and walkers who normally frequented this area.

The Hampshire officers set an outer cordon on the main road into the car park and forest entrance. The inner cordon was set around the grass area in front of the toilet block.

The fact that the body was naked and burnt meant that the officers dealt with this as a murder from the outset. It was unlikely to be a suicide (however bizarre) and this meant that someone else had been there. Was this the murder scene or just the disposal site?

A priority for the Hampshire crime scene investigators was to get to the body, but they rightly decided to use the natural path around the toilet block to allow an access point beyond where the body was. This was to leave undisturbed the grass area between the car park and the body. Whoever had placed the body there (and if they used a vehicle) they would have used this route.

They quickly undertook the general photographing of the scene. The photographs accurately captured the heavy frost.

I was called by the local crime scene manager shortly after the body had been found. We had a missing person and Hampshire had a body. Both forces had appointed their own senior investigating officers. Detective Superintendent Pat Crossan was in charge of the Surrey investigation. There would be a need for cross-border liaison between the CSI teams, which was my responsibility.

Pat Crossan was an experienced, accomplished and thorough senior investigator. An Irishman, he had a soft nature but a heart of steel. He knew his craft and he demanded high standards from all who worked for him. He always thought of the victims. 'We are speaking for them,' he would always remind the investigation team. He had been on the interview panel when I was appointed as head of scientific support. He was firm and deeply incisive, and I enjoyed the challenging questions. He seemed to enjoy my parrying responses when they were needed.

Pat liaised with his opposite number in Hampshire. The identity of the deceased would determine who took over the investigation. If the body was that of Anna, then Surrey would take over the investigation. This was based on the guidelines set by the Association of Chief Police Officers (ACPO). The police force with the majority of lines of enquiry would take jurisdiction. Since Anna had already been reported missing in Surrey, that's where the investigation would be.

Up to the point of identification, Hampshire would continue. They would deal with the scene at Alice Holt Forest and the post-mortem examination. As usual, the body would be removed once all the required examinations had been completed at the scene.

The body was almost completely naked, save for the burnt remains of a cotton garment still clinging to the arms. The body was burnt from underneath and in a semi-foetal position. The Hampshire crime scene manager decided that they needed a forensic biologist to examine the scene. The exposed areas of the body could have contained fibres from whatever and whoever it had come into contact with.

The fire was clearly under the body. There was a single seat of fire and the only question remained regarding the presence of accelerants. This is the term given to any flammable material (often liquid) which will accelerate the process of a fire. It is difficult to set fire to a body. The amount of water present means that the fatty tissue will not burn even with the help of accelerants.

Clearing the path around the toilet block meant that the common approach path was quickly completed to allow the prompt examination of the body.

It was then removed for post-mortem examination to Basingstoke and in Surrey we awaited the cause of death and the identification. The remainder of the scene at the forest was protected for further searches in daylight the following day.

At Farnham Police Station we continued with our investigation of the missing person. Bill had been informed that the body of a female had been found. He voluntarily remained at the police station, but he was not going to be allowed to leave. He sat with a detective.

A search had already been made of the house by two detectives. They were looking for Anna, in case she had hidden there, they even checked the loft.

We made contingency plans to take control of the family house, but until the deceased was identified we had no powers to do so. Pat Crossan asked me to go to the house, which I did. With Bill's mother and child there I concluded that whatever was there would stay there until we had full authority to examine it. It was apparent that Bill's mother had put her grandchild to bed, and was probably doing what mothers do, tidying and fussing. The fact was that the house had been briefly searched by detectives looking for Anna and they hadn't noticed anything untoward. This scene wasn't going anywhere.

Bill was clearly a suspect because of the strange nature of his wife's disappearance from the house. This was extenuated as he had been seen cleaning their two cars before he called the police to report his wife missing. I arranged for a scene investigator and police surgeon to be available and wait in the custody suite at Farnham in case he was arrested.

Shortly after ten pm, Pat Crossan received a call from his

Hampshire counterpart. The description matched Anna; right down to the jewellery and a damaged eardrum (Anna was deaf in one ear). Although this would need confirmation by finger-prints, DNA or dental records, the coroner was content with this preliminary identification. The cause of death was a single blow to the back of the head caused by a round blunt object. Pat Crossan called his senior team together and we reviewed this information. He decided that Bill was to be arrested on suspicion of murdering his wife. This immediately took place. Bill was marched the few paces from the room where he had been sitting with a cup of tea in front of him to the charge room. He was immediately examined by the police surgeon and his clothing seized, labelled and sealed in brown paper sacks. As there was the possibility that an accelerant may have been used to start the fire under he body, all the bags were placed in one large nylon bag and additionally sealed. It may have been too late but there could have been some residues of accelerant present. It was possible that if they had been there they would have evaporated, but the day had been cold and it was better to do this now, even though late, rather than not at all. You never know what you might find.

Officers also attended the family home and gave Bill's mother the bad news. As delicately as possible she was told she and her granddaughter would have to leave as this was now the subject of a murder investigation.

Once examined, Bill was placed in a cell and allowed to have a night's sleep. The clock was ticking but it was not appropriate to question him through the night. I sent the rest of the Surrey CSI team home to rest and told them to report before first light the following morning. I would then brief them. There were now a number of scenes and many issues. The forest scene examina-tion had been started and would be resumed the next day, in better light. The house examination would also be started. Bill was a scene but he had been examined. There were also the two cars, Bill's Mini and Anna's Vauxhall.

I spoke with my counterpart in Hampshire about their continuation of the examination at the forest. I also called the forensic science laboratory and requested that a forensic biologist attend the house scene with our CSI team. One of the reasons for the search and examination of the house was to determine if this was the scene of Anna's murder. Had it been cleaned up recently? A head wound would bleed extensively. If this had been cleaned up we would be looking for signs of that clear-up. I would work through the night preparing information about the search area, maps and plans and a briefing for the CSI team and the forensic biologist.

The question I asked was, 'Which forensic biologist?' One had already attended Alice Holt Forest at the request of Hampshire. This person would normally take on the case as they were called first. But we needed a biologist at the house scene too. If we used the same scientist, there would be a contamination issue. Fibres evidence could play a part later. We would not know this until we were well into the investigation and had looked. Bill could be innocent. We were there to determine that. Anna may have left the house, as Bill had said, and been attacked by someone else. Contamination of blood would be less of an issue but still needed careful consideration. For blood to be contaminated it would need to be in large enough quantities, picked up on a transferable medium and liquid. So the careful changing of gloves and protective clothing would cover this issue.

Following a discussion with the scientist concerned, we decided that he would examine the house scene. He would go home, shower and change clothing and, on his return the following morning, go to the house. He would use protective clothing: white suit, gloves and masks and any other equipment he needed, provided by us in Surrey.

The vehicles would be briefly searched for weapons and anything that the interviewing officer might urgently need to know. But then they would be removed to the laboratory where they would be examined by scene investigators and forensic photographers from Surrey Police and scientists from the laboratory.

At seven am I briefed the assembled team and gave them their assignments. One of the forensic photographers, rather boldly, asked me what my role was in this. I was relatively new to Surrey and he had not had a technically qualified manager like me as a head of department. My role as scientific support manager was new to the force. Although I was his departmental head, this was the first time we had worked together on a major investigation. I realised that this marked a change for the force. Up to that time no CSI actually managed the scene. In fact, up to that time the photographers (they were yet to become forensic photographers) went in first and reported what they had seen. The scene examiners followed in after. This was not acceptable to me. The photographers could have walked over any evidence on the floor. Photography is a tool and the scene needs to be managed. This is so that each expert undertakes their work without disturbing other forms of evidence. The crucial role is that of the crime scene manager. So the local crime scene manager would manage the scene investigation process at the house. That would be repeated at the forest. My role was to coordinate all the examinations of scene, suspects and vehicles and all the crime scene managers and their teams. I prioritised and resourced the forensic science demands of the investigation. I worked closely with the Pat Crossan, the SIO, to ensure his needs were met and that he received timely advice and support. I would take the problem of the scene investigations off his back but keep him fully informed. This was a much better way to investigate the crime scene and it was new to Surrey. In other places it had yet to happen at all.

One asset which was exploding with potential was Ken Williams. Ken was the head of the Photographic Section and what was to become the Forensic Photography and Enhancement Section within the Scientific Support Department. Ken was an expert photographer who joined Surrey Police the year I was born. Nothing had dampened his resourcefulness or motivation. He embraced and sought new technologies which had been pioneered by the first forensic photographer, Ken Creer at the Metropolitan Police Laboratory in the 1980s. Ken Williams had only been head of the Photographic Section in Surrey for a couple of years when I arrived. His talent was stunted up to then. That was about to change; I hope in me he found a champion. Ken and his technology, skills and team were going to become an important asset in the investigation and detection of crime. He often commented that photography was recovering evidence by photographic means. He was right. He would however go on to introduce high-intensity light source and sequential chemical enhancement of finger marks. Later I would nominate him for public recognition for his length and depth of service, his motivation and professionalism for over forty years with Surrey Police. But it wasn't to be. I always thought that it was a great injustice that his life's work was not recognised beyond his immediate colleagues. My words here can only attempt to right that wrong. Ken is an unsung hero and pioneer of forensic photography and its application.

The team briefed, they set out to their tasks. A crime scene manager would lead the team at the home address. Also present would be a crime scene investigator, the forensic photographic manager, a forensic photographer and the forensic biologist. Their brief was to look for any sign of disturbance or assault. They were to locate and examine any site for signs of attack and for any weapons. We knew from the post-mortem examination that there had been a blow to Anna's head caused by a round object. They had to look for blood or signs that it had been cleaned up.

There would be no examination for finger marks at this time, unless they were found in blood. This was because both Anna and Bill lived in the house and so this would serve no purpose. But we did not discount that the story we had could change later and other players could become relevant. So, although there would be no need for a fingerprint examination at this stage, the team would preserve the scene as they went along in case it needed to take place later. Fingerprint examinations usually take place at two stages during investigations of this kind. At the beginning, in the non-destructive search with light and light sources, marks might be found, then, towards the end of the searches (usually on day two or three) and once all the delicate trace evidence has been located and removed, the scene would be examined with powders and chemicals to develop latent marks.

The scene that greeted the investigator was that expected in any post-Christmas home. It was tidy, with Christmas decorations and cards displayed in many places. The sight of toys indicated the presence of children. The house was two storeys. A front door gave way to a small hallway. To the right a flight of stairs led to the first floor where there were three bedrooms and a bathroom. To the left of the downstairs hallway were a lounge and a kitchen at the rear. There was a kitchen door leading to the enclosed garden. The house was detached. Outside the front of the house, on a small driveway, was Anna's red Vauxhall hatchback car. Bill's Mini was parked in the street.

Starting downstairs, the house was searched in a general way for blood and disturbance. Some stains were found when using a presumptive test for blood. The test is not specific for blood. If it indicates a positive result it means that the stain could be blood. This is because other materials (such as coffee) may also give a positive reading. It is a useful way of screening stains but it needs confirmation later in the laboratory. All positive stains will be considered in the investigation. A negative reaction means the material is not blood.

The search continued to the stairs to the first floor. More stains were found on the white-painted woodwork and these had a directional shape, indicating a moving splash. They looked more like blood. These continued up the stairs in small amounts. At the top of the stairs there was a door to the rear master bedroom. Inside the door was a wash and vac machine, it was plugged in. Looking inside the door, the investigators saw to the left a pine double bed. Either side there were small freestanding pine wardrobes. On the right wall there were pine chests of drawers. On the floor there were neat piles of clothing.

There was one sight which soon captured their attention. On each corner of the bed, there was a bedpost. Sitting on top of them were round wooden balls.

The room was searched in detail. The plugged-in wash and vac was particularly interesting. If there had been a clear-up the scene might be largely inside the machine by now. The bed was made, so the bedding was removed and recovered in sequence, eventually exposing the mattress, which was clean. That was until it was turned over to reveal a large area of blood staining. It was still wet. It also contained a blue dye which would turn out to be ink. Was this part of the attempt to cover it up? Things moved quickly, well quickly for scene investigations. Examination of the bed frame at the foot of the bed at first sight looked unpromising. That was until a detailed examination revealed blood in the crevices and edges. The blood had been cleaned up, but it could not disguise what had soaked into the recesses.

The bedhead looked more and more like a potential murder weapon. So it was the subject of a careful examination and detailed search.

Feedback from the forest scene had revealed that there was the remains of a black plastic bag, similar to those used as refuse bags. Under the bed two black bags were also found.

When the loft was searched, a black plastic bag was found containing two blood-stained pillows. Pat Crossan was not happy when they were found. The loft had been searched when Anna was reported missing, long before we were involved. I stood up for the two police officers who had conducted the search. They were looking for Anna and not searching for evidence, even something which now looked obvious.

The forest search revealed only a little more. It looked more and more like a disposal site. One interesting observation was the depression in the frost-laden grass of two tracks. It indicated that a vehicle had been backed up to allow the body to be removed. The rough distance could be measured. We might be able to narrow down the type of vehicle and implicate or eliminate.

A wider search of the forest would be made over the coming days, extending from where the body was found. It would involve cutting back some of the vegetation and gorse. Although some items would be found, they were unconnected with this crime.

Examination of the refuse bags found under the bed, in the loft (the one containing the blood-stained pillows), and a fragment found under Anna's body would all be linked to the same source. When I asked the laboratory at Aldermaston to undertake this, I was surprised to hear that they were not aware of the technology. So I put them in touch with a scientist at the Metropolitan Police Laboratory who enlightened them. When plastic bags are made the plastic is drawn through rollers which leave extrusion marks. Viewed under polarised light the striations form a pattern which extends along the batch. There is always a possibility that if two bags are in direct sequence there may be uneven tears which line up along the perforated edge. Examination of the bags would link them together.

The two vehicle scenes would take a few days to complete. The vehicles were relatively clean. We knew that Bill had cleaned them. However, blood was found inside the car and also on the edge of the boot. The boot was also examined for fibres, in case fibres from Anna's nightdress could be found there. Although there could potentially be a legitimate reason to find such fibres there, I argued that finding them there would be unusual.

A petrol can was found in Bill's car and enquiries were made to see if he had purchased petrol on the day of Anna's disappearance. The laboratory was also asked to compare the remnants in the petrol container with any residues found in the debris under Anna's body. This technology is now more advanced as it is possible to link petrol by its chemical profile and any contaminants back to previous sources.

Enough evidence was found in the first two days for Bill to be charged with his wife's murder. Further examinations would continue.

Two weeks after the initial post mortem, a second post mortem was undertaken. This was to allow a pathologist for the defence to make his examination. We took the opportunity to undertake some further reconstruction. So our preparations included bringing along the bedhead and a mannequin to reconstruct the injuries. In the event they were not needed. Injuries recorded on Anna's head and shoulder showed that the bedhead was the murder weapon. The deputy SIO was present with members of the team and a full CSI team. The defence pathologist noticed that there were two and possibly three blows, more than our pathologist had noticed in the original examination. The head wound had caused Anna's death. Both pathologists were in no doubt. I waited as this sank in and I held back, waiting for the deputy SIO or someone else to ask the next and to me fundamental question. It didn't come, so I then asked, once she had received this injury could she have got up and walked out? The response was equally profound. She had died instantaneously. Bill was the only other person present.

Bill would deny murder. He offered no defence, insisting that he was not responsible for hurting his wife. He was convicted of her murder and sentenced to life imprisonment.

21. A Murder Crime Scene With No Body

Maureen Foot had not been heard from for over a week. Her brother, who lived in the north of England, reported her missing.

The thirty-seven-year-old woman had come to the UK from South Africa in the autumn of the previous year. She rented a room in semi-detached house on an estate on the outskirts of Guildford. Also renting rooms were two men, Neil Sanders, a twenty-two-year-old shed builder, and James Woolf, a twenty-seven-year-old dustman.

The owner of the house lived elsewhere on the estate. The rooms rented by the three occupants were on the first floor of the house with a shared bathroom. Downstairs there was a communal lounge and shared kitchen.

In December, Maureen started a job at a fast food restaurant in the town. On a day in the following March she left work shortly after five pm. The same day she used a cash machine in Guildford. She was not seen again.

Her brother, worried that he had not heard from her, made all the calls he could make from a distance and then, a week after she had last been seen, he reported her missing.

People go missing every day. Many turn up within a day or

so, just not having told their friends or family that they were going away. Others leave a life and their problems behind. Some never return.

The concerns of family and friends are real and deep. It may seem out of character and the police may not immediately appear over concerned but it is a difficult call. With adults, hospitals will be checked and enquiries made at work and with all known friends are the first steps. Adults are responsible for their own lives. A missing child will, however, always call for a wider and immediate search.

Police officers went to Maureen's home and managed to get into her room. It was sparse but tidy. The officers were not unduly concerned, although they noticed some staining on the walls and ceiling which the other occupants put down to a leak in the loft.

No one but her brother was concerned about her disappearance. Apparently she had gone walkabout before, the police were told. The managers at the fast food restaurant where she worked were used to staff taking time off without giving any notice. Even after a week nobody had thought or cared to check with her.

In the following week the officers made their enquiries but no sign could be found of Maureen. She had not accessed her bank account and she had not been seen. A few days later the officers returned to her flat. This time they were more concerns about the staining.

The officers called Trevor Wykes, a crime scene manager, and asked him to go to the scene. They wanted him to have 'a quick look'. Well, there is no such thing as a quick look in these circumstances. Once you have set your foot in the door you are committed and you can't go back. So, as head of the CSI department, I was called. The decision was easy but it had cost implications. There was only one way of doing this and it was the right way. It could have turned out to be a waste of time but there was no way of knowing that until we looked, and to look we would use all the resources systematically and thoroughly examine the scene.

With a sense of urgency, a scene investigation team was put together. No detectives were involved at this stage; it was a simple missing person enquiry. The focus of our search would be Maureen's room. That would be our inner cordon. At this stage we had no reason to search the whole house. To get to her room, access was via the front door and up a flight of stairs, immediately inside it, to the first-floor landing, off which all the bedrooms were situated. An officer would protect the front door entrance to make it our outer cordon. There would be no search of the hall and stairs at this stage. It had been well trod since her disappearance. We would have to deal with that later. The priority was to examine her room and go nowhere else until that had been done.

The officers made arrangements for the occupants to restrict their access whilst we made our examination.

The room was small but that did not necessarily make it an easy task. The search would start with the carpeted floor to allow access to the rest of the room. The walls would be searched without disturbance. The bedding would be examined and carefully removed and the furniture searched methodically. All the furniture would be removed in sequence to expose the whole floor. Once fully examined it would be removed so that the floor and walls could be examined.

Our search would include the use of light sources to examine the carpet, recover any footwear marks and alien fibres. Forensic photographers would work alongside a scene of crime officer under the direction of the crime scene manager. I also agreed from the outset we would involve a specialist in blood pattern analysis. So Roger Mann (a forensic biologist from the Aldermaston Forensic Science Laboratory) was there from the start.

Throughout the scene, investigators would review progress as they made any observations or made any finds.

Very quickly, once the floor had been cleared, the staining on the wall was examined. It was blood. Under the bed a small piece of bone was found. This was sent to a forensic pathologist to see if he could determine its origin. The big question was, Is it human? Once the bed covers were removed from the bed, the mattress looked unremarkable. Until it was turned over. It revealed heavy blood-staining. It was apparent that someone had bled heavily on the bed, and there were stains up the wall. It looked like it could be as the result of a violent assault. What was more, there had been a significant clean-up. Someone knew about this. But who?

The senior detectives were immediately informed and started a major investigation. Brian Woodfield was appointed the senior investigating officer. He was in charge of the overall investigation and I and my team were totally at his disposal now. I would now work closely with Brian, coordinating all the crime scene investigations and forensic science examinations.

A team of detectives continued to make enquiries to see if Maureen could be found alive. There was also a focus on the fact that Maureen could be dead and the knowledge that if she were we would have to find her body. All the men associated with her accommodation (the landlord and male occupants) were under suspicion.

We would eagerly await the results of the bone examination and confirmation that the blood was human, although all of us thought that in a bedroom it was unlikely to be anything else. Nonetheless it needed confirmation and we would expect that within a few hours.

The cordon was immediately extended to the front gate of the house. The results quickly confirmed that the blood was human. This was followed by news from Dr Dick Shepherd, the forensic pathologist, that the bone was human and from a skull.

In the days following the initial search two crime scene investigators (Jon Young and Andy Penson) continued the systematic search and examination of the rest of the house under Trevor Wykes's management. No sign of Maureen could be found. An extension had been built and a concrete floor laid. Enquiries were made to see if it had been laid after Maureen's disappearance. It was determined that it had been completed before Maureen went missing so it was recorded that there was no need to disturb it. The examination revealed that Maureen had been attacked whilst on the bed. Directional blood distribution emanated from this location. The stripped room was pasted with lines of string to indicate the distribution so it could be photographed for presentation in court. The clean-up attempt had been thorough, but it was never going to be thorough enough.

Detectives made extensive enquiries of the owner and male occupants. They were interviewed at length. They were also the subject of thorough examination. There had been a clear-up and one of these men knew something, although there was no evidence to say who at this early stage.

A large team of police officers was involved in searching the area which surrounds the housing estate. The searches were going on everywhere. The objective was quite simply to find Maureen or her body. Amongst the areas which would need specialist search were the local streams and drains. In the middle of the estate there was a pond. It was surrounded by a large green. Houses overlooked the perimeter offering clear uninterrupted views of the green and central pond.

As a senior manager, I had to balance a budget. This and a number of other investigations in the preceding months had severely reduced the funds I had available. I had to make some correctional decisions. Our policy and practice had been pretty firm. Even at the risk or running over budget I would not let cost limit an investigation that needed to take place. We would always look at the most cost-effective way of meeting our goals in a professional manner. Up to that time it was the crime scene managers who knew the criteria and managed the problem of authorising overtime to investigators. They managed this process well. To relieve CSMs of the pressure, I decided to be the sole arbiter for authorising overtime. The final decision would have to come from me. After all, the buck stopped with me. I didn't like doing it because the managers were doing the job well but if I continued to go over budget, I would have to demonstrate the steps I had taken to try and reduce it. I had a department of fifty. Thirty-three were scene of crime officers or forensic photographers of which four were on call to cover events through the night.

On the very day, and within an hour of making the decision and notifying the department, events took place which would mean I would have eleven staff working throughout the night. So much for trying to limit the overtime costs. It looked like the crime scene managers were doing a better job than me!

Having no underwater search unit within our police force we arranged for a team from a neighbouring force to undertake a search of the pond. Accordingly, the underwater search team from Sussex Police was called in. Within forty minutes they had found a body in two black plastic bin liners.

I was at Police Headquarters when Brian Woodfield, the senior investigation officer, called me with the news. Trevor Wykes and his team were nearby but obviously committed, and could not get involved because of contamination issues.

I made my way quickly to the pond. It was only a ten-minute drive from Police Headquarters. I called John Armstrong (who was the crime scene manager on the neighbouring Woking Division) to muster a team. I got to the pond scene first. The Sussex Underwater Search team had set up their equipment at one end of the oval-shaped pond. They had found the two bags submerged under a fallen tree. The green was covered in grass but the edge of the pond was slightly muddy around the perimeter. It was all in full view of the houses around the green. The search team had yet to remove the bags from the water. This would have to be planned and carefully undertaken in such public view. I quickly set a new five-metre cordon around the perimeter of the pond to protect potential areas where the body may have been introduced. There could be shoe or tyre tracks in such an area.

Another problem was that the local senior school was about to turn out for their lunch break. The presence of the underwater search team was drawing the attention of a large number of people and this would soon be swelled with hundreds of teenagers. This could be a disturbing and unpleasant sight. So the recovery had to be as dignified and as simple as possible. The outer cordon in place, a path was cleared from where the search team had set up to the water's edge and a tent erected and brought close to the water so that the bags could be brought into this controlled area.

Putting up the tent went well. This may seem like a strange statement. Only a few weeks before, I had been horrified to see on the TV news a CSI team from another force trying to erect a tent around a body in the full gaze of the cameras. Not only were there poles missing, but they managed to get it inside out. It looked like the Keystone Cops. Seeing this I took the precaution of calling in the Surrey CSI staff to the Force HQ gymnasium to practise in small groups. It paid off and the tent went up without any fuss.

The tent prepared, the bags were photographed and briefly examined within the tent to preserve evidence and then removed to the mortuary for closer examination and post mortem. The bags each contained half of a female body severed at the waist. Dick Shepherd, the forensic pathologist, had already been called and attended the scene at the pond.

An investigator remained at the scene searching inside the five-metre cordon for signs of where the body may have been introduced into the water. It was their job to look for shoe or tyre marks or any other signs.

John Armstrong led the remainder of the crime scene team at the mortuary. We had a number of new, younger staff for whom this was their first murder investigation and post-mortem examination. I went to the mortuary to keep an eye on them and see how they performed as members of the team. John Armstrong was more than capable of leading the CSI team. John carefully briefed his team, and included the message that if at any stage they felt unwell, they should let him know. It was not a problem; in fact it was quite natural. Being present and taking part in a post-mortem examination is not a pleasant experience. It is a necessary part of our work, but not something we should take lightly.

The post mortem had a number of priorities. One was to identify the deceased and confirm or otherwise if it was Maureen Foot. Others were to determine the time, cause and manner of her death if at all possible. This was obviously not a suicide (the body was in two halves in plastic bags). This was most likely a murder investigation from the very outset. The investigators would be looking for signs of violent or sexual assault, injuries and the presence of any material which could have come from her attacker or the person who had dismembered her body and placed her in the bags.

The bags themselves would need careful examination. They were both large refuse sacks. They were bound with clear adhesive tape. A decision had to be made where to open them so that they could be examined later for finger marks and other evidence. They would have to be dried in a clean environment without causing a health hazard.

The bags were carefully opened on a large plastic sheet on the floor and the two parts of the body photographed individually. They were searched for extraneous material and marks and injuries recorded. Then the parts were placed in line. They made the complete body of a female. No limbs or parts were missing. The description matched Maureen's and there really was little doubt that it was her. But that would need confirmation.

Each part of the body was examined in detail. When it came to move the lower part of the body on to the dissection table Dick Shepherd bent down and placed one arm under the buttocks. Placing his other arm under the knees he stood up and took a few paces towards the table. As he did so the outstretched legs sagged at the knee joint. The sight made my heart jump. In a flashback it reminded me of the times I would pick up my own daughters and carry them up to bed. The horror was that there was nothing above her waist.

I had gone to the mortuary to keep an eye on the newer members of staff and I had found myself upset by what I had seen. It is important to maintain an emotional distance from the events in hand. But every once in a while a sight will touch every investigator, no matter how experienced. This was one of those times for me. Of course it is a sound human quality never to forget the victim. That is why we do what we do.

Maureen had a heavy head wound and her skull was fractured. It was the cause or contributed to her death. Dick Shepherd stated that her body had been cut in two in by some-one who 'knew where to cut'.

This information made Brian Woodfield's ears prick up. One of the male occupants of the house at Hazel Avenue, Woolf, had worked in a slaughterhouse before becoming a bin man for the local council.

Further enquiries narrowed down Woolf as the main and only suspect. He was arrested and remanded in custody.

Over the next weeks and months the case against Woolf was built. The search of his room and the rest of the house had revealed a larger than normal number of bin bags with markings similar to those found with the body. Woolf had free access to them in his work. The same types of bags were also given freely to residents of the street. We needed to try and narrow things down. Once again we called on the evidence of the extrusion marks we had used in the Ross case. Detective Inspector Bill Harding, the deputy SIO, made extensive enquiries. There was a link between the bags in the house and those around the body but the process needed to be described so that it could be explained to the jury.

The clear adhesive tape which had secured the bags around the body also revealed further clues. We had examined the tape for finger marks but none were found. What we did find were three human hairs. They did not match Maureen, but they were of a similar colour to Woolf's sample. The bad news for us was that the hairs had no roots. So the main DNA profiling technology of the time (SGM+) would not work. For SGM+ DNA to work, DNA material would have to be extracted from cells present in the root. This result left me with a slight dilemma. There was another DNA technique called Mitochondrial DNA. The mitochondria are the source of power around cells but not within it. They are inherited only from the mother's DNA. Brothers and sisters will have the same mitochondrial DNA as their mother and maternal grandmother. But it is statically low evidence. It also took a long time to undertake and was an expensive technique. The examination of the three hairs would cost £15,000. Although the inclusion of evidence, if found, would have been limited, there was always the possibility of eliminating Woolf as the source of the hairs. So, on this basis, I authorised the examination of the hairs to ensure the results were known before any forthcoming trial. If Woolf was not the source if the hairs we would have to ask who was. He may not have been excluded from the enquiry, but it would open the possibility of another offender or an accomplice. I also reasoned that any good defence lawyer would rightly pick up on this question if we did not answer it. Cost was no excuse. But that wasn't going to help my budget situation.

Two months later, Bill Harding received a surprise call from Woolf's solicitors. Brian Woodfield wasn't available, although he would have raced back if he knew what was about to transpire. Woolf had decided that he wanted to speak to the investigators. He wanted to change his plea to that of guilty and he wanted to tell the police all about it.

He was brought to Guildford Police Station where he admitted he had attacked Maureen on the bed in her room. We already knew the attack had taken place there from the reconstruction of directional blood staining. He also described how he cut her body in two. Late one night he took it to the nearby pond and threw it in. He also told officers that he had wrapped the weapons he had used to kill and dismember her body in a black plastic bin bag and had hidden them under a fallen tree in woodlands ten minutes' walk from his house. The bag, he said, contained an axe and a knife in a sheath.

Once the interviews were completed, Woolf was taken back to the house and asked to retrace the route from the house to the tree where he had hidden the weapons. His steps were videoed as he – handcuffed to a prison officer – his solicitor and a small group of officers retraced his steps. The route led from the house, along the road, into a woodland path and then cut across to a fallen tree. When he got to the tree Woolf pointed to it. Jon Young stepped forward and recovered the package from under the tree. It was taken intact to Guildford Police Station where it was photographed, opened and examined. The process was itself videoed. The package contained exactly what Woolf said it would.

As soon as I got the news I made an urgent call to the lab to hold the mitochondrial DNA examination of the hairs. A few days later, once it was clear that Woolf was going to plead guilty, I cancelled the extra work and saved £15,000 from the precious budget.

Woolf pleaded guilty to the murder of Maureen Foot and remained silent as to why he murdered her. Missed by her brother, she had not been forgotten and doing things right from the very beginning, as the CSI team had done, paid off. Taking the easy route is not always an option when faced with suspicions which turn into serious allegations. It can cost time and money but there is really no other way. If you are going to investigate crime you must do it well from the very beginning.

22. Murder in Mozambique

The disappearance of a family member is a traumatic experience for any family. The feeling of hopelessness is all the more difficult when the loved one goes missing in a foreign country, and especially when that country does not have the resources to deal with it.

In April 1997 Andrew and Caroline McGowan dropped two friends at the airport in Harare, Zimbabwe, before heading home through Mozambique. They had all been on a bird-watching and elephant safari. Leaving the airport, they made their way back along the Tete Corridor, a 460-mile track heading north to their home in neighbouring Malawi.

Andrew was a former British Army officer who was using his own money to fund a Round Table project for the reforestation in Malawi. His wife was a technology teacher at the college in Lilongwe.

They did not reach home and their family back in England heard about it and were worried. Not happy with the actions of the Mozambique authorities, Andrew's brother flew to Harare to retrace their last known steps.

Bandits were notorious in the area and apparently white foreigners could be attacked for what possessions they had on them and their vehicles.

It was a formidable task, but asking for sightings of his brother and sister-in-law paid off pretty quickly. In one village, the locals remembered the fairly unusual event of a white four-wheel drive vehicle passing through with a white man and white woman in it. Only a short time later the vehicle drove back at speed through the village, this time with three local men wearing army fatigues in it. Another village member remembered seeing the vehicle off the side of the road at the bottom of a hill.

Andrew's brother found the vehicle at the bottom of the hill. The vehicle was wrecked. There were no signs of Andrew or Caroline although their passports were still in the car. Also there amongst the broken glass was some blood and three sets of blood-stained battle-fatigue jackets.

Wherever Andrew and Caroline had been left having been relieved of the vehicle was not far away so Andrew's brother headed a little further north. It was not long before he found what he had been dreading. The decomposing bodies of his brother and sister-in-law were in bushes just off the road side. They had been there for a few weeks.

The Mozambique authorities had little or no resources to deal with this matter. The persistence of Andrew's and Caroline's families brought it to the attention of the UK Foreign and Commonwealth Office. The bodies were returned to the UK and arrived in Surrey, where they were brought to the attention of the Surrey coroner, Michael Burgess. Any death of a British national overseas will automatically trigger an inquest by a UK coroner and certainly when the bodies of the deceased are returned to the UK for burial.

The bodies had been returned in sealed caskets ready for burial, but as far as could be determined no post-mortem examinations had taken place. Even if they had, one would have also been carried out by a Home Office pathologist on behalf of the local UK coroner.

Michael Burgess contacted Detective Superintendent Brian Woodfield at Surrey Police HQ to assist with the investigation. That is when I was called to provide crime scene and photographic personnel.

The post-mortem examination revealed that Caroline had been shot twice and Andrew once. They had both been lying down when they were shot. The cause of death in both cases was gunshot wounds.

There was still little interest from the Mozambique authorities who, although clearly concerned, had no resources to investigate the matter to the satisfaction of the families. Not wishing to embarrass the government of Mozambique, the UK Foreign and Commonwealth Office (FCO) offered the assistance of the Surrey coroner and Surrey Police to help them with their investigation.

Brian Woodfield being the senior investigating officer in the case was naturally going to go and he appointed a detective inspector as his assistant in the matter. The FCO were going to fund the additional expenses, above that of salaries for the investigators, which would be borne by Surrey Police.

Brian and I discussed the case and identified potential areas of evidence. Examination of the vehicle was important and so was examining the site where the bodies were found. From all accounts it was an area of bush and trees, but it was most likely the murder scene.

We thought about the potential evidence we could expect or hope to find and how we might deal with it, remembering, of course, that we were assisting the Mozambique authorities and would be dealing with the local police chief.

Towards the end of the meeting with Brian, he asked me to arrange for a forensic examination kit to be put together so he could examine the scene when he was out there. I think he had in mind bottles and bags and the like. But I was not happy with that.

'I wouldn't let you examine a scene here in Surrey, so why should you do so in difficult conditions in a far off and foreign land?' I said. 'So you want a trip, do you?' was his reply. 'No, but I will get you the right person to go with you,' I concluded.

I put together a case for sending a scenes of crime officer

with him and his assistant. It was a complex case and not one which he was capable of examining himself. Brian put the case to the chief constable who in turn put it to the FCO. After a little persuasion they saw the merits and agreed.

Choosing the right person to go was a difficult decision. One of my deputies, a senior crime scene manager, was the natural choice. However, in Surrey at that time all our scenes of crime officers and managers were not routinely photographers of crime scenes, although it was part of their initial training. We had a highly specialised team who worked under the direction of the crime scene manager and head of forensic photography at major scenes. So my choice quickly went to Jon Young who had been trained as a scene photographer and had worked as one before joining Surrey from another force. He was young but mature and had a cool head. There was no doubt he was my first choice, much to the disappointment of his manager.

I had appointed Jon to his post a few years before. He was a big man and knew his job well. I remember at his interview he answered all our questions with ease, so much so I thought he had been tipped off, although this had not been the case. Not only did he not know anyone in Surrey, some of the questions had only been finalised immediately before the interview.

This was a difficult assignment. Although it was exciting it was not without its dangers. Andrew and Caroline McGowan had already been murdered and safety, although 'guaranteed', was not certain. The team was going to a remote part of Africa where there were little resources. They would have to work with the local police chief and try and ensure that any investigative leads were identified and followed through.

I was quite prepared to go myself and I said this to Jon when I spoke to him. He had a young family and asked for a day to consider it and speak to his wife.

Jon accepted the offer. I was pleased; he was the right person to go.

Jon and I met with Brian Woodfield and his DI and once

again went through the details of the case. The team got the necessary inoculations to travel and within a few days they were on their way.

In preparing for the trip Jon had put together a kit specifically for the purpose, the usual examination bag and photographic kit. But it was made clear he would have to be able to carry it. I'm not sure if Brian and his DI ever offered to help but they would have their own luggage. So 'only what you can carry' was the order. Jon being a big guy could carry a lot and he would have to.

As we discussed the equipment list, we identified that he would probably need a metal detector to try to locate spent gun cartridges at the scene. It was then that another aspect to the risk assessment became apparent: land mines. Mozambique was full of them, left over from years of war. The murder scene was off the road and even that was a track. If Jon thought of pulling out he didn't show it. We made plans as to how he would deal with the situation and do his research. Above all he was to take no risk if there was any doubt or lack of information about the areas he was to examine.

I arranged to make regular contact with him. The team was to stay with local British consular officials, who would also accompany them wherever possible. The consul would provide protection as the area contained armed bandits, as the McGowans had found out to their cost. They were going well and truly off the beaten track.

The Surrey team arrived in Mozambique in June 1997. They met the local consular officials and were introduced to the local police chief. He occupied a rundown police station. The buildings were in disrepair and had little furniture. His team of a few officers was poorly equipped, but they had received some guidance. To the team's surprise they were informed that the station had a laboratory. Opening the door to a near-empty room, they found an officer sat at a lonely desk displaying a box with a few sheets of fingerprints in it, their entire collection.

They were introduced to the police chief's driver who sat

expectantly inside a room just off the front entrance to the run-down building. When it came to setting off to the scene it was suggested that the chief's driver could lead until it was realised that he didn't actually have a car.

The McGowans' vehicle had been found, albeit looted. The team first made their way to the scene where the bodies had been found. Any worries about land mines quickly evaporated.

The scene was a grass area a few metres just off the main track. Within a few minutes two shell cases from a rifle were found in the grass.

Jon's examination of the vehicle revealed some finger marks and blood, along with samples of fibres and glass. He also took possession of the battle fatigues which had been found in the vehicle.

The local police chief may not have had much in the way of resources but he had his sources of intelligence and very quickly three suspects were put forward. Left to his own devices he would have resorted to obtaining a confession by whatever means from the suspects, which clearly worried Brian and the team.

A raid was made at the suspects' known address. They were arrested and their home searched. An AK 47 rifle was recovered along with a photograph of the three suspects wearing battle-fatigue jackets.

I made some enquiries with the forensic science laboratory here in the UK. We were hopeful that the pattern on the fatigues and the potential for it to be cut at random in production could make each jacket unique. This was dependent on obtaining information from the manufacturer, wherever that may be in the world. So we were hopeful that comparing the recovered jackets with these in the photographs could prove that the suspects had been wearing them in the past.

As we were only assisting the Mozambique authorities we considered where a laboratory examination would take place. Of course we offered to arrange and pay for the work to be done in the UK. After consultation it was arranged that the items would be examined in nearby South Africa.

The shell cases found at the scene were matched with the AK 47 found at the suspects' address. The battle fatigues found in the vehicle matched those worn by the suspects in the photograph.

Brian Woodfield returned to Mozambique for the trial along with members of Andrew's and Caroline's families.

The trial lasted one very long day, at the end of which the three men were convicted of the double murder. The men were former members of the guerrilla movement. They had camped out for three days waiting for a suitable vehicle to attack.

Both Andrew's and Caroline's fathers addressed the court. Caroline's father explained that she was an only child, so her murder had deprived her parents of grandchildren, and the family line ended with her. This had an effect on the local people, who honoured and respected the importance of the family and its continuity.

The three suspects were each sentenced to twenty-four years' imprisonment. As they stood in the dock one of the victims' fathers took a photograph of them.

The story did not end there. A few months later the convicted men escaped from prison. The lack of resources meant that no official photographs had been taken. The photograph taken at the trial was used to identify the guilty men when they were eventually arrested.

Jon left most of his consumable equipment in Mozambique for the officer in the one-desk laboratory to use. He had my blessing to do so. He came back with lots of memories and the satisfaction he had done a good job. He was the right person for the job and we had worked as a team.

23. Independent

Crime scene investigators, if they are good at their job, are independent; they are driven by where the evidence goes. They are almost exclusively employed by law enforcement organisations. In early 1999 I left the comfortable confines of the police service to set up my own consultancy. The prospect of offering my skills to those outside the police had been an attraction for many years. Consultancy for police forces, training of crime scene investigators and casework for defence work was to be a challenge.

Independence comes with its benefits and problems. Firstly there is the true ability to say exactly what you feel and be your own boss. At least your boss will appreciate you. There are, however, dangers, such as not pleasing your client and losing further work. The truth is the truth and you can't change it. Some people don't like that or are closed to the prospect, for any number of reasons. There is also the danger that you might step outside your field. I was determined to make sure I didn't make those mistakes and my decision to undertake independent work was made because I consciously accepted this. So I stuck to what I knew best – crime scene investigation and management. I would not be involved in any direct comparison work. My skill was in finding potential evidence and putting it in front of a specialist who could realise that potential. As a manager and trainer, I would help others develop.

Telling the truth is obviously something I have valued. It was so when I was a member of the police organisation and it was the core value I took forward with me.

For the first few years I made a living out of offering the exact organisational development I had delivered in Surrey. Of course I listened to the needs of the forces I advised, but the organisational development which many forces needed to start with were the very same I had used in my previous post in Surrey.

Training of crime scene managers was a gift offered to me by Peter Ablett, Director of the National Training Centre based in Durham. Peter had been the first civilian scientific support manager in the UK when he was appointed in West Mercia Constabulary in 1989. He was a pioneer and later went to head up the national programme for crime scene personnel in 1991. I had a long association with the Centre at Durham through the society's diploma. Peter was used as an examiner in the first of the society's diploma examinations in 1991. Having seen the standard, he told me that the society's diploma was for the élite within the profession.

Through Peter I was engaged to deliver the crime scene manager course at the training centre. Its programme was well developed and I was perfectly at home with it. Indeed I had many discussions with Peter and his predecessors, Detective Superintendent Brian Howe and Chief Superintendent (later Assistant Chief Constable) Eddy Merchant, about the need and content. These three men had over a long period of time made a massive contribution to the field of crime scene science. Durham had made a large contribution to forensic science in the UK over the years; Alex Muir, a former chief constable of Durham Constabulary, was a founder member and later president of the Forensic Science Society.

The crime scene manager course allowed me to add my own input and material within the course framework. The course programme had been running for a few years. The custodians at the time were Martin Parker (a forensic scientist) and Geoff

Knupfer (a retired detective chief superintendent). The course was only five days and had only nine students. Apart from myself and a deputy, there were three facilitators, practitioners from other forces. The first day was spent in the classroom where the common needs, goals and practice of crime scene management were discussed. The real work was done on days two, three and four. This was where, divided into three-person teams, each student had the chance to be a crime scene manager in a developing investigation. All those involved in the day learned something from it, not just the scene manager but the team, facilitator and me. Trainee forensic scientists and senior investigators also got the opportunity to come along and play their part. The commitment of Keith Fryer (then deputy director) and Shaun Mallinson (then head of crime scene training) ensured that the course continued to develop with the greater participation of other practitioners.

The most valuable lessons learned on the course were those of listening, evaluation, planning and review. With this came communication and balancing investigative needs and the role of forensic scientists and other experts who would be called to the scene. The last day was left for a final debriefing. The scenes were as real as possible and always challenging. The managers had to lead and their two colleagues undertake the scene work under their direction. Nothing was notional. On one occasion a student crime scene manager was trying to speed things up asking for some notional resources. However, he failed to plan and make provision for his team's lunch and so when he decided to break for lunch he found his lunch too was notional! I bet he never made that mistake again. This was the place to make mistakes and learn from them, safe in the knowledge that there isn't a single right way of doing things and a simple change in the weather can alter plans. There is, however, a wrong way of doing things and that is when the manager doesn't listen, evaluate, plan, action, record and review.

My other work as an independent consultant for defence

solicitors may have sat awkwardly with some of my students and training colleagues. I, however, found it a strength. I always declared this work at the opening course introduction to see if it raised any response amongst the students or visiting facilitators. Sometimes it did and over the course I managed to expand on the work openly. To some police personnel it is a matter of taking sides, prosecution or defence, police or accused. I hope I offered some enlightenment. It is all a matter of truth for the crime scene investigator no matter who employs or instructs you. There are no versions of the truth, only the truth. By undertaking defence work, I was offered a window to see how the truth is sometimes obstructed or missed by the practice and application of the police and so I was able to introduce this to the training of my police students. It was a unique opportunity and most certainly in the interests of those who seek truth.

The defence work I undertook was often a challenge and I had to learn the needs of the instructing solicitor and their client. Not that I was there to meet their need but to test their needs in relation to the case against them. It is not the defence's job to investigate, to show who is responsible for a crime. It is the defence's role to defend the defendant and nothing else. No longer was I there to investigate, this was the police and prosecution role. This was the hardest challenge for me and often I was only allowed to look at and challenge work that the police had found. Sometimes there was an opportunity to question or comment on the investigation itself or perhaps the lack of it. So there were opportunities when the police had failed to investigate or had not sought to eliminate the defendant when there was an opportunity to do so. I too would often praise in my reports to the defence the work of the crime scene investigators or police, in particular when they undertook a piece of work in a way I would have done or would have been proud to be associated with.

As a defence expert, your work is only for the defence unless they offer it to the police. So if you find incriminating evidence which the police have missed there is no mechanism or right to inform the police. Indeed this would be a break of contract with the instructing defence solicitor and liable to legal action from them.

Finding the truth is something which some (and only some) defence solicitors fail to appreciate. This often leads to the lack of follow-up casework. On a number of occasions I have been pleasantly surprised by the need and brief given to me by a defence solicitor. In one case where a young man was accused of the violent and ritualistic murder of an elderly victim, the defence solicitor asked me to test the police case and if was strong and sound to say so, so that he might encourage his client to plead and take psychiatric help in order that he could mitigate on his behalf. I found this to be a sound search for the truth without neglecting the defence's role to test the case.

No so the solicitor who was defending a man for the rape of a young woman. The defendant claimed that the woman had consented to sex, climbing on top of him as they lay on the grass. The woman stated that the suspect had pushed her on to the grass and it was he who jumped on top of her. The police investigators had only submitted the swabs which proved that sexual intercourse had taken place, which was not in dispute. Both parties agreed that it was a matter of consent. The suspect denied any assault. I arrange for the clothing to be examined for damage and staining. This proved that the woman had indeed been pushed on to her back whilst the man knelt. This evidence was never seen by the court and the man was acquitted of rape. The solicitor seemed pleased that the client had been acquitted, that he had done his job in defending his client. However, I felt that the victim of a rape had been denied the truth. This challenged my professional commitment to stick to establishing the truth and leaving the subject of justice to others. The truth, however, had not been heard and that was the fault of the original investigators, not the defence team. It was not my place to do anything, but it did not sit well. I wrote an article in *The Police*

Review, without identifying the case, in a general effort to pass the lesson on. Titled 'Where Have All the Detectives Gone?', it unfortunately fell on stony ground. The point I wanted to convey was that police officers who were not, by rank at least, detectives had failed to ask the right question, instead using science to prove something which everyone already knew and accepted. They had failed to investigate and they could have used the same material as I had to prove the case. After all, it was in their possession. No detective or supervisor had noticed or corrected the matter.

My work for defence teams, often at appeal after conviction, has led me to believe that many miscarriages of justice occur when the original defence team fails to test the evidence at the first trial. Defence must be rigorous and complete. So I approach my work as a sceptic, not a judge, but one who tests the thought process, asks the right questions and seeks the right answers. These features have always been present in my work for the police and are used by sound and professional investigators but they are also neglected by some. They take on a new profound meaning when they are the last hope of the individual who is innocent until proven guilty.

Unfortunately, defence work is almost exclusively used to counter the specific evidence which the police have found. Any need or wish on my part to completely view the scientific investigation is seen by those officials who monitor the funding of defence work as an unnecessary fishing expedition. So in this regard I do little work like this for the legal profession. In my experience it only comes to light when a pressure group or TV documentary team fund the work. Only then can an alleged miscarriage of justice be examined from a scientific investigator's view.

It must be somewhat unusual to deal with two cases in one career where the deceased share strange parallels and the same family name, even though one occurred in Mozambique and one in the heart of England.

The first case was that of Andrew and Caroline McGowan, a white couple who went missing in Mozambique, discussed in the previous chapter. The second case was of Errol McGowan, a black man living in the heart of England. He had been the subject of racial threats, but when he was found dead the police treated it as suicide and refused to look further, even when they were reminded of the threats.

The love of their families and their tenacity in seeking justice may not be unusual. In the two McGowan cases there were striking similarities from apparently diverse geographic locations and cultural expectations.

This raised questions for me about the way we treat the dead who we feel have been the victims of crime, and our expectations of the justice systems abroad and at home.

24. Justice Delayed

Errol could not be found. He was not at work and he had been depressed and worried. Errol McGowan was a black man living in Telford in Shropshire, a quiet town in the Midlands. In 1999 it was remarkable for its ordinariness, getting on with daily life in the heart of multicultural England.

Joyce McGowan had come to Britain with her husband and eldest children from the West Indies, seeking a better life. Her younger children and her grandchildren were born here and they had made a respectable life. They worked hard and prospered as a family.

Errol was the eldest. He had a variety of jobs in a factory and he also worked as a doorman to supplement this income. This particular job had exposed him to racial abuse and threats. He was the target of abuse in the street and had received threatening phone calls. He was so concerned that he reported his fears to the local police. It appeared there was nothing they could do. His fears played on his mind and his family were worried about him.

When he had not turned up for work, his family had genuine concerns.

Errol had agreed to look after a friend's house whilst the friend visited the USA on holiday. Jimmy Ross lived in a small terraced house in Urban Gardens, Telford. Errol would go there in the evening to switch some lights on and draw the curtains and return again the next morning to switch the lights off before going to work.

When the search to find Errol began, Urban Gardens was naturally the first place to look. When his family got there they found Errol's white van parked outside. There was no answer at the door. Fearing the worst, they called the police, who forced the door open.

The house was a typical two-up two-down. From the front door a flight of stairs led straight to the first floor. To the right, a glass-panelled door led to the front lounge, which was crowded with furniture. At the rear was the door to the kitchen.

An armchair obscured the bottom half of the kitchen door and behind it lay Errol's body. The length of flex around his neck was tied to the door handle.

An ambulance was called but there was nothing the paramedics could do. More police officers, including a detective, came to the scene.

The family was grief stricken and they left the police to do their work. The family's grief was to increase when they were told that Errol had obviously committed suicide. But what about the threats that had been made to Errol, threats that he had reported to the police only a few days before? The family went to the police station that evening to protest and remind the officers of the threats. They were concerned and sure that someone had done this to Errol. They were told it was a simple and tragic suicide, plain and simple. There would be no further investigation. The police were firm on this. However, they had underestimated the strength of the family. Their concerns about the racial abuse which Errol had reported were ignored, but they would continue to fight to be heard.

Over the following weeks and months they continued to engage the police, and sought support from the local community and press.

It had a result; Peter Hampson, the chief constable, recognised the concerns of the family and ordered a new investigation under the direction of a detective superintendent. The family sought the support of the Home Office and even saw the Home Secretary, who promised the police would do all they could.

An investigative news team, from Channel 4, agreed to produce a documentary on the case and I was called in to offer advice to the news team.

I met the news team at the Moat House Hotel in Telford. It was early evening and getting dark, the autumn evenings were drawing in. The producer, Ian Hunter, had briefed me on the phone and we had discussed the case, based on his knowledge of it, at length.

His concerns, echoed by the family, were that the police had not been interested. I met Errol's sister Doreen and a younger brother. They were nice people, they were good people and I felt their grief and frustration, still strong some ten months after Errol had died. I also met Errol's mother, Joyce. It was apparent from the outset that she believed her son had been killed, and nothing would change that. I promised her that I would try and find the truth, and I would look and look hard, but the truth might be unpleasant and painful to hear. She would have none of that; her son had been murdered, and that was final. My words struck Ian as a little hard, but I felt compelled to say them. Doreen and her brother were genuinely grateful that at least I was listening.

I agreed to go to the house where Errol had been found. Negotiations with Jimmy Ross were delicate. He was unhappy with all the attention he and his home were getting. However, he was good friends with the McGowan family and he would not turn down any request from the matriarch, Joyce. He had too much respect.

The following morning we went to Urban Gardens and were met by Jimmy. He led me in. Although the scene was ten months old and I was entering to give advice, I still felt some trepidation. I was entering an alleged crime scene and I was not in the usual protective clothing. It didn't stop me from instinctively sticking my hands in my pockets, an impulse taught in my early days as a scene investigator, long before the modern techniques and routine white suits we now use.

The house was small. A large three-piece suite took up most of the cosy front room. My first thought was to look in the immediate vicinity of the door where Errol had been found hanged. I was struck by its cleanliness. The white paint was a little old and the wallpaper clean but also old. Not a trace of any fingerprint powder. Even after cleaning, I would expect to see some of the tell-tale signs. Some traces in the cracks or edges. But there were none. Perhaps the doors had been removed and taken away for examination at the police headquarters laboratory. I knew West Mercia Police had a good scientific support department with committed staff, some of whom I knew. Had they ever been called? Had they even attended? I wondered. I looked at the door hinges to see if there was any disturbance to confirm their removal. There was none. The hinges were still painted over. Jimmy Ross confirmed that the doors had not been painted for a few years. The wallpaper also showed no sign of treatment with chemicals.

It dawned on me with some horror that this central part of the scene, possibly the whole scene had not been examined. This in spite of the new investigation called within a few months of Errol's death. What about the assurances of the chief constable and Home Secretary that everything possible was being done?

I felt embarrassed. I should not be there. How had I got to this scene, ten months after the event, but before the police who are investigating it? How could the family be let down in such a way, and how could a police force, one with a good reputation, committed staff and an excellent scientific support department let themselves down in such a way?

My interview there and then showed my shock and disappointment. My inclination was to throw the film crew out. I had done that at least once before in my career as an investigator when I found one in a scene. This was very different. Our presence there was because of the lack of proper investigation.

The scene had waited ten months. In my opinion it was still worthy of examination. This was because only Jimmy lived there and although we were present and perhaps others had been in the intervening months, we were unlikely to leave our finger marks on the door and wall in any quantity without specific activity there. In any event our marks could be eliminated. I was struck by the thought that perhaps a suspect (if Errol's death was suspicious) may have touched the door or the wall in a struggle and their finger marks might still be there. Even with the passage of time they could still be present. In any event, if nobody looked we would never know. It was later suggested to me that any marks would have disappeared, but that is simply not true. Marks can be found months or years later on a suitable surface and both the door and walls were just that. Even ten months after the event, evidence was still potentially there. I put myself in the position of the scene investigator. If I found the finger marks of a white man on the door, a man who had no legitimate reason to be in Jimmy Ross's home and who had made threats against Errol, would the senior investigating officer be interested? My answer, you bet he would.

I gave some advice to Jimmy, not to paint or disturb the door unnecessarily and to keep visitors away from it until the police examined it. I was determined the police would. They had by far the best facilities and it was their job. I knew their boss and some others; I had probably helped train some of them.

The documentary would be shown within a few weeks. I was aware that the police had no idea what the documentary would show and what my views were. This gave me real concerns. If the documentary produced an increase in the investigation activity, I would hope that it would include re-examining or, more accurately, examining for the first time the house at Urban Gardens. My deepest concern was for Jimmy and his safety. If in fact Errol had been murdered, his murderer would know that the scene may contain some incriminating evidence. Not wishing to be melodramatic, stranger things had happened and I knew that, having worked within the police for a number of years. I feared that someone might try to burn the house down with little regard for Jimmy Ross if he were still inside. So I faxed Ian Hunter and demanded that he made the police aware of the content of my views.

By coincidence, Peter Hampson, the chief constable, had been my boss when he was assistant chief constable in Surrey. He was a good, honourable man, an absolute gentleman and a talented and competent leader. He was a great supporter of forensic science and it had been a pleasure to work for him in Surrey. He is exactly the type of person you would want to see as a chief constable. This made it all the more remarkable that his force was being criticised in such a way. It was my personal view that someone, somewhere, had let him down. Such was the honour of the man that he put steps in place, trusting others under his command to put it right and to his absolute credit apologising to the family for the original investigation. It went against the strong view held by many police that they should never apologise, never explain. It was, however, the right thing to do.

On the morning after the screening, the police attended Urban Gardens and removed the door and other items mentioned in my report.

A few months later, as the date of the inquest approached, I was contacted by the McGowan family's solicitors who asked me to formally look at the case on their behalf and prepare a report for them, one which they would send to the coroner. I agreed and received a pile of documents and statements which I requested for the review.

Much of the detail I had received was confirmed as accurate and I set about reviewing the investigation as best I could. My thoughts about the lack of examination at Urban Gardens were also confirmed. However, in a rebuttal of my view that the doors may contain some fingerprint evidence, the head of scientific support for West Mercia, Tristram Elmhirst, disagreed. He had reviewed the case at the time of the first re-investigation and concluded that there would be nothing there after such a time. I had a lot of personal respect for Tristram, but I felt that he was wrong on this matter.

My statement was submitted to the coroner and I was advised that I would be called to give evidence at the inquest.

The atmosphere in Telford became more intense following the death of Errol's nephew on New Year's Eve. He was found hanging from railing outside a pub. His death was being dealt with as a suicide but the family were further convinced of foul play. The police were under pressure to demonstrate their commitment to finding out the truth.

The inquest was to be held at the Moat House Hotel in Telford. The coroner's court was too small for the purpose as there was likely to be a large press presence. The Moat House was centrally located and large enough to fit the needs of what, for all intents and purposes, was a very public event. I was advised that Ronald Thwaites had been instructed to represent West Mercia Police at the inquest. This too surprised me. Ronnie Thwaites was no lover of police. I had come across him many times in my time with the Flying Squad where he had defended suspected armed robbers. It was the view of many police officers that he believed that all police officers were liars. Indeed, shortly afterwards he was the subject of an article in *The Police Review* where he openly stated that it was his job to attack both the evidence and the witnesses' credibility. All was fair game as far as he was concerned. The irony was not lost on me. There was Ronnie Thwaites representing the police and there was I appearing on the 'other side', so to speak. I was not looking forward to the encounter, but I was firm and felt safe on my ground, not that Thwaites would have any respect for that.

Early one evening I got the call from the family's solicitor that I was required to give my evidence to the inquest first thing the following morning. It was accompanied by the view that Thwaites was after me.

I decided to travel straightaway and stay at the Moat House. The drive would take me a few hours and I wanted to be fresh and rested the following morning, ready and at my best and most alert for Mr Thwaites. Having confirmed a room was available, I set off.

Many rooms at the hotel were occupied by interested parties, members of the press, police and other witnesses. I ran into an old colleague from the Metropolitan Police. Ron Woodland and I had worked together at City Road and Forest Gate. He was an extremely competent detective and I enjoyed his friendship. He had a great sense of humour, and working with him had been enjoyable and fun. Ron was now attached to the Racial Crimes Investigation Squad at New Scotland Yard. They had been formed after the death of Stephen Lawrence and had a nationwide remit and interest. Ron had read my statement and knew of my appointment with Ronnie Thwaites the following morning. He for one was looking forward to the engagement, and he told me so with gleeful relish.

The inquest was being held in one of the larger ballrooms of the hotel. After a light breakfast I made myself known to the coroner's officer.

The spacious location allowed for large numbers of press and public to occupy the rows of seats behind counsel who were representing the police and the family. The coroner sat on an elevated position on the ballroom's stage and the inquest jury along the far wall opposite the witness box.

Tristram Elmhirst had already given his evidence the previous day. Peter Herbert was the counsel for the family and it was he who took me through my evidence in chief. This mainly concerned my visit to the scene and the view that the scene had not been examined and was still worthy of examination. It also included that, at various times before my visit to the scene, the police had ample opportunity to review and consider that the scene should have been examined.

Apart from the examination of the door and the wall, I also emphasised that it was never too late to resurrect an investigation when new information was received and even old information realised. All it took was to review the information and act to find out what could still be examined and investigated. There had been an underlying failing in the police investigation, graphically indicated by the scene still not being fingerprinted ten months after the death of Errol McGowan.

Having completed my evidence in chief it was Ronnie Thwaites's turn and he did not disappoint. True to form, his first attack was on the witness not the evidence. He questioned my qualifications and right to offer such an opinion. He compared me with Tristram Elmhirst, the head of scientific support for West Mercia Constabulary. I had held the identical post in Surrey for eight years. Tristram was a graduate whereas I had a Higher National Certificate vocational qualification in chemistry awarded by the Royal Institute. Tristram held a bachelor's degree in a pathology science, from recollection. This was all very impressive but not necessarily any more relevant to this field than my own qualification. Thwaites was not going to give up. I then hit upon the idea of having a bit of fun, it would be tricky but the outcome could be worthwhile if I could get away with it. It would go something like this:

'It is true, Mr Thwaites, that I do not have a degree in pathology and neither do I have a more relevant qualification such as the prestigious Forensic Science Society Diploma in Crime Scene Investigation,' I would say.

'So, Mr Millen, you have no qualification in this field. Can you explain why not and why we should listen to you?' Thwaites would seize the opportunity.

'Well, I set up the Forensic Science Society's diploma and ran the examination board for seven years!!' I would close.

I knew Thwaites would have done his homework and

probably have been briefed by the police, which made me wonder why he was taking the approach of attacking my qualifications. In case he had not and as he seemed keen to attack my qualifications it was worth a try. I felt I could not lose.

It was the sort of fun Ron Woodland was expecting and I could see him grinning in the public area. But in any event it wasn't to be. The coroner, Michael Gwynne, wasn't going to allow any such criticism of my right to express my view. He intervened and stopped Thwaites in his tracks. The coroner had already heard my evidence in chief and found what I had said made perfect sense. It had. It was good practice.

In the interest of truth, the coroner asked for Tristram and me to confer outside the court and agree common ground.

We met outside the court and went with a coroner's officer and representatives of counsel into a side room. I was firm and was not prepared to concede on the matter. When I visited the scene, it was still worthy of examination. This had been strengthened by the fact that the police subsequently removed the door. The fact that they had found nothing, no finger marks at all (not even Jimmy Ross's) I accepted, albeit with a little disappointment. Tristram had to agree that the finding of marks after such a time could not be excluded until they had looked.

Our agreement was fed back via counsel to the coroner and I was not required to give any further testimony.

At the end of my evidence I was approached by members of the McGowan family, including Errol's younger brother, who thanked me. They had just wanted someone to look and they had got that.

The inquest concluded that Errol had received racial abuse but his death was suicide. It was a painful pill for the family to swallow. Errol's mother would never accept it and the delay had only worsened that view. Justice delayed was justice denied as far as she was concerned.

In his closing remarks at the inquest, the coroner commended my views, recommending to the police that they should 'give some detailed thought to the views of Mr Millen, which seemed eminently sensible to me'. That was the last I heard of the case. So what, many might think. The path of justice had prevailed, the outcome could not be judged until all the matters known were explored to their natural conclusion.

The greater tragedy was that at a time of deep grief, a family had to fight to get their concerns investigated. All they had wanted was for someone to look.

I would like to believe that if the allegation of Errol's racial murder (as the allegation from the family was) had happened in Mozambique and his body returned to the UK, as Andrew's and Caroline's had, the coroner and the police would have launched a proper investigation. That is based on the hope that the coroner and senior investigators would see their responsibility, as I'm in no doubt they would.

Both families expected, indeed demanded, that the death of their loved ones be investigated, that someone looked and that someone cared. They wanted justice. However, justice delayed, in the face of answerable questions, is often justice denied.

25. A Cockney at the Source of the Nile

Glancing down, I saw the student adjust a piece of paper under his seat. I had caught a student police officer cheating in an examination. The response perhaps should have been automatic dismissal. My response was immediate, but a little wisdom was needed. This was Jamaica and I had been running a crime scene investigation course for the Jamaican Constabulary Force. Funded by the UK Department for International Development, it was part of the international commitment to bring the island's police up to date.

The competition amongst the students on the course was immense. They relished the new skills which they were being taught and they were all highly motivated. I was committed to help them develop and this mid-term test was to see how both they and I were doing. So I was a little upset that this fine student had not heeded my words of encouragement. I wanted to know what they had taken in. What surprised me further was that the student in question was one who I knew was committed. He had ensured that he sat in the very front for the test. I could not fail to recognise his nervous glances down to the piece of paper under his seat. Cheating is something that cannot and must not be tolerated in a police officer. In the police work environment there is no greater sin than dishonesty. I had to consider how they would learn, and how to respond to the needs of a developing nation. Should I cut away and make an example? This environment and situation was new territory for me. Cutting away is OK, but how much do you need to cut before you have firm ground on which to build, will there be anything left and what happens to the rejected? Do they go somewhere else, not treated, to fester and cause more problems for society later? Is it not better to treat and heal the problem? That is OK provided no one else gets hurt in the meantime. Evolution not revolution was the stance I took. I knew that the student in question was a good one. He was a sound and active participant in the class work. So I decided to remove the offending piece of paper and let him continue. After the test, having marked the paper, which he comfortably passed anyway, I decided to give him the biggest dressing down I could. He took my harsh words, but he shuddered with guilt and embarrassment as he realised exactly what I felt of his conduct. I had already considered the fact that all the students carried their service issue side arms at all times. During the dressing down I particularly noticed that on the side of his belt he wore an automatic pistol. I was in full flow by then and it was too late to change my tack. Had he been offended or angered by my words he could have reacted differently. Perhaps by then he realised I was not going to take the matter further. I left him in no doubt about his responsibilities and the position of trust which he held. Although my words to him were in private, the rest of the class knew what had gone on. I used the episode as an example of trust, honesty and growth, which seemed to benefit the whole class. The future of their own community and how it was policed was in their hands. He went on to be a sound student and there were no signs of any repetition, by him or any of his classmates, in the final tests. I hope our conversation worked.

The backdrop to the course was the increasing illegal drugs trade, itself being felt back in the UK, and social unrest, mainly in Kingston, the capital. The country had an extremely high murder rate in the community, something that did not affect the tourists who visited the island beauty spots and who never got to hear about it. The first weekend I was there, there were riots in parts of the capital. Many were killed, including at least one police officer. It resulted in a curfew and the bodies of many of the dead were left lying in the streets overnight, as it was too dangerous to recover them. I was given a police escort, sandwiched between two police cars in my hired white jeep, from the training centre back to my hotel. It was during this that I realised that my guard and I were the sole occupants of this middle vehicle, but by then it was too late. We drove a long route, avoiding the main hot spots but we still drove through barricades. I stuck to the lead vehicle like glue but lost the vehicle behind me before I entered my hotel's gates safely. It was a difficult few days and crystallised the training needs of the students and the environment in which they would be working.

It also crystallised for me the need for joined-up aid. Crime scene training was, rightly, an important part of the development of the island's police, but it had to be seen in the context of wider planning. Crime scene investigation, and training in it, does not sit on its own. It is part of a much wider programme of development which includes detective training, pathology, forensic science support and the legal and social environment in which it operates. These all needed serious consideration and support in Jamaica. There was home-grown talent, particularly at the government's Forensic Science Laboratory, headed by its director, Yvonne Cruickshank. She and her staff were making progress in delivering and developing sound forensic science with limited funds and high caseloads.

In contrast, by the end of the course, I managed to take a trip around this beautiful island, leaving the problems in the main behind in Kingston. The reconstruction work undertaken since then has made a marked improvement in the situation.

The need for crime scene training is usually identified by a senior police officer, often a retired chief officer who undertakes a review of the customer in question. Training is often the first offer of aid from governments such as the UK. Training does not exist in isolation. It fills the gap between where the students are at the beginning of the process and where they are at the end. Training in an area devoid of organisational development is like building on sand. It is common to be asked to design and deliver crime scene training without any help in establishing the exact need and context of the work environment. It is rare for a training needs analysis to be undertaken in a foreign country by someone who will design the course, as this costs additional money. Where it is done, the course is much better suited to the needs of the customer and the students. So although a course can be designed with limited information, there is often a need to focus on the students' needs on the ground once more research has been done. The course programme may not seem to change much – that would probably alarm the customer – but the content and how it is delivered might. Not to review and make changes would be neglecting the needs of the students.

The main issue for me in delivering a three-week crime scene investigation course was not what to put in but what to leave out. As always, it is a matter of context and meeting the needs and expectations of the students and their managers. The students often had detective experience but were new to crime scene investigation. Three weeks is a very short time and so the focus was on forensic and fingerprint evidence types, methods of crime scene search and recovery, preservation and note-taking. Photography, although requested, was not possible for two reasons: lack of time and also the lack of likely availability. For me, note-taking took a higher priority. In running the course I worked with Suzanne Chapman, an extremely competent crime scene investigator and a top-class trainer. Suzanne was on a career break from her police force back in the UK and we made a good team.

The head of the crime scene unit in Kingston was Mackenzie,

an inspector and veteran of the force for almost forty years. He had studied at the National Training Centre back at Durham in the UK. At first he appeared a little suspicious of me. I was careful not to come across as a 'know all' from the UK (which he might have suspected and indeed I may have seemed to be) and tried to give him the respect he deserved. That respect was easy and he did deserve it. Any misgiving he had or I felt quickly evaporated and he complemented the course with his visits and participation. Part of my brief was to arrange for the supply of a number of crime scene kits. These had to be robust and meet the investigative needs of the users. A number of kits previously donated or bought were located at the main head-quarters building in Kingston. They were rare and highly prized and were used by only a select few. This was understandable, given the lack of funding and resources. So I hoped that the kits we were supplying would have a good impact in the stations around the rest of the country.

The course was held at the police training centre some ten miles outside Kingston. The establishment had a colonial feel to it and could have benefited from a lick of paint. It was a good environment in which to learn and to teach. Outbuildings provided a good source of scene houses for practical exercises and examinations, of which there would be many. The students would be expected to work in teams and individually, both good attributes for crime scene investigators.

The course went well and a lot of ground was covered in the relatively short period of time. The lessons on evidence types, search, evaluation, intelligence and notes and diagrams built up to final written and practical examinations with all the key components. The very planning of the course followed my model of listening, reviewing, planning, acting and once again reviewing, and Suzanne and I were flexible enough for this. Visits to the crime scene department and the forensic science laboratory found committed individuals doing their absolute best with limited resources and high caseloads. It was no good just trying to plant UK CSI techniques into their environment. One simple example was that of glass evidence. This is a significant and common source of evidence in the UK. But in Jamaica there is much more wooden-slatted ventilation than glass in the vast majority of premises. The basis principles remain the same, though, and that is what we taught.

There was a rather grand closing ceremony for the course, attended by senior chief officers, at which many fine words were said and the students presented with their course certificates. I felt that the course was a success, particularly as the students could apply what they had been taught in their work environment with the few resources they had.

Within a year I was to receive another call, this time from the British Council Anti-Corruption Programme in Uganda. The setting for the course was at the Hotel Triangle on the shores of Lake Victoria, only two hundred metres from the source of the Nile. It was a magnificent setting for a memorable course. I managed to persuade the British Council that two trainers were needed and, having gained their agreement, I called on Suzanne to once again work with me.

I very nearly didn't get there at all. I prepared three heavy extra-large holdalls full of crime scene training and investigation equipment and consumables to use on the course. These would also be donated to the Ugandan police at the end of the course. They weighed over 130 kilogrammes which made them many times my baggage allowance. I had arrived at Heathrow two hours early to make sure the bags were checked in OK. I had taken a similar amount to Jamaica the year before with only a small excess baggage fee. This time, however, the official at the Kenya Airways check-in was less amused and requested £1,000 excess baggage fee. We were flying Kenya Airways all the way to Nairobi first and then on to Entebbe. I knew this would eat into the fee. I phoned Suzanne (who was on her way) in the hope that I might be able to use some of her baggage allowance. But she had packed lots of children's clothing to donate when she got out there. Suzanne had worked before in Africa and knew that such a gift would be valued in the areas where we were going to work. When she arrived she was over her limit too. There was only one thing to do. Negotiate! There was little movement with the Kenya Airways official. I even pleaded with them that this was British Council Aid and was going to be donated when we left, but this cut no ice with them. They were Kenyan and we were going to Uganda, they reminded me. I then suggested that relations with their neighbour might be soured when this got out, but to little effect. I didn't move an inch. In the end the official called the supervisor for Lufthansa who was overseeing the baggage for the airline. I repeated the story and pulled out every card I could. Eventually they gave in and I got our entire luggage on at no extra cost. It felt like a grand achievement and a good omen for the course.

Once on the ground at Entebbe, we were met by British Council officials and Chief Inspector Willie Punaha. He was the contact point and the senior student on the course. We drove through Kampala, making a detour to Willie's house to pick up his clothing. It was a salutary lesson seeing how the police personnel and their families were billeted on a police housing compound. Willie was lucky as he had a house for his family but the conditions were very poor. We were made extremely welcome.

It took an hour or so to make the journey to Jinja on Lake Victoria. As we approached the hotel gates I could see a large banner draped across the entrance announcing the course and our arrival. For one second I was frightened that there was some large official welcome, or even a band. Well, there was no band but there was a wonderful welcome which ended a long day's travel.

The students began to arrive the next morning. They all took advantage of staying at the hotel, which was luxurious compared to their own homes. At the end of the first week some were to bring their partners to stay.

The class was large, over thirty students, and once again the expectations were high. There were only three students who had done any crime scene investigation before. Apart from the basics, they wanted photography, crime scene management, and fire and bomb scene management too. In the pre-course check, Suzanne established that no one owned or used a camera and there was little chance that even if they were able get hold of one, they or their employer would be able to afford the consumables.

So Suzanne and I tailored the content on scene investigation and some management. One of the experienced scene investigators was very approachable, but one of the others pretty negative, so much so we didn't realise his skills until the course developed. As it did, he came out of his shell and became a great contributor to the course. Once again we took time to develop note-taking and diagram skills, building on them as the course developed until by the end many of the students were proficient.

I felt a sense of unease with the resources that even the experienced guys would have. I didn't doubt their ability to undertake a competent investigation within their job role, but I didn't know where they would get help in the way of forensic science support. I left them with the knowledge of what they could do and what science offered beyond their own resources. I also left details of contacts within the UK, from laboratories to training organisations. If they ever got a high-profile investigation, particularly with international dimensions, there would, I hoped, be support to see they got the investigation right. They were committed to this but resources might compromise that commitment.

Suzanne and I hosted a drinks party at the source of the Nile for the course. For the cost of a couple of beers back home we managed to keep the entire course happy for a few hours. On our weekend off we had planned to hire a car and visit the local sites, including the famous Bujagali Falls. When a few of the students heard about it they too expressed their interest. Although only a few miles away, most of the students had not seen the falls either. So Suzanne and I traded our hire car for a coach to take everyone. On the morning of the trip, I was very unwell. I was feeling the effects of the sickness and diarrhoea which both Suzanne and I had suffered all week. In class we had managed to quickly hand over so our discomfort went unnoticed. There were many times when I felt like throwing my food straight down the toilet, cutting out the middleman! However, the trip to the falls was too good an opportunity to miss. So I mustered outside the hotel as a rickety old coach, just big enough to hold the entire course, arrived. I was given the pride of place seat at the front of the coach next to the driver. The back of the seat folded forward but was broken, so I found myself hanging on to the seat and the contents of my intestines for the whole trip. The falls were beautiful and this was mirrored in the expressions of the happy students. We went back to the hotel for lunch. I retired to my room whilst Suzanne and the students went on to another excursion at a local fish factory for the afternoon. On Sunday, Suzanne and I took a boat trip with two of the students around Lake Victoria to the source of the Nile, the place where the lake bubbles over exposed rock to make its journey over a few thousand miles to the sea. The source was marked by a plaque where Speke had found it a hundred and fifty years before.

During our stay we were informed that there was to be a national census and we would have to fill in our details on the day in question for the government inspectors. The record would show our presence in Uganda at that time and record it for posterity. Two questions stood out in my mind. The first was my marital status. Having been happily married for over twenty years I was not impressed with the options: single, currently married, divorced or widowed. The nearest option to reflect my status was currently married but this didn't sound too hopeful for me. So I crossed out currently and declared that

I was married. The second question asked me what tribe I was from. I thought about this for some time before proudly declaring my London roots and that I was a cockney. I hope to look at the records in the years to come to see that there was at least one member of the cockney tribe in Uganda in 2002.

Epilogue

My work as a crime scene investigator has taught me many things. Firstly, there is the absolute need to accurately and methodically record the crime scene, then to observe and listen, plan, act, reflect and review. There is a need to maintain the integrity of notes, photographs and any material that is recovered. This will ensure that the investigation can be examined and re-examined. On this foundation, no matter what scientific practice is applied or subsequently becomes available, there is a known starting point, an anchor. It may alleviate or even stop the most determined conspiracy theorist.

I have been both fortunate and troubled to see the horror and grief of man, humanity at its worst and also at its best. When people rise above the trauma, it is a gift to witness. The search for the truth, although demanded by the vast majority of victims, can also add to their pain.

This was the case with the young woman who had awoken in her basement flat to find a man beside her who then raped her. She was certainly not comforted by the fact that, two months before, a young neighbour, two doors away, had suffered the same fate. Had he been returning to attack the same victim again? It was quite possible. My examination of the scene revealed fingermarks outside the rear window of her flat where the offender had climbed in. Blood grouping obtained from semen found on a vaginal swab taken from the victim revealed that the rapist was a group B secretor, as in the earlier offence.

At the earlier scene a colleague of mine had found only one area of a palm print. He had recovered it from the surface of a vacuum cleaner which the offender had pushed away during the violent struggle with the victim.

A dedicated fingerprint expert at New Scotland Yard managed to identify the grubby finger mark which I had found on the outside surface of the window frame. It led to a closer examination of the palm mark, which was also then identified. A suspect was arrested and blood and saliva samples obtained. He was a group B secretor. He denied the offence and stood trial at the Central Criminal Court. On the day of the trial with both victims present, I witnessed him plead guilty to the first offence, the second remaining on file. This meant he was not convicted of raping the second victim and the victim was denied her justice. The fact was that the marks which I had found were outside and although in an enclosed, quite private garden, they still only placed him outside. DNA evidence was many years off. The only comfort was that had I not found the finger marks he would not have been identified as the donor of the palm mark at the earlier offence. This is because it was on an area of the hand which could not at that time be searched.

I still recall the look of despair on the victim's face as she tried to make sense of what she was going through. The suspect was sentenced to a term of imprisonment for the offence of which he was convicted. The second offence probably would not have added any more time, but that was of no consolation to the second victim. He had not been convicted of raping her. Some twenty three years later as I prepared to write this book, I heard on the radio about a man who had been convicted of a rape in the same area in very similar circumstances. Science, I was told, had convicted him. I immediately recognised the name of the convicted man. It was the same man and my heart sank to think that yet another woman had suffered at his hands.

It is times like those that makes even the most dedicated investigator wonder whether it is all worth it. But it is. Justice cannot be dispensed if the truth is not found and not known. The deficiencies, or what might seem to many as safeguards, of our legal systems are not the business of the investigator and it is best to detach oneself from them.

The scale of the investigator's task often seems overwhelming. The only way to overcome this is to break the problem down into bite-size questions to which bite-size answers can be found. That is the way to build up a picture which others can see and recognise as sound even if there are weak spots. That is equally important.

The search for the truth is a noble cause. However, not all crime is detected and not all offenders are brought to book. The truth is out there. For every contact there is a trace. For every action there is a reaction and in the reaction there are artefacts. There lies the evidence.

The detection of crime is solely in the hands of the investigator, their skill, tenacity and often luck. If you search hard and wide enough, that luck will also be found.

For those offenders who manage to evade justice on earth there is one last catch. Those who choose a life of crime should remember that there are always two people who will know the truth. The first is the offender. For those of faith there is a second. Although the evidence for the existence of a 'superior being' may not meet with earthly legal standards, there is hope and faith. It may seem strange that a man of science may be drawn into such feelings. I draw a distinction between that physical evidence which I would expect and demand in a court of law and that which I feel in my human emotion.

Although some offenders escape the attentions of mortal investigators, there is comfort for the pained and troubled victims of crime, even when there seems no hope of closure. For me there is always a second and final person who knows the truth, the innocent and the guilty, and there is no escaping His investigation and His justice. He is the final arbiter. That person is God.